SANCTUARY

SANCTUARY

GLOBAL OASES OF INNOCENCE

MICHAEL TOBIAS & JANE GRAY MORRISON

A DANCING STAR FOUNDATION BOOK

COUNCIL
OAK BOOKS

SAN FRANCISCO & TULSA

In Loving Memory of William Tobias,
and Bruce Morrison.

CONTENTS

FOREWORD

Sanctuary: Global Oases of Innocence lovingly addresses the convergence of conservation biology, ecological sciences, animal rights and public policy, occurring throughout the world. With over 114,000 protected areas on earth, human endeavours to protect sacred places have spawned an environmental and spiritual renaissance. *Sanctuary* profiles dedicated examples of that remarkable collective passion and suggests that our need to revere and celebrate nature may be a key to our survival as a species.

Beginning with the world's largest protected area that spans contiguous portions of Alaska and Canada and continuing with profiles of extraordinary individuals and their work in 19 other nations, *Sanctuary* offers a singular vision of a world at peace ecologically.

Bhutan herself is strikingly emblematic of this "sanctuary movement." Bhutan's visionary Fourth King, His Majesty Jigme Singye Wangchuck, enshrined over 60% of the nation as inviolable primeval forest. It is a land dominated by a cultural commitment to non-violence, mutual tolerance and respect for all sentient beings; where the measure of the economy is not merely per capita earning power, but the degree to which the nation's people are enriched by a high quality of life. Here each and every individual can find deep and lasting forms of spiritual, as well as pragmatic sustainability. It is an example for concerned citizenry and policymakers of the world.

In *Sanctuary*, the authors have chronicled a very special expedition into one of Bhutan's most pristine habitats, its newest Wildlife Sanctuary in Sakteng. A land inhabited by mountain people, the Brokpas, whose lives exhibit many of humanity's finest qualities: generosity, community cohesiveness, spiritual integrity and a true innocence in the form of a deeply abiding connection to the natural world that has been nurtured by forward thinking Bhutanese conservation policies. The Brokpa, like indigenous peoples everywhere, are tied to nature. The authors point out that conservation can never exist without engaging the participation of and securing a future for those closest to the natural world.

Other nations have contributed their own unique visions of progressive, non-violent conservation. *Sanctuary* looks at the continuing legacies of such animal welfare luminaries as Brigitte Bardot, Michael Aufhauser and Gene Baur whose efforts to strengthen animal protection legislation are exemplary and indicative of a global sea change. Their effective voices remind people that nature regards all creatures as equal and that it is our challenge as a powerful species to be modest, gentle and compassionate towards others. This is where conservation biology and animal welfare must come together to work in favor of all sentient beings, without discrimination.

In Poland's exquisite old forest of Bialowieza, ornithologists have rallied to protect woodpeckers, an indicator species for the health of dead wood forests disappearing throughout Europe. In South Africa, Howard Buffett with his wife Devon struggle to save cheetahs from extinction, while working to alleviate poverty and disease and to provide clean drinking water for millions of people. Sanctuaries in the Nilgiris of South India, in Indonesian Borneo and on the island of Socotra in South Yemen, protect both indigenous peoples, like the Todas and the Dyak, while saving rare endemic orchids, orangutans and cinnabar trees.

Combining a persuasive overview of animal rights as a necessary precursor to global conservation initiatives, *Sanctuary* offers methodologies for merging science and policy with spiritual ecology. With data gleaned from some of the most exquisite refuges in the world, Michael Tobias and Jane Morrison provide blueprints for hope. *Sanctuary* advances the causes of the heart while embracing methods to ensure that critical habitat and endangered species are safeguarded.

Sanctuary is an ambitious and important book. Its authors have traveled the world in search of many of the most astonishing, little known and important ambassadors for conservation and animal welfare. In over 20 countries they have profiled inspiring examples of what is working and how good people make a difference.

It is fortuitous that the 2008 Smithsonian Folklife Festival in Washington, D.C., worked with the Royal Government of Bhutan to celebrate Bhutanese culture, history, and conservation at the very moment that this book officially emerged as part of that Festival. With Bhutanese conservation being an important hallmark of this work, we have compelling synchronicity. As Bhutan herself presents a beacon of conservation for the 21st century, *Sanctuary: Global Oases of Innocence* celebrates that movement in its international context.

Not only will *Sanctuary* prove invaluable for policymakers and scientists, but it should provide inspiration for the next generation of young ecologists wanting to make a difference in the world. And it is for readers everywhere who wish to be reminded that the world of nature is beautiful and precious; and each of us has the opportunity, everyday, to help make profound changes that can bring peace and happiness to all living beings.

I congratulate the authors and deeply appreciate their extraordinary work.

HER MAJESTY ASHI DORJI WANGMO WANGCHUCK
QUEEN OF THE FOURTH KING OF BHUTAN

HER MAJESTY THE QUEEN

THE LOVE AND PROTECTION OF INNOCENCE

He is called by thy name,
For He calls Himself a Lamb.
He is meek, and He is mild;
He became a little child

From William Blake's poem "The Lamb" in
Songs of Innocence and of Experience, 1789

"Every time I look into their eyes, I recall the original inhabitants of the Garden of Eden," famed primatologist, Dr. Biruté Galdikas quietly told us. She was speaking of her extended family of orangutans with whom she has been living for over 35 years in the tropical peat forests and swamps of Borneo. There, during one of the two dozen journeys profiled in this book, each to remarkable remnants of the original world that have been preserved with the dedicated help of humans, we sat in the dusk watching a few remaining female orangutans consuming their rambutan fruit (*Nephelium lappaceum*) before we departed back to our camp through the knee deep balm of cooling black water. "They are so innocent, free, pure," she whispered.

Whether orangutans or lambs or human children of the world, innocence conjures in its origins a call to the heart that is unmistakable. The 19th century French painter William-Adolphe Bouguereau depicted innocence by intimating sublime trust and tenderness in the guise of an infant and a lamb held protectively by a beautiful maiden in the painting aptly titled *L'Innocence*. Thus, he invoked the words of both Blake and the Prophet Isaiah, who spoke of the wolf, the lamb, the leopard and the goat in harmony together.

This ideal survives in our deepest instincts: not those of fear or flight, but of loving engagement and protection in the natural world. Paleontologists might debate the human propensity for peace or violence, and biologists have argued the evolutionary

advantages of competition versus cooperation. Do tough-minded survivors gain the most over the long run or are their tender-hearted counterparts the ultimate winners? But the act of celebrating nature is more deeply woven into the human heart than any other intellectual conceit. The notion of Adam and Eve in the Garden continues to fuel great ideals, to invoke the passions for beauty and kindness, as well as interdependency, a hallmark of all ecological communities.

The harsh realities of life and death remain, but these are clearly mitigated by all the poetic truths of biodiversity and what we think of as sacred in nature. *Sanctuary: Global Oases of Innocence* is a modest record of some two dozen places on Earth where humans have recognized ecological importance and devoted huge energy to ensure their survival and integrity. The combination of science, legislation, community and individual activism, non-violence, animal rights, conservation biology and spiritual ecology is a convergence of forces the authors have sought to observe and enshrine. The emergent paradigm we call the *sanctuary movement.*

For thousands of years, protection of ideal harmony—in countless paradise evocations all around—has elicited a constantly revised consensus as to our role as a species, including our duties to each other, to other creatures and to all of nature. In every invocation of innocence, as with love, there has been a universal understanding of its most enduring nuances. And while the overall message morphs amid the turbulence of the human condition and its escalating damage to self and to nature, innocence poignantly reminds us what the world feels like if we are willing to believe in her, trust her and act in accordance with that faith.

Those actions toward some measure of redemption have emerged as critical watersheds of global biological survival, as our species trespasses in ways so burdensome to the natural world. That weight is upon us as we each struggle to survive and to become re-enchanted with nature. Sustainability begs us to leave as light a footprint as possible. But beyond treading lightly, many feel the call to take action to create and preserve. The major thrust of the "sanctuary movement," as we term it, concerns people taking steps toward the assistance and protection of 'others': of individuals of our own species and those with whom we share the planet, indeed with all life. There are no limits.

Early efforts to protect landscapes are easily traceable. In India, Japan, Sri Lanka and England, wildlife and forests were safeguarded going back 2,500 years. Today's Epping Forest, London's 6,000 acre contribution to global biodiversity, also heralds an historic connection dating to the 12th century and Henry I, a time when this primeval wilderness enjoyed a unique level of protection. In 1832, 47 hot springs in the Ouachita Mountains of Arkansas were protected, followed by the Siebengebirge Nature Reserve in Prussia.

It has been said that the soul speaks when it is spoken to. The creation of Yellowstone in 1872 spoke to a large constituency whose motives were free of bias. This national impulse to create sanctuary was soon emulated: first with the Royal National Park in Australia, then Banff National Park in Canada, followed by the deeding of the sacred volcano, Tongariro, by a Maori chief to the people of New Zealand. It was to be the first of that country's 14 national parks. Meanwhile, other national areas of protection were being created in the U.S. and elsewhere. Europe's first parks were engendered in 1909, when Sweden designated nine such regions with one piece of legislation. Today, Sweden contains 28 national parks (out of 350 total in Europe), 2,500 nature reserves, 1,000 wildlife sanctuaries and 150 nature management areas. Although this seems like a lot, it constitutes no more than 10% of the entire country.[1] These definitions can become nebulous. For example, Canada provides full protection to

only 9% of its nation, although 63% of Canadian nature has partial protections in place and 3,500 separate reserves.[2] While a mere 6.3% of England's 8,238 square kilometers actually enjoy full protection, the U.K.'s rural legacy, from Wordsworth's "Tintern Abbey" to the nation's contemporary rural landscapes, proffer an incalculable ecological force on the world stage. France, a country with a huge rural heritage and possessing 40% of European flora and 1,153 protected areas, only in 1963 created its first national park at Vanoise in the Alps. The apparent gap between the sheer number of protected areas and the overall size of a country, translates into biological fragmentation. To the extent those fragments can be connected, ecological corridors are created.

Those fragments include private property. In the United States there is a certification program for wildlife-friendly backyards. The vast collective of private gardens, rural estates, tiny urban fragments of biomass, particularly cemeteries, provide increasingly critical habitat in a world where greenery of all kinds is disappearing. Urban rooftops turned into gardens; balconies hosting native plants—all of these unlikely mechanisms for botanical regeneration have become more than relevant. In those instances of proactive and compassionate forward-thinking, scientists at zoos committed to returning species to the wild have also effectively provided another piece of the puzzle. This has been the case with the European bison, profiled in this book, as well as snow leopards bred under the umbrella of the Species Survival Program. The small North American native red wolf has also benefited from zoo collaboration.[3]

The delineations of park, refuge, reserve, sanctuary, wilderness, buffer and dozens of other categories indicate greatly varying degrees of protection. Sanctuaries abound in the form of private and community gardens, city, state, regional and national parks, private refuges devoted to domestic animals, rare breed societies, land trusts, various biological so-

cieties and multitudinous clubs and conservancies that work to save living creatures. They are the subject of much debate over the principles of choice, the ethical compromises and the priorities with respect to habitat types, or specific species or genera, biological families and orders, and entire ecosystem dynamics; not to mention how legislation must find ways to accommodate human needs. In England, for example, there are at least 24 different national designations for protected areas, including Local Nature Reserve, Green Belt, National Park, Site of Special Scientific Interest, even Nitrate Vulnerable Zones.[4] On all continents, humans are working hard to save that which they love in nature.

For this book we sought out examples of some of the varied ways the reality of sanctuaries manifest themselves in today's world. In one instance, the impulse to save life emerges in the high-profile endeavors of a movie star in France who has devoted her life to the protection of dogs, cats, horses, bears and seal pups; in another a conservationist in Africa who sees clearly that unless the crisis of hunger is alleviated, the cheetah will more than likely go extinct. We see that passion exemplified by a Namibian family taking in orphaned lions, wild dogs, and baboons, among others, and saving them from a desert of pain, trauma and certain death. In Poland one brave ornithologist has worked for over 35 years in that country's oldest national park, Bialowieza, to protect woodpeckers and preserve their forest.

We follow a botanist on a difficult expedition in India to find methods to help save the last vegetarian tribe in the world, their unique culture and the miraculous wild habitat they worship and upon which they depend. And, we profile an animal protectionist in New York State who created one of the first farm animal sanctuaries in the West and who has devoted his life to rescuing these gorgeous, sensitive creatures.

There is the King of Bahrain who was determined against a tide of rapid development to protect a precious piece of land within his island country so that it remains intact, providing comfort and sanctuary to endemic and native species of the region.

There are many such incarnations of the human impulse to love. Myriad approaches to that catalogue of passion have arisen in response to our growing realization of the extent of peril in which we have placed the rest of the Creation and the urgent need to meld science with governmental, legislative and community priorities for nurturing or sparing life. *Sanctuary: Global Oases of Innocence* pays homage to just a few of these endeavors.

The World Conservation Union (IUCN) based in Gland, Switzerland defines these oases and the environmental urgencies that have resulted in their protection, according to a biological hierarchy of imperatives.[5] The IUCN has denominated numerous types of areas of special protected status in which biological diversity—and other natural and/or cultural resources—can be said to be legally maintained at an effective level, with six duly recognized types of protection: nature or science or wilderness reserves; national parks; national monuments; habitat and species management areas; landscape/seascape protected areas; and sustainable use ecosystems. The IUCN is also the international consortium (involving most nations of the world) that "Red Lists" levels of vulnerability among Rare, Threatened, Endangered and Critically Endangered species of which 16,116 were known as of 2006.[6]

The endangered species are everywhere, inside and out of protected areas; in cities and in the wilderness. For example, in a country famous for being "clean green," namely, New Zealand, approximately 50% of the known 5,822 native species are Threatened, while not even enough data is yet known to determine the status of the country's other remaining 50%. The rate at which biological organisms are succumbing to this tragic predicament, commonly called extinction, is between 100 to 1000 times the natural background rate for disappearance of taxa, depending upon the species in question. That means that a species of mountain go-

rilla, Spix's macaw or Amsterdam albatross is likely to go extinct 1,000 times faster than it would have barring the types of system-wide planetary disturbances, such as a supervolcano or an asteroid hit, that have triggered the previous five known mass extinctions. The human population explosion of both rich and poor consumers must be balanced by a human response which is the essence of conservation. Without any certainty as to where this demographic winter will end, certain principles have emerged that both define conservation biology and animal protection. At the core must be a love of life, unstinting and unconditional. That is the heart of the sanctuary movement. We feature one such passion, that of Dr. Biruté Galdikas, for the organgutan and for their home, Borneo. Dr. Galdikas' marriage to a tribal elder and engagement with her adopted country, both with the local people and the government, is an apt demonstration of how compassion and care for humans and our near relatives are one and the same.

Cooperation with indigenous peoples, and respect for their tribal customs, religious and ethnic orientations, is critical to the success of the majority of the strategies conservationists call for in the name of rapid preservation; the creation of protected areas and wildlife sanctuaries, corridors, connected ecosystems and the like. Several hundred million such people live near or within the very areas under ecological scrutiny so their partnerships for the long-term are the only possible solutions.

The "hotspots" matrix at the heart of much of the work done by Conservation International (CI) and its many partners recognizes that an overwhelming share of the world's most diverse biological heritage is actually consolidated in 2.3% of the terrestrial Earth, or 3,379,246 square kilometers. Each hotspot contains at least 1,500 endemic vascular plants found nowhere else. This number also recognizes that at least 70% of the hotspots' habitat has already been lost.[7] Protect that 2.3% of remaining rare ecosystems and humanity shall have protected not just the charismatic species like tigers and kakapo, but the subtle and equally significant ones: trees bearing critical fruits, fungi, insects, leaf matter

and deadwood critical to many other species. Equally pronounced in the hierarchy of biological imperatives, if seldom explored from a biodiversity perspective, are the multitudinous parasites, viruses and bacteria without which life on earth would vanish. All are essential to a strategy that merges love with science. One remarkable sanctuary in Suriname is the love child of Russell Mittermeier, whose seminal work on hotspots has given him a keen appreciation of the unique places he is helping to safeguard.

Dr. Mittermeier and team have also advocated two other key designations for varying types of protected areas, namely, "wilderness" and "megadiversity." These designations invite the consideration of those political entities within whose boundaries are assembled the largest biological aggregates of species and habitat type.[8] The highest megadiverse nations include Brazil, Columbia, Indonesia, South Africa and Australia.[9] The science behind designations such as "hotspots" and "megadiversity" provides great opportunities for residents, governments, donors, and ecologists in general to be better equipped and informed in their efforts to help make a difference. There are many ways to preserve and cherish life and the creation of sanctuaries inside the identified hotspots is one such approach. Many have or are being created by NGOs and governments.

Another type of assessment is called *gap analysis*; efforts to fill in blanks on the biological map. In human-dominated landscapes, such as exist throughout much of the world, one case study showed that "more than half of Costa Rica's native land birds" were relying on "deforested agricultural countryside."[10] How long this dependency had endured could not yet be determined, but the fact that so many tropical birds had made these trees or shrub areas home, suggests a behavioral latitude, which could be translated into sanctuary paradigms particularly apt during an era of global warming.

New and broader guidelines for appreciating and safeguarding biodiversity have emerged. In 2002 190 parties committed to the Johannes-burg World Summit on Sustainable Development (WSSD) on curtailing "the current rate of biodiversity loss at the global, regional and national levels." Also goals were set for the year 2010 by the European Union's Natura 2000 Alliance, which seek to create larger protected areas and designate more species as Endangered.[11] The World Wildlife Fund has come up with a priority list of 200 Global Ecoregions "of the Earth's most biologically outstanding terrestrial, freshwater and marine habitats."[12]

Some regions have made great strides in recent years. New Zealand, for example, has managed to hold on to some 30% of its forest estate, with 19% of that remaining in high-level protected categories. In Bhutan, more than 62% of primary canopy can be said to be intact, a fact we explore in our profile of Bhutan. Within the United States, less than 10% of our original forests are still standing, though second and third growth forests have rebounded—lacking, however, the biodiversity that once blessed North American forests.

According to the Worldwatch Institute, "wilderness" requires a minimum of 4,000 square kilometers of undefiled, pristine terrain. By that criterion, Nepal has zero "wilderness" remaining. India is in an equally dismal situation although we discover how sanctuaries can survive in a country without wilderness. Safe harbors offer differing criteria or visions of what constitutes biological robustness both in micro- and macro-settings. Nearly all of the approaches to creating sanctuaries—whether small private reserves or huge national parks—depend not only upon fine interdisciplinary science, but also political and economic common sense, altruism, compassion, and a large degree of imagination.

World Heritage Site protections were inaugurated in Paris in December 1975 under the auspices of the United Nations Educational, Scientific and Cultural Organization (UNESCO). As of late 2007, 644 cultural, 162 natural and 24 other combined World Heritage Sites from 138 countries had been designated. Three of the sanctuaries in this book—in Alaska, Poland and Suriname—are so recognized; and that status for a fourth, in Yemen, is currently under consideration.[13] Often, a World Heritage site

may encompass multiple parks, as in the case of Te Wahipounamu, which takes in 40 different reserves and parks in southwestern New Zealand.[14]

Other UNESCO efforts include the Biosphere Reserves, part of the Man and the Biosphere Program, where unique ecological biomes of global scientific importance are duly recognized. One such reserve is profiled in this book, in the Nilgiris of South India. While there is no binding legislation upon nations allied with UNESCO, the recognition itself has been sufficient to increase substantially the level of protection afforded by governments.[15]

In the United States, the U.S. Fish and Wildlife Service (USFWS) has established 548 National Wildlife Refuges across 50 states and more than 96 million acres expressly for the purpose of preserving habitat and bringing back endangered species. Writes USFW, "Wildlife refuges are home to more than 700 species of mammals, 250 reptile and amphibian species, and more than 200 species of fish [providing] habitat for more than 250 threatened or endangered plants and animals."[16]

Begun in 1903 by President Theodore Roosevelt with his designation of Florida's Pelican Island, the National Wildlife Refuge system provides profoundly important wildlife experiences to some 40 million visitors each year. Only 2% of the entire refuge system is off limits to the public, except under strictly monitored "special use" permits. One such sanctuary is profiled in this book. First established in 1909, the Farallon National Wildlife Refuge, 28 miles west of San Francisco, is the most important sea bird breeding area south of Alaska in the United States, as well as a critical marine mammal habitat.[17] The spring of 1909 marked a frenzied time of protection for Roosevelt: it was the final few months of his second term as President and he was determined to imbue America with a conservationist ethic that would last.

Also, across the U.S. 58 National Parks and 330 other national park service "units"—among them the Statue of Liberty and Smithsonian Institution Mall in Washington, D.C.—occupy over 84 million acres.

National Parks are places where our footprint has been tempered. This was also the message inherent to the *United States Wilderness Act of 1964*, which provided places where human solitude could be found, natural ecosystems sustained in an "unimpaired condition." "At least five thousand acres of land" were by definition to be incorporated within that wilderness.[18] "In wildness is the preservation of the world," wrote Thoreau. That has been the goal of most American parkland legislation though perhaps it has not always been articulated with the same uncompromising vigor and directness of the great poet of Walden Pond.

Wilderness areas are meant to remind us of the past, though we want them to be here in the present and stay with us into the future. We cannot possibly know what we will be like as a species in the future, any more than we could have predicted an American population that has multiplied ten-fold, from 30 to 300 million people, since the time Abraham Lincoln signed legislation protecting the Yosemite Valley and Mariposa Grove of Giant Sequoias on June 30th, 1864—the first such legislation in Congressional history.

Congressional funding for the park service, since its creation in 1916, has never kept pace with the modernizing impacts of a democratic constituency, however. Indeed, the notion of visits by as many people as possible was written into the earliest memos accompanying parkland legislation. The railroad business through Yellowstone was hugely abetted by park nationalization and Stephen Mather, a champion of industry who would become the first superintendent of the parks, made it clear that he wanted those parks to provide Americans with a high level of amenities. Millions of automobiles would venture into Yosemite at the very moment that its last Native Americans, the Southern Miwok, were being systematically extirpated from their ancestral home.

Mather echoed the sentiment earlier expressed by William Wordsworth when he described his own beloved Lake District in England as a place that should become the "property" of every interested person. John

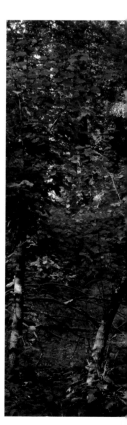

Muir also believed in this democratization of nature though he detested the notion of "utilization of natural resources." Ingrained into the park concept, then, is an ongoing debate as to what constitutes true protection and whose interests are to be served. Is it possible to preserve wilderness while allowing humans to enjoy its solace? What balance if any can be achieved? What is clear is that parks are still one of the greatest ideas fostered by humanity as islands of ecological integrity amid turbulent sprawl and destruction. Parks provide a physical set of coordinates, a landscape of idealism whose inspiration is the pristine natural world.

The U.S. Bureau of Land Management (BLM) controls another huge swath of nature in the U.S. with nearly 264 million acres compared with the National Park Service's 83.6 million acres. Of the BLM holdings, 26 million acres have been incorporated into the National Landscape Conservation System (NLCS). Parts of this acreage are called Conservation land, others National Monuments, National Trails, Scenic Rivers, Wilderness and Wilderness Study Areas. A few BLM Monuments have been turned into National Parks, such as Zion and Olympic. Other BLM lands fall at the opposite side of the protection spectrum, allowing various levels of public and corporate use or exploitation. A common *currency* of conservation and protection, one that has true legal teeth, is yet to be worked out.[19]

Despite the multitude of perspectives swirling across the ecological playing field, the fact remains that over 100 nations have embraced the protectionist ethic. Since the formation of Yellowstone National Park, over 1,200 other national parks have been created. Some of these are merely on paper, particularly in Africa and India, which continue to see poaching and illegal lumber extraction, notwithstanding solid national legislation and international conventions like CITES and other treaties designed to inhibit trafficking in Endangered and Threatened species. Approximately 12% of the Earth's terrestrial surface has some protected status.[20] As of 2007 there were 114,007 protected areas in all catego-ries: 1,961,398,989 hectares or more than 4.7 billion acres, according to the World Data Base on Protected Areas, a critical tool developed by the United Nations Environment Programme and the World Conservation Monitoring Centre.[21]

But what about the future? As global warming unleashes new and sudden forces in nature, how will parks and sanctuaries recover, or stay ahead of declines under new and unprecedented pressures? Some have begun to speak of proactive micro-management of evolution. "Perhaps we could help plants respond to global warming by moving southern, more drought-adapted individuals into northern populations." This "inoculation" approach "to foster rapid evolution" as a defense against destruction was recently proposed.[22]

In tracking critical types of sanctuaries throughout the world, we have paid particular attention to common themes emergent in the parks and reserves of the future. In each instance, people endowed with tolerance, kindness and an ardent conviction to save what can be saved, to spare what can be spared, are at the forefront of the sanctuary movement. These individuals and communities are in touch with humanity's extended family tree, which includes individuals of all other species.

We cannot ensure against future pandemics, over-population and corresponding consumptive chaos—including the extinction of experience—without knowing how things were: seeing a squirrel scamper up a tree, for example. Sanctuaries are vital to our survival as a sane species and equally critical to the maintenance of the biosphere we share with the rest of creation.

Conservation biologists rarely speak of individuals, except—as with the Florida Panther or New Zealand Kakapo—when the numbers are so low and the species so close to extinction, that each and every individual is necessarily known by name. Merging conservation biology, which seeks to protect various populations, while valuing principles of animal rights, is a major focus of the sanctuary movement: the goal of saving

habitat *and* individuals (including domesticated creatures like our-selves); and, the development of a deep understanding of non-violence that embraces *all* creatures.

The number of known species on the planet is still a mystery, but estimates from throughout the scientific community range from 10 million to 100 million, an estimated 30% of which are thought to be under threat from global warming. It is essential that we curtail our high demographic growth rates, seek benign alternatives to fossil fuels and trade our consumerist habits for more sustainable and prudent choices. We can all help to avert extinctions. As of the year 2000, a known 11,166 species worldwide were under threat of extinction[23] and less than five years later, that number increased by nearly 6%.[24]

There's much work to be done, and little time left. We've heard such warnings before, but never has the data been so refined, the picture of destruction so clear.

The reconciliation of conservation biology, ecosystem protection, with compassion towards individuals, is a work-in-progress. The sanctuary movement is one of the most pragmatic operating counter-measures to rectify ongoing anthropogenic (human-induced) assaults on biodiversity; and to halt the global epidemic of cruelty towards animals. Eco-tourism to those sanctuaries represents a potential annual trillion-plus dollar industry. Increasingly sophisticated approaches to adventure and ecological travel have resulted in self-sustaining lodges that focus upon conservation of the natural world surrounding them. One such sanctuary profiled in this book is Al Maha in Dubai, the brain-child of South African conservationist Tony Williams, where he and his staff scientists spend much of their time documenting the remarkable, rarely seen denizens of this dune environment.

Other sanctuaries profiled are restricted scientific areas of global im-portance, inhabited by indigenous peoples who are doing their part to save critical habitat and all the species therein. Without a corresponding respect and investment by these knowledgeable stewards, such refuges would never satisfy the needs of *all* the resident species. Three such sanctuaries are profiled here: Eastern Bhutan, home of several yak-herding communities; the Nilgiris of India where a remarkable ecologist, Dr. Tarun Chhabra, has spent much of his life recording endemic orchids and impatiens flowers while working to preserve the indigenous Toda culture; and the Guyana Shield, representing a protected rain forest that spans several contiguous South American countries and is home to numerous indigenous tribal groups, like the Trio Amerindians.

In Kyoto, thousand-year-old Buddhist temple gardens afford protection not only of their glorious spiritual and aesthetic traditions, but of rare bryophytes (particularly moss species) as well as rich suites of forest and plant communities lost outside the temple walls. In this ancient, sacred city, we follow a recent Ph.D. graduate, Dr. Yoshitaka Ooishi and his venerable mentor, Dr. Hiroyuki Akiyama who have spent years on their hands and knees with high-powered macro-lenses examining mosses across the city's greenbelt of nearly 10,000 historic, religious gardens.

A wonderful melding of the best of human creativity with nature, garden traditions are implicit in millions of acres of protected landscape in country after country, as beautifully described in *The New Garden Paradise: Great Private Gardens Of The World* [25] Wild gardens also thrive when cultural traditions have laid claim to rationales of protection, as on the unique Socotra Archipelago in the Indian Ocean where we venture into the high mountain haunts of the Socotri indigenous people, surrounded by unique bottle trees. In the Thar Desert of Rajasthan, populated by Bishnois, is the remarkable vegetarian city of Puskhar, where we investigate innate conservation sensibilities that have for centuries protected life.

Species that might have suffered by our excesses and indifference such as European lynx, bears, bisons and wolves have been honored by those who deem it their duty and pleasure to make amends. In Portugal, the scientists working at an Iberian wolf reserve endeavor to promote understanding and care for these endangered canines. A mere thirty minutes from Utrecht, in the Netherlands, a group of devoted bear aficionados have been working passionately for years to rescue these gorgeous, sociable mammals from circuses and cages throughout Eastern Europe. With endurance and courage, they have gone through the bureaucratic hurdles to transport the bears to a forest in Holland and there provide a world of freedom, where these marvelous and sensitive beings can live out their lives with a measure of joy and safety.

From Central Park's gregarious legacy of artistic and biological heritage, to San Francisco's key biological cornerstones; from the wilds of the well-protected jungle of Brunei, to the surprising sanctuaries in Bangkok, Singapore and Kuala Lumpur, we have tried to present a cross-section of exceptional individuals, kings, biologists, private citizens, and city planners among others. Their ambitious initiatives are emblematic of thousands of other such refuges that cannot be encompassed in one modest volume. But we have learned that love and innocence are at the heart of all of these efforts.

The sanctuary movement has shown us that each project has a critical role to play; each individual can make a huge difference. The legacy we leave this Earth should celebrate kindness and compassion; gestures of virtue that do not discriminate between an endangered parrot or a domestic chicken. While the authors subscribe to the necessity of saving those species that are endangered, with all due force, rapidity and weight of law, we acknowledge that all life deserves respect. Every living being is inherently valuable by dint of the miracle of its life. These components motivated our selection of sanctuaries. With the success of these many unique and complex efforts by so many good people, we understand that the 21st century has given us a blueprint of compassion-in-action

Individuality itself is a critical concept that transcends the traditional population dynamics model of thinking about ecology. It allows us to work one-on-one, whether with a tree, an epiphyte, a beetle, or an elephant.

Above all else, the sanctuary movement yields a vivid, if experimental, study of the human facility to do Good. Our responses to nature are the basis of our survival. Our ability to celebrate all of nature defines our humanity, as does the reasonableness and inspiration by which we reverse biological and social crises with dignity and grace. We do not "call the shots" in nature; nor have we much of a clue what's really going on. E.O. Wilson, in his book *The Creation: An Appeal To Save Life On Earth*, walks readers through three steps in divining the complexity of the biological sciences: 1) the complete life cycles of individual species; 2) mapping their diversity; and, 3) the complete history of life, from the gene to entire ecosystems. Then, he adds, "Try now to envision simultaneously the reach of the three dimensions of biology. You cannot, I cannot, no one can . . . ."[26]

What we can do is judiciously toss and turn through the reams of scientific data, and then place everything on a pillow before the more generous human heart, which will act to save life regardless of the complexities involved. The dizzying ecological challenges, what the Jain faith has described as "a whirl of pain", now promise to bring forward the very best in humanity, the memory of innocence reminding us what is possible, who we are and why we are here. When those diverse oases become connected, we shall have restored harmony on Earth.

A LITTLE BIRD IN THE LARGEST PROTECTED AREA ON EARTH

WRANGELL-SAINT ELIAS NATIONAL PARK AND PRESERVE, ALASKA

Peering out an open window from a Cessna 185 at the third highest peak in North America (after Mount McKinley and Canada's Mount Logan), 18,008-foot Mount Saint Elias presents the single largest elevation gain in the world, an ice-enraptured massif towering above the Gulf of Alaska. Mount Everest, by contrast, reaches more than 29,000 feet, but its real fall-line commences just above the so-called Nepalese Base Camp, at over 18,000 feet. This math favors Mount Saint Elias in terms of sheer verticality. The centrifugal forces surrounding this giant are expressed as ice floes. They encompass a daunting percentage of all the ice in North America, known by such historic attributions as the Bering Glacier, the Bagley Ice Field, the

enormous Seward and seemingly extra-terrestrial Malaspina glaciers, as well as tens-of-thousands of additional miles and cubic volumes worth of glacial crevasse and tumult. Sixty feet of snow fall in any given year on Mount Saint Elias, whose summit, called by local Tlingit Native Americans *Yaas'eit'aa Shaa*, or "the mountain behind Icy Bay"[1] was documented early on by the Russian explorer Vitus Bering (July 16th, 1741). The mountain, when one is fortunate enough to see it in its dazzling splendor, is named after the 9th century BC prophet Elias who was, according to the Old Testament, "taken to heaven in a fiery chariot."[2]

Icy Bay happens to be our destination this day. Ominously, when John Muir visited the region in the Summer of 1879, Icy Bay was barely a blip on the map.[3] Since that time a vast cirque of deep water has accumulated at a rate that would seem to exceed even the most dire prognoses concerning the state of global climate change. All that ice, rock and water is in flux, just as Alaska herself portends of rapid transition, some of it cataclysmic.

Author John McPhee once wrote that if thieves had stolen Italy and were searching for a place to hide it, it would be in Alaska. Moreover, inside Alaska's vast complex of mountain ranges, tundra, rugged coastline beyond compare, and 50% of all ice in the world outside of Greenland and the Antarctica, 39 mountain ranges containing an estimated 100,000 glaciers, 99.4% of them unnamed, Icy Bay harbors a diminutive but emblematic problem: a little bird whose fate, as measured by the number of estimated living individuals—14,000 to 24,000 in the U.S. where it is endemic, and probably others in Russia—hangs upon both known and unknown forces.

The bird is called the Kittlitz's murrelet (*Brachyramphus brevirostris*), a loyal member of the Alcidae family, with its 22 species of penguin-like auks, murres, and puffins.[4] The problem as described by U.S. Fish and Wildlife biologist Michelle Kissling could not be starker. In the last 18 years, 80% of the little bird's population appears to have vanished and the Fish and Wildlife Service was petitioned

3

to list Kittlitz's as an Endangered Species. Following preliminary research, it was entered onto the "candidate species" list for the *U.S. Endangered Species Act.* Michelle feels that, along with the Steller's, spectacled and king eiders, as well as the yellow-billed loon and Eskimo curlew (not seen since 1924), this little murrelet is quite possibly the most critically endangered bird in all of Alaska, and the least understood seabird found anywhere.

It is also one of the most tenacious birds in the world, based upon data thus far obtained, and a fitting icon for the largest protected area on the planet and the conservation passions inherent to such status.

Wrangell-St.Elias National Park and Preserve, at 13,188,024 million acres, is six times larger than Yellowstone National Park. If that weren't superlative enough, at least another 20 million acres of protected area adjoins it, both in the U.S. and Canada, including Glacier Bay and Kluane National Park/Reserves/Sanctuaries, the Kluane Game Sanctuary, the Tetlin National Wildlife Refuge, the Tatshenshini-Alsek Park and the Tongass National Forest. From the air, nearly everything between Anchorage and Juneau appears to be wild and untrammeled, an assessment further borne out on the ground. But it is the actual protection status of so much land that triggered the United Nations World Heritage status conferred upon it in a designation that reads like a dream: "the largest internationally protected wildland on Earth."[5] Here an astounding array of North America's most orgiastic geological tumult, an ongoing collision of tectonic plates, with the resulting highest peaks and biggest glaciers, capped

by the severest weather and inhabited by much of the most elusive wildlife on the continent all begs ecological discovery and enthrallment. Mount Wrangell, writes Jill De La Hunt "is frosted with 250 square miles (64,750 hectares) of ice. Nine of the sixteen highest peaks of the United States rise from the lands of the park."[6]

But it is the power of protection itself that settles most majestically in the enquiring mind: protection for at least 48 known mammal species, many hundreds of native vascular plants, 212 known bird species, far more bears than human inhabitants, wolves, wolverines, lynx and herds of caribou for whom the local Ahtna Indians have at least 20 differentiated names based upon gender, size, and behavior of the animals.[7] The numbers themselves, by comparison, say, with European or tropical inventories, are scant. But in this glacial wilderness, any living creature stands out as a kind of miracle.

Says Meg Jensen, the newly-appointed Superintendent of America's biggest park, "Wrangell-St.Elias is like no other place. It's in a league of its own."

And so is the Kittlitz's murrelet, with its penguin-like bark, graceful eyes, hearty countenance and flippant little butt. For eight months of the year, after breeding on sheer cliffs and tidewater glaciers (those that hit the ocean) it vanishes. Michelle and her colleagues, including chief biologist for Wrangell-St.Elias National Park and Preserve, Mason Reid, have no idea, as yet, as to where this bird disappears (possibly to the Aleutians where dozens of the birds have been discovered), or what it feeds on during much of the year. And, there are a hundred other unanswered questions

fundamental to understanding who this bird is, and why she appears to be heading towards the brink of extinction when, for example, so many other birds breeding the same time of year in remote places like Icy Bay, are not. Those would include "Wilson's and orange-crowned warblers, Lincoln's sparrows, hermit thrush, semipalmated plover, black turnstone, Arctic tern, Caspian tern, glaucous-winged gull and mew gull" as well as the "black-billed magpie."[8]

One thing is clear: the retreat of the glaciers at Icy Bay has provided opportunistic habitat for forest cover which, in turn, has ushered in nesting sites for peregrine falcons and golden and bald eagles. Michelle has seen predation on the murrelets by peregrines (based upon the specific feather types at the base of so-called plucking posts, where the falcons consistently de-feather their meals prior to consumption). That might be one pressure forcing the Kittlitz's (named KIMU for short by Michelle's research team) to seek more and more inaccessible glacial terrain upon which to nest. This question remains unsolved, at present.

Kathy Kuletz, a biologist with the Nongame Bird Management program out of Anchorage, summarized data on the Kittlitz's in 2004 and declared, "Kittlitz's murrelets (also) have many unique characteristics which have enabled them to survive global climate changes since the Pleistocene. Their association with glacially affected waters may make them one of the better barometers of climate change. . . ."[9] Michelle and her team (Leah Kenney, Nik Hatch and Jonathan Felis, along with critical input from Mason Reid and others) have managed to net 37 birds out in the Bay, where between 1,800 and 2,000 murrelets have been counted (nearly 18% of the entire known global population). Once caught, Michelle writes up the birds' medical vitals and takes weights, wing measurements (on average the adults have a single wingspan of 141 millimeters, or 5.5 inches). When reasonable she affixes a radio transmitter (thirty birds thus far have been radio tagged, each with a different frequency to enable aerial monitoring) and then releases the bird. The tracking devices weigh very little and enable Michelle and team to assess at least 30% of the bird's annual reproductive cycle. That includes an incubation period of 28 to 30 days. One month before a newborn can make it on its own, both parents take part in sitting on the egg(s) and going out for food.

Once the KIMU is released out in the Bay with its numerous fjords where the birds are caught (the holding period usually lasts between 15 and 40 minutes), the Kittlitz's frequently makes three large swoops in the air with each loop giving them another 1,000 vertical feet. Some have flown up as high as six thousand feet onto the glaciers of Saint Elias. When they fly back to the water from their nests, the 250 gram bird lifts off like a helicopter. "You have to be amazed by the water temperatures and conditions that these super small birds can survive in," says Michelle.

Upon arrival on a gravel beach, we take off again with the skilled pilot Les Hartley of Alsek Air out of Yakutat for nearly four hours of flying over ocean and glacier, back and forth across the maze of ice fields embroidering the steeps of Mount Saint Elias, tracking several of those tagged birds. One of the nests, perched at nearly 5,000 feet on a sheer wall, is identified by its frequency signature. The parents will fly 25 kilometers out into the Bay four to five times daily, to bring food back to the one or two chicks. This effort translates to hundreds of kilometers per day. In Kuletz' 2004 overview, she suggested that "lack of food" may be one culprit leading to "poor reproduction" as well as "marine vessel traffic," "gillnet fisheries" and, as with other seabirds, "low biological productivity in fjords with receding glaciers, as a result of increased sedimentation and lowered salinity" which would diminish the number of possible species and individual fish available as food sources, the three principal prey species being capelin (*Mallotus villosus*), Pacific herring (*Clupea pallasi*), and sand lance (*Ammodytes hexapterus*). Dietary hard data is now one of the priorities of Michelle, whose team nets tiny pockets along the shorelines in search of what is out there. Deep water netting is not a financial option for her research, as yet.

The extinction factors affecting this and other seabirds have previously been thought of largely in terms of potential oil spills, but there are countless other considerations which include what biologists call the "scale area curve."[10] That refers to a bird's potential geographical range and whether the densities of birds that could be sustained in those ranges are being realized. In the case of the KIMU, it is impossible to say, as yet. As of May 2004, only 25 nests had been discovered in a century, though Michelle and team, in the midst of a bare bones multi-year research project focusing on KIMUs, have increased that number. But the work to be done is daunting. For ex-

ample, among the birds caught, hormone research indicated that there were numerous fecund females but very few ended up actually nesting. Is that due to disease, hunger, immune system problems, or some other mechanism altogether? "We need an understanding of the bird's natural history as a species in order to prioritize where we need to go, what steps we need to take in order to help the species survive into the next generation," says Michelle.

Even more complicated is the fact that the Park does not protect the water, only the land. Michelle hopes that Icy Bay and environs become gazetted as a U.S. Fish and Wildlife Marine Reserve within the National Park/Preserve. That would make fishing off-limits entirely. The traditional Eyak tribe (related to the Athabascan) that lived closest to Icy Bay along the so-called Lost Coast used to hunt the omnipresent harbor seals and glaucous-winged gulls. But those days are over and there is, sadly, but one speaker of the original Eyak language alive today. There is no commercial and virtually no recreational fishing in the area anymore. It is too remote, too filled with dangerous drifting icebergs. It should be a perfect candidate for complete "no kill" protection status. And, by focusing on KIMUs, Michelle's proposed marine reserve would thus protect countless other avifauna, including the pigeon guillemot, loons, mergansers, terns, black oystercatchers, scooters and phalaropes. Moreover, it would complement the National Oceanic and Atmospheric Administration (NOAA)

Aleutian Islands Habitat Conservation Area in Alaska, one of the largest in the world at 280 thousand square nautical miles. The irony is that this latter reserve protects 25 species or subspecies of deep-water corals from various extraction methods (trawls, dredges, pots, et cetera) but does not protect birds on the upper surface of the ocean from deadly longlines. So, while much of Alaska and Wrangell-Saint Elias National Park and Preserve in particular, abound in scale, there are inevitable loopholes for breaching the protective shield. Tragically, at present, the KIMU is ensnared in one such gap.

"Right now for this species it's sort of like protecting their legs but not their wings. Estimating the KIMU's trends and abundance over the next twenty years isn't an option. At the rate of decline we don't have twenty years," Michelle emphasized. Icy Bay and environs are among the last great wilderness on Earth. And this little bird its chief Ambassador. Above one of the glaciers closest to Mount Saint Elias, at six in the morning, the team climbs a mile up tallus slopes to reach a solar-powered video camera trained on one of the nests. Its engineering has proved to be a remarkable achievement for Michelle and team, all the more so because on this day a little chick has been born, the first ever filmed. It is raining but Michelle's tears are unmistakable as she stares down from a discrete vantage upon the sole feather ball of new life.

Later in the summer, Michelle will contact us with deeply unsettling news: this one chick has made it, but the compilation of her research over the brief summer months reveals the startling fact that since 2002 there has been a 53% decline in Kittlitz's murrelets in Icy Bay. Is it an aberration or a systemic trend? Nobody knows for sure.

As we head towards Park headquarters at Copper River Center far to the northwest, the interior presents an entirely different side to the protected area. While the horizons are bridled by glaring storm clouds and by the glaciated giants Mounts Wrangell, Zanetti, Drum, Sanford and Blackburn, it is the black spruce-dominated permafrost, with alder, quaking aspen, cottonwood and other broadleaf that stands out in stark contrast to the coastal zone. The grizzly bears here are also said to be quite different from those on the ocean—hungrier, according to some. When several million acres of Alaskan tundra burned in the massive conflagrations of 2004, according to Smitty Parratt, the Park Interpretation Chief, the ground "wept." Water literally flowed from the unprecedented wounds of the afterblaze. This fragility is easily missed by the nearly 40,000 visitors who make their way to America's largest protected area (about 1% of the millions of people who annually visit the more famous national parks). But if you try and walk anywhere off trail, you instantly sink up to your knees in tundra, moss, permafrost, and a thousand other little plants hanging together in the fragile, cooperative lifeforce that embodies Arctic biology. It is soft to the touch and as vulnerable as the human heart.

Fragility is key to understanding not only the plight of a rarified murrelet, but the vulnerability of every living creature, including the many indigenous tribal people who still inhabit the Park and Preserve. There are nearly one million private acres of land on the inside, and some of the human occupants still subsist as their ancestors did for thousands of years. Their customs, languages and belief systems are as endangered as the other biological species.

There are numerous holes in a park this big, just as modern day conservation strug-

gles to get it right. As Michelle and her team are challenged by the many mysteries of Kittlitz's murrelet, Park Biologist Mason Reid, and his Canadian counterparts are struggling with the plight of the caribou, whose herds have also declined drastically. As for bears, nobody knows how many brown bears exist in Wrangell-St.Elias. There is no invertebrate or amphibian database. Grass species, flowers, epiphytes—each require an expert and this largest of all Parks has a budget for but one staff biologist and a second botanist.

On a glacier beneath Mount Blackburn, little balls of moss literally roll like tumbleweed as their growth warms and sculpts their thin soil underpinnings, until they topple, only to the start the cycle all over again. Their ecodynamics are a mystery, as are the glacier fleas, and a minute species of spider, called by locals a wolf spider, that races across the silt and debris that accumulate on the glacial surface. Atop the myriad nunataks rising as granite pyramids out of the ice are to be found mostly unstudied Pleistocene islands of life whose protection may one day yield up unexpected clues to our own survival as a species.

At night we watch a fly following the flight patterns of the bees, only later in the evening to avoid competition, one assumes, as it, too, pollinates. One could look upon a park such as Wrangell-St.Elias and succumb to the overwhelming sensation that we humans know next to nothing. But such gaps in data are surrounded by one thing we are surely capable of getting right: acknowledgement of our humility and a sense of the presence of sanctity. In spite of countless unknowns, the Park ideal is unambiguous: the act of compassion magnified into a geographically awesome whole far greater than one's self, which defines the very concept of sanctuary, and is fittingly at home in the place called Icy Bay.

A CITY CALLED SAINT FRANCIS

FARALLON ISLANDS NATIONAL WILDLIFE REFUGE AND MUIR WOODS,
SAN FRANCISCO, CALIFORNIA

With well over seven million residents, the San Francisco Bay Area— named for the patron saint of ecology, Saint Francis of Assisi, the friar who spoke to birds, a kind of Doctor Dolittle of Christianity—represents the complex overlay of human pressure characteristic of all big cities. The modern surge of municipalities has left many species vulnerable, their habitat usurped, their lives eclipsed. Sealers, eggers, lumbermen, gold prospectors, developers and non-human bioinvasives are just some of the historic realities threatening the city of mists and dreams. Her beauty lives on, of course, layered in a lyrical fusion of remaining wildness, of which there is much. San Francisco, in part, invented conservation. She was peopled by many wilderness believers, activists and poets. She numbered among her avant garde numerous artists devoted to illuminating places like Yosemite with great painting and photography and thereby promulgated a picture postcard industry, setting hearts aflutter throughout the world with visions of Arcadia.

The city's and regions' ecological vulnerabilities prompted President Theodore Roosevelt to wisely enshrine four fog-enshrouded rocky outcroppings of islands, with a combined size of 211 acres a mere 28 miles west of the Golden Gate, as one of the first National Wildlife Refuges in the United States. Throughout America, Roosevelt safeguarded some 230 million acres, an achievement unequaled in human history.[1] In this case, he had targeted inaccessible towers of storm-lashed granite, covered throughout parts of the year by numerous breeding species of gregarious birds and all of their guano, raucous marine mammals and a few other remarkable rarities as well. A primeval abundance first described as the Farallones in a map dated 1603.[2]

From the air on a clear day one can discern that these jagged peaks rising from a choppy sea are part of an extensive undersea mount, the Farallon Ridge. Michael grew up among the hills of San Francisco able to look out at these mysterious isles and always dreamt of someday going there. We learned that the U.S. Fish and Wildlife Service maintained a strict set of guidelines for visitation. Whale watching boats are allowed to come fairly close. They provide significant wildlife viewing experiences for those yearly 3,000 enthusiasts who brave the three hour journey each way, depending on weather. Actual landings upon the rugged isles is strictly off-limits to all but a few. These fortunates are government representatives, just a few invited ecological advocates each year, and the permanently-placed Point Reyes Bird Observatory scientists who had entered into a long-term contract with Fish and Wildlife to research, monitor and maintain the historic farmstead-research center and the oldest lighthouse on the Pacific Coast. Both structures are situated on the Southeast Island.

In July of 2007, with Refuge Manager Joelle Buffa, we headed out through four-meter troughs aboard the "Superfish" under the expert marine guidance of skipper Mick Menigoz.

The near approach yielded rising fog with a veiled hint of sun and azure sky yet as ominous as Skull Island in the film *King Kong*. At one time Coastal Miwok had a name for the Farallones which translates roughly as "Islands of the Dead." It was a

feared place. The mists swirl, the sea slams, but the real energy is concentrated in the hundreds of thousands of birds that steadfastly guard their nests. Life abounds. Two hundred thousand common murres are present, says Russ Bradley, a resident ornithologist from Point Reyes Bird Observatory (PRBO). Not to mention all of the Cassin's auklets, Brandt's cormorants, double-crested cormorants, pelagic cormorants, pigeon guillemots, tufted puffins, rhinoceros auklets, and Western gulls: at least 300,000 breeding birds in the month of July—the largest colonies in North America outside of Alaska.[3] Including so-called "vagrants," over 400 species of birds have been found at the Farallones. In addition, there are five species of pinnipeds: the California sea lion, Steller sea lion, Harbour seal, Northern elephant seal and Northern fur seal. And, there are the four species of sharks guarding the islands, including great whites, leopard, blue and soupfin, plus various whale species, dolphins and porpoises.

Russ Bradley and his colleagues are looking at reams of information which they have been collecting for years profilng population shifts, reproductive habits, diets and El Niño-Southern Oscillation-related sets of data.

"The Northern fur seal had gone extinct here. They were hunted down to the last one. It took 150 years but they started to come back and are now growing exponentially," Russ explains. "This is a big story." In 1968–69, Southeast Farallon Island,

which we are now traversing, was added to the National Reserve. Four years later Congress designated all of the Farallones, with the exception of Southeast Island, to be a Wilderness, off limits to all of human kind.[4]

Even with such laws in place and a full-time staff of at least two people on the Southeast Island, the boldest of poachers still made their mark and some fishermen continue to hunt illegally within the 948 square nautical miles of the Gulf of the Farallones National Marine Sanctuary (GFNMS) that was created in 1981. Notebooks from the 1970s kept inside the field research house show comments from biologists who still had to contend with hunters sneaking to the Farallones to shoot sea lions point-blank. The murre population had declined by that time to fewer than 6,000 individual birds and there were no Western gulls. But, by 1979 when an ornithological survey was conducted, there were "60,000 common murres, 105,000 Cassin's auklets, 100 tufted puffins, 100 rhinoceros auklets [they had renewed breeding on the Farallones in 1972], 4,000 ashy storm-petrels, 1,400 Leach's storm-petrels and 3,000 pigeon guillemots."[5] Nature had found a way to ensure a comeback.

But, in the 1980s, explains Russ, many of these seabirds, particularly the now abundant murres, were impacted by additional problems: oil spills, gill net fishing, and the continuing poaching of both eggs and birds themselves. A single hunter could wreak carnage.

U.S. Fish and Wildlife made this monument a priority and avifauna and marine mammal populations have spectacularly rebounded, with the exception, perhaps, of Cassin's auklet which has been showing a mysterious and massive decline. Russ and team are trying to figure out what has gone wrong. This particular bird, Cassin's, feeds primarily on krill, the veritable base of the marine food chain. While California legislated a fifty year ban on fishing krill, the causes and consequences for a disappearing species like Cassin's auklet and the blue whale (seen less frequently in the region) are not as yet understood, especially as sympatric species are doing well.

As we attempt to walk along a single trail, the vulnerability of all the creatures crowded everywhere in mass reveals what reckless human intrusion can accom-

plish. Some years ago Russ ran into two trespassers who had shipwrecked in a cove and climbed up a ridge to safety, marooned for the night. "If they'd kept going straight they'd have walked over a ridge right into the sea lion colony not knowing that there were also 900 breeding cormorants that would have flown off leaving defenseless chicks. Gulls would have come in and mass carnage and pandemonium ensued," Russ explains. Another time, trespassers fled upon being detected by scientists, and as they ran down a hill, the trespassers crushed masses of avian burrows.

Such needless harm adds to nature's challenging odds of survival, if you are a bird breeding at the Farallones. A Western gull lays only three eggs a year. Breeding success across an entire colony amounts to no more than one bird per nine eggs. Staking a claim, surviving on these highly competitive nesting sites, requires luck and ruthless competition for survival. The Farallones themselves are lucky to have been recognized by the U.S. Government in time to save their wildlife from total destruction. That conservation impetus is felt and witnessed throughout the San Francisco Bay Area.

Joelle Buffa, supervisory wildlife biologist with U.S. Fish and Wildlife, manages the seven National Refuges in the region, in addition to the Farallones, which include Antioch Dunes, Don Edwards San Francisco Bay, Ellicott Slough, Marin Islands, Salinas River and San Pablo Bay National Wildlife Refuges. That complex abounds in riches: salt marshes, vernal pools, mudflats, the largest heron and egret rookeries in the State, saline ponds, sand dunes, riparian corridors, millions of shorebirds, waterfowl, a black legless lizard, whales and butterflies. The complete list of species represented is vast, and there are Federally-listed Endangered ones, as well. The Don Edwards National Wildlife Refuge alone includes 30,000 acres of "upland, salt marsh, salt pond, mudflat and vernal pool habitats." Joelle's office looks out over that landscape and on a good day she might see the rare salt marsh harvest mouse, or California clapper rail.

These seven National Refuges are only the beginning of the San Francisco greenbelt story, however. There are redwood canyons, forested mountains, grassy head-

lands and exquisite beaches within the 118 square miles (75,500 acres) of the Golden Gate National Recreation Area.[6] San Francisco culture helped shape world conservation culture, in large part due to the influence and lasting legacy of one of the Bay Area's most famous residents, John Muir. Scottish born Muir eventually settled in Martinez, California having married Louise Strentzel in 1880. Their large farm was owned by her family, and Muir settled in, wrote his books, raised two daughters, continued to explore the world and was the proactive genius behind Yosemite National Park in addition to other parks and monuments. In 1888, Muir edited and mostly wrote a book of enormous appeal, *Picturesque California and the Region West of the Rocky Mountains from Alaska to Mexico*.[7] Among the hundreds of illustrations by great artists such as Thomas Hill and Thomas Moran, was an exquisite photogravure from a painting by Julian Rix of Southeast Farallon Island, with its notable lighthouse atop its rocky pinnacle. This represents the celebratory mysticism of Muir to the core. Gretel Ehrlich, in her exquisite profile of Muir, writes "A favored haunt for thousands of sea creatures, the wave-lashed Farallon Islands . . . made the kind of wild Pacific scape that Muir loved."[8] In February 1872, several years before Muir's *Picturesque California*, the great German American landscape painter, Albert Bierstadt visited the islands and made numerous sketches and paintings of the rugged beauty he witnessed.[9]

When the Sierra Club was founded in 1892, John Muir was the first president of the organization. Twenty-two years later, Muir died in a Los Angeles hospital. This was the same year the world lost Martha, the last of the passenger pigeons. These two events occurred in 1914, the year America entered World War I.

Today, Muir's house in Martinez, just northeast of San Francisco, is a National Historic Site within the National Park Service and open to the public. Its elegance remains undiminished, notwithstanding a freeway behind it. During his lifetime, Muir himself maintained an optimism that was infectious. He nurtured the American environmental movement. In fact, the man who created legislation that would engender the National Park Service in 1916, William Kent, named a gorgeous forest grove within the San Francisco Bay Area after Muir: Muir Woods.

Kent had purchased the thickly studded redwood canyon just eight miles north of the Golden Gate in 1905 for $45,000 at a time when the lumber industry was closing in fast. Mount Tamalpais, whose gorgeous summit rises above Mill Valley and Muir Woods, had failed to gain Park status and a railroad line was veering towards the canyon Kent had acquired. The forest's days were numbered. But Kent was a formidable personality and he would persuade the U.S. Chief Forester Gifford Pinchot to get to Roosevelt and have him name the Kent bequest a National Monument. January 9, 1908 this was achieved. Kent then named his gift for John Muir.[10] Today, Muir Woods provides millions of visitors a serene, even solemn experience. It is "the best tree-lover's monument that could possibly be found in all the forests of the world," wrote Muir in a letter of thanks to Kent.[11] One of the coast redwoods (*Sequoia semper-*

virens) within the park stands 254 feet high. Deer wander beside tourists unafraid. Rubber boas cross silently through thick carpets of bryophytes on the forest floor, while flocks of colorful warblers and thrushes migrate in the spring and fall. In the winter, silver salmon and rainbow trout spawn up Redwood Creek, where John Muir was once photographed standing on a bridge in the heart of the woods he so loved.[12] Years later, Jimmy Stewart and Kim Novack would enact a scene from Hitchcock's *Vertigo* there, mesmerized by the primeval quality of the redwood forest.

Mount Tamalpais eventually became a State Park contiguous with Muir Woods and other parks and monuments throughout the Bay Area: Angel Island State Park, Alcatraz Island (with its large bird colonies), the Marina Green, Fort Point, the Presidio, Coastal Trail, Baker, China, and Ocean Beaches, Lands End, Lake Merced, the Bay Area Ridge Trail, the Philip Burton Memorial Beach, and, of course, the 1,013 acre Golden Gate Park, designed by the extraordinary William Hammond Hall in

23

1868.[13] These are just some of the punctuation marks in the Bay Area oasis. Add all of the regions to the immediate North of San Francisco, including Point Reyes National Seashore, Stinson Beach and the Bolinas Lagoon, the sixteen-mile-long Tomales Bay, and one can understand how the earliest indigenous peoples thought of this region as paradise.[14]

Joelle gets out to the Farallones quite regularly, but it is never easy, she says. Most of the time, boats have to turn back due to tumultuous seas, high winds and poor visibility. The islands may languish fewer than 30 miles from the Golden Gate Bridge, but they are unto themselves another world entire.

Speaking about the enforced isolation of the Farallones and the U.S. Fish and Wildlife Service, Joelle looks out to sea and declares, "Our management philosophy on the island has been a hands-off approach in terms of trying to reduce human disturbance as much as possible and still maintain some sort of presence out there. We only allow visitors in very rare circumstances." And she adds, "Teddy Roosevelt is one of my heroes."[15]

A VISION OF URBAN ARCADIA: CENTRAL PARK

NEW YORK CITY, NEW YORK

As early as 1844, when New York City's human population hovered at 312,000, poet William Cullen Bryant called for a park to save the city from "commerce [which was] devouring inch by inch the coast of the island . . . if we would rescue any part of it for health and recreation it must be done now." And he referenced other cities with venerable public park traditions, such as Paris, Vienna, Mexico City, Madrid and London.[1]

When the earliest legislation creating Central Park was enacted July 11, 1851, the land in the Nineteenth Ward was known as Jones' Wood, and it was "to be a public place." That was all. John Jones, a successful tavern owner had purchased the manicured 150 acre "country" estate from the heirs of a smuggler. His family was in no mood to sell their coveted paradise to the city of New York. To their chagrin, the city aldermen promptly snatched it through an act of immanent domain.[2] By

1853, with court hearings, controversies and strident editorials calling for the fusion of rich and poor, the homogenization of all classes into one glorious ecological unison, the vision for this public area had added the Twelfth and Twenty-second Wards, with specific language encompassing "Fifth-ninth-street" to the south, "One Hundred and Sixth-street" to the north, "Fifth-avenue" to the east and "Eighth-avenue" to the west.[3] Three years later, a loan of $2,867,000 at 5% interest was ordained to secure funding for the newly-named Central Park. By April 28, 1858, Frederick Law Olmsted and Calvert Vaux's "Greensward Plan" had been selected by the Board of Commissioners of Central Park, a design that would result in what has unambiguously been hailed "an American masterpiece."[4] Olmsted would write, "Every foot of the park's surface, every tree and bush, as well as every arch, roadway and walk has been fixed where it is with a purpose."[5]

Due to a long history of landscape architecture and the public enjoyment of parklands in Europe, many designers had become celebrities in their own right, like William Kent for Rousham Park, Oxfordshire; Lancelot "Capability" Brown, Master Gardener at Hampton Court Palace; Henry Repton for Woburn Abbey; and André Le Nôtre for the gardens of Versailles. However, Americans had not yet fully embraced the possibilities of creating a uniquely American style of park based on the "Hudson River School" of romantic landscapes. While Mount Vernon and Monticello represented the earliest English landscape-style of gardens (along with the gardens of Williamsburg, Virginia),[6] the concept for New York City was an altogether new and daring undertaking. This was particularly so given the countless conflicting ideologies

at work, and the on-the-ground reality, which included the total reinvention of the landscape along with the simultaneous removal of homesteaders and squatters—the very people some park theorists enthusiastically proposed to merge in a gloriously neutral socio-economic Elysian Field.

Today, that vision bears provocative fruit in the work of such artists as Bruce Davidson, whose black and white photographs unstintingly depict the human diversity which inhabits the park.[7] And, as Doug Blonsky, President of the Central Park Conservancy, says, "I'd like to think that Olmsted and Vaux would be pleased with the park today," adding, that Central Park, one of more than 103 parks in metropolitan New York City, has literally revitalized Manhattan.

The Park is globally stellar in every respect. Imagine the following: 843 acres including 21 playgrounds, 26,000 trees of 200 species, 50 sculptures including the great *Alice In Wonderland* bronze by Jose de Creeft, so generously commissioned by George Delacorte in the late 1950s, and the ever popular *Balto, 1925* by Frederick George Richard Roth, commemorating the heroic husky sled dog who brought desperatedly-needed diphtheria serum one grim winter to the benighted residents of Nome, Alaska.[8] Also found in the park are 5,400 fish representing 11 species found in just one section of one of the bodies of water in the park (including banded killfish, golden shiner, brown bullhead, large-mouth bass, carp, bluegill, pumpkinseed and large goldfish). Fourteen fresh-water vertebrate species are known to live permanently in the Park.[9] Ten mammals include big brown bats, Eastern red bats, Eastern gray squirrel, raccoon, Eastern cottontail, deer mouse, common raccoon, woodchuck and Norway rat

and, recently, a wandering coyote.[10] At least 172 insect species are resident. A modest but omnipresent reptile and amphibian population includes snapping, Western and Eastern painted turtle, Florida cooter, bullfrog, green frog and red-eared slider; and a prodigious suite of 43 different fungal species: among them, a fawn mushroom (*Pluteus cervinus*), and carbon balls (*Daldinia concentrica*), also known as crampballs or King Alfred's cakes, a black fungus that grows on the bark of dead logs, preferably oak. A bite of this is likened to eating a "lump of coal."[11] Surely as intriguing are Central Park's water scorpion, pond leech, water flea and giant pond snail. Crayfish are frequently found meandering over the trails from one source of water to another. We encountered two elderly ladies walking on a path when a large dusty crayfish crossed before them. They had never seen one and were absolutely mystified, wanting im-

mediately to "rescue" the poor fellow before being assured that the large *Procambarus* genus species knew exactly where he or she was going.

Among the butterflies present in the Park are an orange sulphur, Eastern tailed blue, pearl crescent, question mark, red admiral, mourning cloak, silver-spotted skipper, Zabulon skipper, Monarch and three species of swallowtail. The sight of any one of them is sure to make anyone's day.

The plants of Central Park are off the charts. During a 24-hour biomarathon, 837 species were recorded.

Even the microbes and algae are now being investigated. One of Central Park Conservancy's long-time initiatives concerns environmental education and basic scientific research. Native tree and shrub recruitment is studied alongside those non-

natives that were planted in the Park. Wildlife migrations take up a huge part of the study; also, soil analysis, flora and fauna disease vectors, the monitoring of plots to observe regeneration, and the everpresent possibility of finding new species that have made their way into the Park. There is a tradition of introducing bioinvasives in Central Park. One "eccentric New Yorker and Shakespeare fanatic named Eugene Schiffelin felt compelled to introduce all the birds of Shakespeare to the United States."[12] Among those introductions were 60 starlings, not native to the U.S. Today, says Joe DiCostanzo, an ornithologist with the American Museum of Natural History, which faces the Park, those same birds, along with non-native pigeons, and house sparrows, have multiplied to over 200 million in the United States. They "might be considered the Adam and Eve of North American starlings."[13] Some research work is done in collaboration with the Central Park Conservancy's partner, the Black Rock Forest Consortium, based at the 3,830 acre wilderness in the Hudson Highlands, 50 miles north of New York City.[14] One question that fascinates Doug Blonsky and his research associates is why, for example, they're losing ash trees in the Park, whereas the oak and poplars are really doing well.

But it is the 270-odd birds found in Central Park throughout the year that magnificently obsesses a large following of visitors. Consider, for example, the story of Pale Male, a red-tailed hawk who built a nest across the street from the model-boat pond, and brought scores of amateur ornithologists to the site of an on-going saga that became the basis of a marvelous book by Marie Winn.[15] Following birds in Central Park has long been a national pastime. Every season has its share of wonders and loyal nest observers. Spring sees arrivals along the Atlantic Coast Flyway, including the Baltimore oriole. Summer has the ruby-throated hummingbirds. In Fall scarlet tanagers and belted kingfishers grace New York, while winter has been known to provide a setting for a rare boreal owl who sat in the middle of a meadow for three days, mystifying all who saw her.[16] One of those aficionados, an extraordinary (and

generous) ornithologist, and unquestionably the finest photographer of birds in the history of Central Park, is Cal Vornberger (his book *Birds of Central Park* gets a featured cameo in the movie *Night at the Museum*).

We followed Cal Vornberger for a day, throughout the Park, starting at the Boathouse and concluding at the Northeastern corner of the Harlem Meer. He was carrying his immense and heavy arsenal of Canon cameras, 600 mm f/4 image and 400mm f/5–5.6 stabilized lenses, teleconverters, batteries, extenders, Gitzo carbon fiber tripod and Wimberley tripod head.[17] Cal's daily birdwatching forays—a ritual he has maintained for years—are graceful immersions storied by innumerable tales of wonder. He follows the fruiting plants, the seeds, the seasons, and he knows the birds' preferred haunts. That is where he dwells. As for so many New Yorkers, this Park offers time out, a place of dreams and solace into which millions of people disappear, as the birds, frogs, crickets, squirrels, raccoons, herons, as well as legions of dogs all take over.[18]

If you want to be alone in the middle of New York City this is the place. Sit on a quiet park bench, call it your own and ruminate on all the mysteries and beauties of this world. Here the wilderness conjured up by Olmsted and Vaux remains consecrated ground. The sense of a sacred wilderness in the middle of busy lives was partly expressed by Ralph Waldo Emerson; lived by Thoreau (his little cabin at Walden Pond did not prevent his near daily visits to Concord); and pictured with extraordinary lushness by Hudson River resident, Frederic Church (1826–1900): Church's *Heart of the Andes*, an enormous masterpiece that blesses the Metropolitan Museum of Art, which abides within Central Park.

Church was one of the founding directors of that Museum, as well as an appointed member of the Department of City Parks of New York. His commitment to wilderness in art, along with his equal force in shaping New York's own domestic wildness, remains an unmatched legacy within the United States. Americans were not unmoved

by this challenge to their senses and feelings. When *Heart of the Andes* was first unveiled on April 27, 1859 at Lyric Hall in New York City, "its appearance was recorded as one of the landmark events of the American art world."[19] Among the thousands of visitors to come see it was Mark Twain who made repeated pilgrimages to view the painting and wrote, "your third visit will find your brain gasping and straining with futile efforts to take all the wonder in."[20]

Part of the Central Park experience is guaranteed by Doug Blonsky and his staff of 300 employees within the Conservancy. People like Regina Alvarez. Regina began work in the park as a seasonal gardener well over a decade ago. Now, while completing a doctorate in urban ecology, she manages the North Woods, the Ramble and Hallett Nature Sanctuary woodlands. Her enthusiasm, as we spoke beside robins bathing and raccoons playing in full daylight, speaks for itself.

Among Regina's equally enthusiastic colleagues are the police whose task has improved, as the millions of parkophiles increasingly work it out for themselves with occasional hiccoughs as when 40 guinea pigs were found abandoned. But, if ever an arcadian blueprint were to evolve, involving people, lots of people, this would be the laboratory: a living blueprint for how Rousseau's social contract might best be modified and brought to closure. Of course, just when one is ready to wax utopic, the odd purse gets snatched. Ultimately, though, there's no question that the most ardent defenders and disciples of Central Park are the people of New York themselves—and their dogs.

While we urged Cal to consider doing a book on the dogs of Central Park, he wasn't leaping at the idea. He prefers birds and his knowledge of the avifauna here is exquisite. He knows exactly where, in winter, the long-eared owls are likely to appear: "low in a tree near Bow Bridge;"[21] or where the robins are going to build their home: "in the statue of Romeo and Juliet that stands in front of the Delacorte Theatre near the Great Lawn."[22]

Cal's patient love for these avian lives has resulted in an internationally-prized collection of images that speak to the soul. Cal's birds—whether the gentlest spotted sandpiper walking along gravel near The Pool, the indigo buntings at The Ravine, the amazing male Blackburnian warbler hanging out in Tupelo Meadow, or the char-

ismatic female Baltimore oriole "feeding on wisteria" in the North Woods—all tell of nature's bounties and of one man's passion to chronicle these miracles. That such natural beauty can exist in the heart of New York City suggests that humanity—all the 30 million or so visitors who venture to the park each year and those who are uplifted living near to the Park, catching glimpses of it, just knowing it is there—is proof that we can get it right as a species. Proof that the sanctuary concept works. If we can share love with a red-winged blackbird, provide a safe haven for Swainson's thrush and be consistently celebratory about the Eastern bluebird (New York's official State bird),[23] we might just possibly get through another millennium, ensuring that the rest of the Creation gets there with us.

PASTURE OF GREAT SPIRITS: FARM SANCTUARY

UPSTATE NEW YORK

The nature of biology and the biology of nature presuppose not merely an affiliation between humans and other species (what Eric Fromm, in his 1964 book *The Heart of Man*, first called "biophilia," a concept later expounded upon by E. O. Wilson) but our recognition that all life forms are linked together and therefore precious. As a species endowed with a conscience, we have the unique opportunity to appreciate and to act on that appreciation. Though some may feel that an ant is less special than an elephant, Wilson's own Pultizer Prize winning work *The Ants* demonstrates that others see these tiny beings' unique value. The question of whether a chicken deserves less consideration than a blue whale is not going to be answered here, or anywhere else, except in the arms of those who have saved whales from beach strandings and other forms of doom, and saved chickens from slaughterhouses. These are the people who have created safe havens without discrimination. According to nature, all creatures great and small are equal. On the

ground, in the seas, up in a tree, even swarming in our intestines and eyelashes, there is life that has exquisite reasons for being. In the case of so-called farm animals, their lives have been diminished in the long process by which humans have forced them into submission, and onto dinner plates. Unlike their more fortunate domestic counterparts—dogs, cats, and other doted upon animal companions—cows, sheep, pigs, turkeys and chickens are the animals most likely to bear the brunt of human insensitivity. Fifty-two billion farm animals are known to be killed every year for human consumption, according to annual United Nations Food & Agriculture statistics. More recent data by evolutionary biologist Marc Bekoff places the tally at over 30 billion per year *just* in the United States (if one includes fish). No tally exists for the global toll of marine species taken by humans, but it is unquestionally huge given that most fisheries are in precipitous decline. For mammals whose lives will be usurped by humans, the majority of these multitudinous individuals are forever condemned to the unnatural world of factory farming, a mechanical model imposed on a living world. The luckier ones spend their brief lives on small organic farms where they are allowed the good food, fresh air, and freedom of movement all animals (including the human ones) require. But a very, very fortunate few find themselves blessed by sanctuary.

Wild and domesticated animals are inseparable, their genes connected. "Wildness" cannot be entirely bred out of a cow or a chicken, any more than it can be totally eclipsed in a human. That these animals could be viewed and treated with the same wonder and admiration humans mostly reserve for the rare and the free is a personal wish of ours.

In the United States, the *Humane Slaughter Act of 1958* was an important step in the recognition that farm animals should also benefit from anti-cruelty measures. However there is still much more work to be done for these billions of lovely, sensitive creatures; as much or more than for any other group of animals. As governments lag, that work has been the task of individuals, particularly those focused on animal rights and animal welfare, which collectively we call "animal protection."[1]

And, that is also why the farm sanctuary movement has fought a battle like no other. Indeed, conservation biology—the world of national parks and reserves with

their struggles to save endangered species and habitat—have an easier time by comparison.

One of the champions of the animal rights revolution is Gene Baur who lives in Upstate New York where he created one of the first sanctuaries to receive rescued farm animals in the United States. In the beginning, Gene and his former partner Lorri went to stockyards and slaughterhouses to see for themselves what writers like Upton Sinclair had been reporting on for decades. They discovered one story after another: animals left for dead in piles, in trash cans or sprawled across the killing floors in their own blood and feces, still breathing, still capable of being brought back to a rich life. Frequently farmers, ranchers and especially those employed in the industries pertaining directly to the transport and slaughter of animals would beat the animals to stand up, to move into or off trucks and toward the assembly line of death. Gene vowed to do whatever he could to change these outrages about which most honest folks were ignorant.

Gene's efforts began in 1986 with a single gruesome discovery of a sheep he and Lorri named Hilda, one more statistic in a pile of animals left for dead. Hilda had passed out from injuries and heat exhaustion in a cramped truck that had taken her to be slaughtered. Now she would be rescued and rehabilitated at Gene's home in Delaware, in his backyard shed. As the number of rescued animals grew, it became clear that more land was needed. In 1989 he was able to purchase 175 acres near Watkins Glen, New York. Nearly two decades later, Farm Sanctuary has proved a paradise for tens-of-thousands of rescued animals, and a model for the shift in consciousness occurring throughout the world.[2]

The revelatory literature regarding the nightmare that is factory farming is considerable. This was not the case when Gene founded Farm Sanctuary. Details have arisen, in part due to consumer fears about tainted meat and transmissible diseases that were less known a generation ago. Gene, who studied agricultural economics at Cornell College in Ithaca, New York, has come to the realization that factory farms are inherently wrong. "There's no reason for them in this day and age. People are made sick by eating 200 pounds of meat, another 200 pounds of milk and at least 200

eggs per year, on average, in the United States. Meanwhile, the animals have been tortured and slaughtered and the environment is being destroyed as a result. It's a losing scenario for all concerned."[3]

Gene does not lay blame. It is a systemic evil. "Laws need to have social support," he has long stated. "A social context . . . I don't want to put down the guy at the slaughterhouse, but that guy's got to figure out another way to make a living because what they're doing is absolutely wrong and it's bad for them, too."[4]

The grounds and residents of Farm Sanctuary in Watkins Glen (and at their sanctuary in Orland, California) are open to visitors. Families are able to get up close and personal with cows, pigs, chickens, ducks, sheep, goats, and some equines. Those intimate encounters are worth everything. They change minds and hearts. One of the sanctuary's neighbors used to be a hunter. After several years of knowing Gene, he gave up his profession and now grows vegetables. Gene sees the small farming revolution as one answer to big agriculture; a revolution that would involve the near equivalent of "petting zoos" though he refrains from calling them that. Places where people and other species can become reacquainted. Livelihoods can be economically nurtured without recourse to killing, he insists, and Farm Sanctuary shows how that can happen. With annual revenues exceeding $5 million, it's clear that the model of non-violence that the sanctuary movement espouses can be economically viable.

Gene and colleagues also actively engage in education and legal reform work. In the year 2006, Farm Sanctuary sponsored a ballot initiative that was passed in the State of Arizona "outlawing gestation crates and veal crates."[5] Farm Sanctuary spon-

sored events in 44 cities throughout the U.S. devoted to a Walk for Farm Animals day. Farm Sanctuary rescued 120 "broiler" chickens from an abandonment case in Brooklyn, New York; campaigned in Chicago against the cruel practice of foie gras production; issued a scientific report pertaining to "The Welfare of Cattle in Beef Production"; and provided an oasis of peace and love for 1,500 more animals between its two refuges that year.

At the same time, Gene has continued to campaign to prevent the suffering of downed animals; to promote more humane standards in New Jersey; to institute a national ban of battery cages and gestation crates; and other reforms he views as essential within the American Veterinary Medical Association. That's for starters. Farm Sanctuary issues "go vegetarian" checkbooks which also read: Stand Up For Animals. They sell vegan cutlets, soy milk, books and videos; and they provide information on where to dine vegan within their area (a remarkable 31 different restaurants throughout the Ithaca region).

With resident ambassadors Charlotte (a pig), Phyllis (a chicken), Grace (a sheep), Snowflake (a hen), Hannah, Gideon and Isaiah (turkeys), Linda (a cow), and Dagwood (a rabbit), to name but a few of the educators who inhabit Farm Sanctuary, this wonderland is an ultimate icon of love and respect that could inform environmental and social justice movements worldwide. What Gene and his colleagues teach is that humans have the capacity for unconditional love. This might be the solution to our other woes as a species. If we can make peace with the Lamb of God, then perhaps we can learn to respect and cherish each other.

At sunset, we sit with Gene looking out over pastures consecrated for these resident animals and we chat about the sanctuary movement, what he hopes to accomplish, as well as some of the difficulties.

He begins, "I guess that prayer you know, 'give me the strength to change things I can, the serenity to accept the things I can't change and the wisdom to know the difference.' That really is a very important way of maintaining your composure in doing this work for a long time when there are things that are completely ethically intolerable and you are nearly incapable of changing them."

Gene points out that there is "this amazing fear" within the agricultural industries themselves, a knowledge that "deep down [they] know their behavior is harmful and violent." All that violence is obscured by profitability and the fact the industry is entrenched. By that he means connected to a system of tax exemptions and subsidies

and other preferential treatment by the government, like cheap access to water. The companies are exempt from anti-trust laws and even "the minimum wage is lower than the normal minimum wage," he adds.

In the end, while dreaming of the day when the entire world might become a non-violent community (which would include a widespread vegan diet for all Americans) Gene is especially ardent in his commitment to combating the whole system of factory farming.

His optimism is uncommon. He actually posits his Garden of Eden where, he says, "We would live along with other animals. We would go down to the river to drink and the deer would be there drinking and the deer would not be afraid and we would not be afraid."

What about international pressure on consumers, we ask. "I think that consum-

ers play a huge role and they need to be more aware and more involved in their food choices. Unfortunately, we're social animals who tend to do what others around us do. And a lot of us are behaving in very bad ways. We need to figure out how to reach people and just sort of wake people up."

To Gene, we suggest the following scenario: Imagine Upstate New York and the rest of the country having 500 farm sanctuaries where people visit the way they go wine-tasting, staying at B&Bs like the one at Farm Sanctuary. It would be like the New Zealand farmstay, with a twist. People would pay to have joyful commune with cows and pigs and sheep and turkeys (like Chickey, one of our favorites from earlier that day). Wouldn't that be wonderful for the whole family and all of nature!

"I love the sound of that!" Gene exclaims.

DR. RUSSELL MITTERMEIER AND THE LAST GREAT TROPICAL RAIN FOREST

CENTRAL SURINAME NATURE RESERVE, SURINAME

"Trees never feel themselves really trees nor perform their duty until they are there in numbers. Then, at once, everything is transformed: sky and light recover their first deep meaning, dew and shade return, peace and silence once more find a sanctuary."[1]

Those calming words by Belgian botanist, and Nobel Prize-winning poet Count Maurice Maeterlink are not entirely to be trusted, one must acknowledge, as Dr. Russell Mittermeier pauses, then gazes into those same trees with palpable

apprehension. One by one large cracking sounds explode through the air. We start to run as an avalanche engulfs the forest all around us, coming close enough to convey a strong sense that we are all about to die.

Finally, Maeterlink's blessed silence resumes, but not before a huge tree, probably 40 meters tall, had seized this moment to collapse.

Says Mittermeier, "That is by far the greatest danger of all in the rainforest."

That, and industrial trespass.

Back in 1973, Russell Mittermeier was working on his thesis at Harvard University, hoping to obtain field data on two rare South American primate species, the uakari and saki monkeys. Virtually nothing was known about them in the wild. After examining the necessary logistics (Mittermeier estimated he'd need five years, living in remote, flooded jungle areas of Brazil to find them and do justice to his thesis), he ended up in Panama, instead of Brazil, where he heard from a Dutch scientist about a remarkable location in Dutch Guyana ("Suriname" since its independence in 1975) where a population of bearded saki monkeys could be found.

With another scientist who planned to study spider monkeys, Mittermeier decided this was the place for his research, along the Coppename River with its rapids, small waterfalls, and adjoining tepuis, or flat topped sandstone mountains, like those of the Tafelberg. For the next three years he spent much of the time in a wet

tent beneath an enormous granite cliff, or inselberg, the 250 meter high Voltzberg, observing all eight primate species co-habiting the region botanically known as Amazonian Hylaea (referring to the forest type, "luxuriant" by ecological standards).[2] Mittermeier spent months following and watching the monkeys, and also observed local hunters, visited their camps and the dumps behind villages largely unknown then to the outside world. There he developed the ability to identify skulls left over from human meals. A grisly, disheartening task, this experience gave Mittermeier inspiration for his commitment to conservation. He also learned Sranan-Tongo, also known as Surinamese, or Taki Taki.

When he obtained his Ph.D. at the end of 1977, he returned to Suriname for another two years of research further fueling his resolve to find ways to help Suriname protect its remarkable biological heritage. At the same time, Mittermeier was extending these beliefs into a global doctrine which would ultimately become his signature, the conservation concept of "hotspots."[3] That scientific method for saving the largest aggregates of endemic species at risk would take Russell Mittermeier to more than half of all the nations of the world, and propel his organization, Conservation Inter-

national (CI), into a position to actually help nations save tens-of-millions of acres of precious habitat, which is exactly what he has done.

While Suriname is not in the Amazon Basin, there is Amazonian connectivity with Guyana to the west, French Guyana to the east and Brazil due south. But Suriname's rivers, like the Coppename, are independent of the Amazon, all flowing from the south to the north and into the Atlantic. It is there, on the coast, where Suriname's capital, Paramaribo is to be found; with a central district that is now a UNESCO World Heritage Site containing the oldest synagogue in the New World.

The river systems of Suriname are so pure, and there is so much water, that this country has more drinking water per capita than any other nation. The country's population was under 500,000 as of mid-2007, and projections indicate the demographic profile will not change even in the next half-century.[4]

Moreover, more than 95% of the country's natural habitat remains untouched across the nation's nearly 40 million acres of land, a region of nearly 163,265 square kilometers, equivalent to the size of Java, Wisconsin or Bangladesh. But consider, in the case of Java and Bangladesh, populations well over 100 million people, compared with Surinmame's half-million. Explanations for such differences are rooted, among other things, in cultural norms with respect to perceptions of ideal family size, women's educational opportunities and economic advantages. With a per capita income of US $8,120 and 10% of the country's pristine territory enshrined under the protected umbrella of the Central Suriname Nature Reserve (CSNR) where Mittermeier researched for his Ph.D., Suriname offers a near nationwide sanctuary. No other country can come close to matching its conservation commitments or cultural paradigms. One can easily see why Mittermeier has called it home since his days at Harvard.

So did one of the most famous botanists in history, Daniel Rolander, who spent seven months in the jungles in 1754, at the urgings of his friend and mentor, the great Swedish botanist Carl Linnaeus. Rolander would complete a 699-page overview of Suriname, *Diarium Surinamicum*. Mittermeier's own dissertation was closer to 800 pages. Unlike Rolander, who returned to Sweden never to see Suriname again, Mittermeier would return again and again, transforming his personal love affair with the country into direct assistance enabling the nation to set aside the 1.6 million hectares as the CSNR. He would accomplish this near-miracle with deep knowledge, passion, and all the resources and global partnerships he could muster as President of Conservation International (CI), based in Washington, D.C. Because of Mittermeier, and the extraordinary data he has been able to reveal to the scientific and philanthropic communities, CI has been in the fortunate position to be able to spend approximately US$15 million dollars on its conservation work there.

Populated by Amerindian tribes, including Carib, Arawak, Waiyana, Trio, Wayarikule, Wama and Akuliyo"[5] as well as Creoles, Hindustanis, Javanese, Chinese, European Jews, and the varied descendants of slaves who obtained freedom under the Dutch during the 18th century, the geopolitics, like Suriname's biodiversity, yields a startling palette.

When we joined him in the fall of 2007, Dr. Mittermeier was in Surimame to accomplish two noteworthy goals. First, to turn over the CI-managed CSNR to the government in a formal ceremony at Raleigh Vallen, an eco-tourist lodge not far from Mittermeier's old jungle research basecamp, and named after Sir Walter Raleigh who allegedly traveled there searching for the original Garden of Eden. Second, he would meet with the granman, or chief of one of the Amerindian tribes, the Trio, located in a village called Kwamalasamutu far to the South, outside the CSNR, on the remote Sipaliwini River, to try to convince the chief that he and his 700 or so people could profit economically by setting aside thousands of hectares of their territory as conservation reserve lands. His goal was to try to persuade the chief that there would be future revenue streams in the form of carbon sequestration subsidies on the world market. He was not sure, as yet, how to explain such intricate economic machinations to a Trio chief, when he, himself, was not exactly certain how or when the whole deal would work. But, he knew it was hope for their future, just as he divined the importance to Suriname of setting aside such remarkable sanctuaries, as the CSNR back in the 1970s. If anything, Mittermeier is a visionary whose kinetic genius is infectious, generous and childlike.

Mittermeier's methodical frenzy to get land set aside and provide economic options for indigenous people dwelling therein is part of his vision to ensure protection for the entire Guyana Shield. His target region comprises upper Amazonian forest that spreads contiguously across some six hundred thousand square kilometers. If Mittermeier succeeds in getting the various world leaders and tribal chiefs to agree on these proposed protected areas (and he is nearly there) he will have helped put together deals resulting in the largest tropical rain forest protected corridor left on Earth. "Helped" is how Mittermeier would put it. Mittermeier, himself, is the author and tireless architect behind this remarkable conservation achievement, of which

Suriname's CSNR is the heart and soul, with conservation tentacles extending all the way to Amapa State in northern Brazil, French Guyana, Guyana, and parts of Columbia and Venezuela.

Later, as Mittermeier climbs the Voltzberg in his socks (providing traction on granite after a downpour where one slip is certain death), the origins of his passion emerge. As a kid, he explained later that night, with a tremendous lightning storm all around us, he was absorbed by the Tarzan books. Unaffected by heat, humidity or the instincts, which, in most people, translate into fear of snakes, biting insects and disease, Mittermeier shows only an abiding love of the jungle, although he admits he has gotten nearly every disease one can get in the tropics, other than malaria. He's been lucky with reptiles, and pirhannas. Nothing serious. His mother shared his love of the jungle and would read to him about exploration when he was a kid. The message sank in. By November of 1977, when he finished writing his dissertation, he got a grant from the World Wildlife Fund to work on the Atlantic forest primates of Brazil, and also started writing what would become a 300-page document entitled, "Global Strategy for Primate Conservation." After about 18-months with the New York Zoological Society, Mittermeier became a fulltime scientist with the World Wildlife Fund (and, eventually, Vice President for Science with direct responsibilities for the programs in Brazil, the Guyanas and Madagascar). He held that job until he was asked to become President of the newly-formed Conservation International in the spring of 1989. To his chagrin, a few weeks after arriving at CI, he discovered they were in financial trouble. But Mittermeier's remarkable grasp of global conservation issues would help the organization turn its future around, and into a 100—million-dollar-a-year success story.[6]

Initially, that success arose as CI embraced corporate donors who recognized the importance of joining forces with a conservation organization that knew how to save land and people's lives, especially in areas of high biodiversity. Now, that same collaborative zeal has infiltrated corporations who know it is in their best interest, and that of the planet, to become carbon neutral. Countries like Suriname offer such companies a handhold that is the perfect fit: incredible forests still remaining, unique species and a rich cultural heritage. All that Suriname asks in return for conserving its forests is a revenue stream that can mitigate adverse economic pressures within the country. When that formula is realized, or grown into a global strategy with the same market base as other forms of equity, then the carbon enigma shall have been overcome.

For the past year, Mittermeier has been immersed in trying to figure out how the Kyoto Protocol can become an economic bonanza for such countries as Suriname. Now, he thinks he's on to it and the Chief Business Correspondent from the *Chicago Tribune*, David Greising, who joined him on this trip to meet the Trio Chief and climb the Voltzberg, is anxious to understand how such ecosystem services and the much discussed asset-laden concept of "avoided deforestation" will play out. Not only in terms of the 25% or so of carbon which destroyed rainforest emits into the atmosphere, but the tropical forest soils, which have now been seen to contribute carbon, as well, based on research done at the South African National Biodiversity Institute (SANBI.) This combined burden of CO2 ups the ante, as far as Mittermeier and other scientists can tell. It means that with every lost hectare of rain forest, or, conversely, every hectare that is saved, the carbon equivalent is sizeable.

CSNR was named a UNESCO World Heritage Site in 2000, thus boosting the country's commitment to "conservation-based development" and providing its political cadre "a new leadership role in global biodiversity conservation."[7]

Part of that leadership comes from the indigenous peoples who depend on their traditional lands. For the Trio, that means ensuring protection for that land because there are no provisions, as yet, within Suriname law for demarcation of the different tribal holdings, as there are in Brazil. New conservation or carbon concessions, or different ways of thinking about traditional resource use categories, are mechanisms, says Mittermeier, than can help the indigenous people gain title to their lands, as well as providing financial incentives to protect them.

These people get hungry, like anyone else. When leaf-cutting ants devour their cassava, or their farms are flooded out, rice does not fill their bellies, they tell us. To date, their micro-slash and burn agriculture, which we see from the air, seems of little consequence. There is no road for hundreds of kilometers. Access is by river, by foot through jungle for weeks if not more and an occasional plane lands on an unlikely clearing after flying two hours from the capital. Fuel is prohibitively expensive. The outside world has scarcely ventured here. In the early 1960s, when the Trio first encountered Caucasians, they fled into the jungle, thinking them cannibals. Today, they seem more accustomed to outsiders and that makes their future considerably more uncertain.

The stakes are huge. Mittermeier knows that Suriname, both the areas that are protected, and those that are not, contains what he terms "fully intact faunal assemblages." That means the biodiversity reflects the "full range of species in their original abundance un-impacted by the presence of humans. You find all your predators there, healthy prey populations, perfectly functioning intact forest system. There are just not a lot of places where that exists. In many regions the big predators have been killed, or exist in extremely low numbers, and that changes completely the dynamic of the system. So, not only is this precious area important in its own right, but it's also important to be able to measure it in relation to what is happening in other more heavily impacted areas." Remarkably, the entire Central Suriname Nature Reserve is devoid of inhabitants. The Trio tribe lives far to the south of it.

Our five days together in the jungles of Suriname underscore the stunning meaning of "intact faunal assemblage." We would fly in a small charter aircraft from Paramaribo South, 45 minutes to a dirt landing strip at Raleigh Vallen, head up river to the CI research station, where a scientist from Florida has been doing his studies, and spend the night beneath the Voltzberg, visiting a rocky area known for some forty resident spectacular orange cock-of-the-rock avians (*Rupicola rupicola*) and find them almost immediately at their year-round courtship grounds (known as a lek). Mittermeier had discovered the site back in the 1970s. It is still a place cloaked in virtual invisibility. Without a guide, nobody could ever find it, let alone retrace his footsteps. It was in this spot that the tree avalanche occurred. More sensible people might have taken this near miss as a cue to call it quits for the day. But we all agreed, despite a thunderous downpour of rain, making all the rock faces dangerously slippery, to attempt an ascent of the famed Voltzberg with its native succulent cacti, sheer faces and phenomenal glimpses over the endless, untouched canopy of the Nature Reserve in all directions. With so much water flowing down the granite walls, our only option was to climb in our socks, a means of providing more traction. Mittermeier had

done it this way before and his confidence paid off. The team was safely off the cliff by darkfall.

The following day, we flew nearly two hours further south over undeviating pristine jungle, no evidence whatsoever that a human being had ever been there, landing at the sudden circular clearing known as the village of Kwamalasamutu. Surrounded on all sides by endless tropic, this was the place Mittermeier had come for meetings late into the night with the Chief and his allies. We would also take a dug-out canoe with outboard motor west along the Sipaliwini River and then trek several kilometers to a series of caves discovered in 2002. Known as Wherephai, the cave system contains hundreds of stone carvings, some 5,000 years old. Among the more than 300 petroglyphs thus far discovered here by the only people ever allowed to venture near are spider monkeys, parrots, men and women, and an artful conscience at work. Some of the species configured in the rock may well be new to science.

During our various journeys throughout Suriname, the abundance of species either seen, or heard, was astonishing. The country itself has a large number of species: 722 birds, 185 mammals, 152 reptiles, 95 amphibians and 790 fish species, of which about 3% are endemic, with a majority of these found within the CSNR.[8] During our time there, we encountered an adult red-footed tortoise (*Geochelone carbonaria*), numerous lizard and frog species (the latter, of the *Phyllobates* genus), a rarely seen blind snake that lives underground (of the genus *Leptotyphlops*), spider, squirrel, howler and capuchin monkeys, white-eyed parakeets, smooth-billed anis, black vultures, white-throated toucan, black nightjar, screaming piha (the most ubiquitous sound in the forest), a white hawk and osprey, a black curassow, and numerous scarlet and red and green macaws, in addition to a pet mealy parrot. For starters.[9]

On the night of October 16, 2002, just shortly after the Wherephai caves were discovered by a Trio Indian named Kamania looking for his lost dog, CI scientists had placed a camera trap there. On that one night, the camera recorded jaguars, ocelot, giant anteater and armadillo. During our trek to and from the caves, it's likely that a jaguar was in front of, or close to us: fresh feces and the remains of devoured peccary made it abundantly clear. The jaguar knew we were there and was probably watching

us the entire time we trekked in the area. This magnificent trail, thick in leaf litter, was his. He owned it.

Insects and amphibians, as well as the occasional reptile, were not shy about showing themselves. Some of these, particularly among the insects, were unknown to Mittermeier, or anyone else on the team. But this is not surprising. In June of 2007, an expedition by 13 CI scientists to the Nassau Plateau in remote eastern Suriname uncovered 24 new species.[10]

Mittermeier believes that the interior of Suriname may well be "the most pristine, the least disturbed piece of tropical rain forest left on the planet. It probably is already," he says, as we reach the summit of the Voltzberg near to sunset, mists roiling across the jungle on all sides of us. Not only the most pristine in terms of lack of human disturbance, but also among the largest untouched stretch of tropical forest. While only 13% of Suriname is fully protected within 14 reserves, including CSNR, the majority of the country, including so-called multiple-use areas, remains incredibly wild. Only around the capital city, Paramaribo, is there evident desforestation and riparian pollution. Suriname contains more rainforest than all of Central America combined, and more than all but perhaps two countries in Africa (the Democratic

Republic of the Congo and Gabon). Borneo is losing its rainforests quickly, and New Guinea has high indigenous populations and levels of threat to its mountain rainforests. Suriname's tiny population and uninhabited reserves are coupled with very little threat in the distant future. The country's exports are dominated by alumina, oil and gold, but as of 2006, alumina (bauxite deposits being the principal ore of aluminum) accounted for 46.2% of the nation's total exports, and these were principally confined to two mines, outside the existing forests.[11]

But, as the country's Minister of Physical Land Planning and Forestry, Dr. M. John Tjie Fa, admits, the pressures are mounting for more and more income and the challenges to sustain Suriname's spectacular conservation gains to date will intensify in coming years. That's why Tjie Fa is also particularly anxious to see what the global marketplaces are going to do with standing forests, and how they are likely to assign market values to biodiversity. He wants to be able to benignly profit from his country's restraint and points out that in his view, even the so-called sustainable 20 cubic meters per hectare of forest extraction—the global mantra—is meaningless in a tropical rainforest, where any disturbance whatsoever is problematic. To hear him speak of the Central Suriname Nature Reserve as the original Garden of Eden is indeed encouraging. He wisely appreciates what his country still has; but he is under unsettling pressure, given the 21st century's demands for production and profit. The World Bank, for example, recently cited Suriname as "among the 17 potentially richest countries in the world" due to its natural resources, mostly unexploited as of yet.[12] It was BHP-Billiton Maatschappij Suriname (BMS) and Suriname Aluminum Com-

pany LLC (Alcoa's subsidiary, Suralco) that sponsored the CI-led expedition which discovered all the new species in June 2007. The stakes were difficult to imagine: two major companies looking for new motherloads, and the country's foremost conservation organization leading the expedition, driven by a sense of responsibility for shaping the future sustainably.

Eco-tourism will certainly play a role. But at present, fewer than 50,000 tourists come each year. CI is working to change that, by providing the resources and training to encourage an increasingly user-friendly and sophisticated eco-tourism infrastructure in the country. The wonderful facilities at Raleigh Vallen are one example.

But ultimately, the sheer value of biodiversity, and the pristine forests so crucial to that ecosystem integrity, will need to be defined and appreciated by the financial communities of the worlds. In the meantime, despite increasing pressures, the Suriname model is certainly working, with 90% of the country's tropical forests in place. Both Minister John Tjie Fa, and the Granman, Chief Ashonko Alalaparoe, are optimistic.

On our last night in the jungle, I asked the Chief how he would characterize Dr. Mittermeier. He thought about that, and finally declared, "Russell is a man who helps others."

THE IBERIAN WOLF SANCTUARY

PORTUGAL

When Francisco Fonseca was four years old, he was sleeping in the backseat of his family's car when his father skidded to the side of the road and shouted "Wolf!" The boy gazed upon the hazy ghost of what appeared to be a large friendly dog disappearing in the forest beside the highway and forever vowed to learn more.

Today, the 54-year old professor of biology at the University of Lisbon, is co-founder of Grupo Lobo, the conservation biology/animal welfare organization of Portugal devoted to saving the *Canus lupus signatus*, the Iberian wolf, from extinction.

"I simply love them. I admire them. Sometime I wish I could be one of them—absolutely free, wandering throughout the mountains, pure and untroubled," he says, reminiscing on that moment in childhood, as we prepare to enter the large forested enclosure at the Lobo Iberico sanctuary about 45 minutes north of Lisbon (depending upon traffic), near the hilly farming villages of Picao, Gravil and Malveira. Fonseca's colleague, Filipa Marcos, a 29-year old Portuguese biologist, tosses three kilos of fresh chicken meat over the nine-foot-tall chain-link fence

that extends around the multi-hectare enclosure. Inside is Prado (his name means open clearing or pasture in a forested area). Prado is an 11-year-old alpha male. He has mixed feelings about Filipa, she admits, without knowing why. Apparently Prado is not entirely thrilled with any human females and will growl and pretend to threaten them should they dare to come inside. He seems to love men.

"I cannot guarantee his behavior," says Francisco, a polite way of suggesting we remain outside the enclosure. "Last week the veterinarian made his rounds and the wolves hate veterinarians. It takes many days for the trauma to wear off. Prado might associate you with the vet."

Francisco goes inside, not in the least worried. Prado has known him all his life. Not needing to go inside, we remain with Filipa.

The 40 kilogram male, about as large as an Iberian male wolf ever gets, is not visible. He rests in the shade up on the hill beneath a dense forest of native cork trees. The cork tree is in serious decline, says Francisco, because international bottle makers are replacing one of Portugal's oldest industries—cork stops for wine—with plastic.

As the demand vanishes, fewer landowners find cork trees (a species of oak) valuable and let them go before the onrush of new types of development and forest clearance. Here at the wolf sanctuary, the cork trees, like the wolves and a host of other native species, are carefully nurtured.

The shade provides a welcome relief in the summer, when the wolves shed most of their coat, except around the neck, and suffer in temperatures that can approach 50 degrees celsius. It was such heat combined with a serious drought that triggered the outbreak of fires all over Portugal in 2003 and 2005. Abbetted, it is widely believed, by pyromaniacs. "Portuguese often engage in neighborly disputes by wantonly setting fires," remarks Filipa.

The 11 wolves and 17 hectares which comprise the Grupo Lobo Iberian Wolf Sanctuary sit beside the Tapada de Mafra, the historic summer palace of the kings of Portugal, on a 1,000 hectare preserve once used for hunting. In the fires of 2003, the estate was caught up in an intense conflagration, where fires on five fronts swept through the native pine and non-native eucalyptus, killing wild boar, red and fallow

deer and asphyxiating two Iberian wolves lent to the park by the Wolf Sanctuary. This tragedy was not the first.

The region itself, from the perspective of wolves, has presented an enormous challenge to their survival. A map of Iberian wolf distribution throughout the country, detailed by Francisco and his research associates, shows that as recently as 1930 there were Iberian wolf packs (typically consisting of between five and eight individuals) throughout most of the country. As of 2003, the last census, those figures were markedly diminished with the total estimated number of wolves in Portugal at no more than 300. Eighty percent of the wolve's territory has been burnt, developed, paved or fragmented. In addition to Portugal's wolf population, there are approximately 2,200 wolves in Spain. That is the entire remaining extent of this rare sub-species, listed as Vulnerable by the IUCN. But in Portugal, the species is Critically Endangered, particularly south of the River Douro in the far north of the country where no more than 30 wolves remain. The other 270 are scattered between three national parks and buffer areas to the North of the river.[1]

"The Portuguese farmers hate them. Traditional Christians hate them. And Portugal is a Christian, farming-based nation," says Francisco.

Prado does not show himself yet. Francisco comes back outside the fence, and we wait for the gloriously beautiful male to appear. He does so, taking his chicken meat with a kind of restrained, almost embarrassed dignity. While standing in the windy spring morning, the professor explains many of the problems that will make or break the future survival of this absolutely magnificent, stunningly precocious animal that he so adores.

"Our religion equates the wolf with the devil and the sheep—which wolves occasionally consume—with God." Never mind that humans kill sheep in vast quantities and wolves, by most national estimates, take no more than 1% of any flock. In the early 1950s, a wolf attacked and killed a Portuguese, injuring another. Those who witnessed the attack have never forgotten it. Firstly, it is the only documented killing of a human being by a wolf in Portuguese history. And second, those who saw the attack knew there was something wrong with the wolf. They decapitated the animal and had it medically tested. Sure enough, that wolf had been deathly ill, stricken with rabies. "Otherwise," says Francisco, "such an attack would not have happened." Indeed, Portugal's nearly 10 million inhabitants have nothing to fear from the 300 remaining wolves.

"What is at risk here is the wolves' own existence. And should we lose them, which is possible, we shall have lost one of the most iconic species. The fact is, farmers set traps for them, poison them with strychinine, which is illegal, and shoot them, which is also illegal."

Professor Fonseca was instrumental in obtaining legislation from Parliament that safeguarded the wolf in Portugal as of 1988. But the law is only on paper. The building of highways, subdivisions and hydro-electric plants has always proceeded at a pace little moderated by lawmakers in this country, where economic zeal now has the added burden of finding a way out of increasing economic marginalization, particularly since the country joined the European Union. This quasi-socialist nation has a low minimum wage and a large number of poor people, their monthly salary averaging 400 euros. The country is ranked behind Greece in all of Europe, at the economic nadir, along with the island of Sicily. Such statistics do not make wolf protection any easier. Moreover, eco-tourism in Portugal has hardly begun. Most tourists come for the beaches, the Madeira wine and the Azores. They are not yet looking for wolves in the mountains.

The Iberian wolf is debated by taxonomists, some arguing that there are only two sub-species, *Canus lupus lupus* and *Canus lupus familiaris*. But, many scientists recognize the Iberian *signatus* as a bona fide subspecies. And indeed, the physiological differences are ascertainable at a glance. They are smaller, their teeth and markings and fur are different. There may be other differences, as well, but the behavioral ecology of the species is little known, despite Fonseca's lifetime of devotion and observation. They have one litter a year, usually in May. Gestation is over 60 days, the burrow often times very shallow. Pups number typically five, but can be as low as two, as high as six. By two years of age the alpha and omega males will likely go different directions, but not always. The others are intensely loyal, dutiful and loving to their young. The packs are close-knit, and not infrequently more than one pack will reside

together. In the early 1900s, a Portuguese hunter who loved wolves reported seeing 18 wolves together.

Filipa's mother is an English teacher and her father an air conditioning engineer. But their parents, and several relatives, are sheep farmers. "They absolutely detest wolves," she says. "Always they are asking me how on earth I can work with wolves. One of these days a wolf will most certainly attack and try to kill me, they insist." She smiles ruefully, "If I cannot persuade my own family to change their viewpoint, imagine how difficult it is to alter the mindset of strangers; farmers who for many generations have hated and tried to kill wolves."

It is indeed a challenge to change peoples' minds about the noble wolf, but it is to this challenge that Francisco is committed. He has taught farmers about the four species of guard dog that can help mitigate the infrequent wolf attacks. Hunters and environmentalists, he says, are now fairly aligned in their love and admiration of the wolf. It is the city dweller and sheep farmer who have a long way to go.

"The uniqueness of the Iberian Wolf (endemic to the Iberian Peninsula) is, in part, its ancient relationship to humans," says Francisco, "dating back at least to the Meso-lithic period, five or six thousand years ago. While there are indeed misconceptions among farmers about wolves and systematic wolf killings, Grupo Lobo has been working hard to correct many of the misconceptions. People and wolves can live side by side. No problem. By introducing the guard dogs to farmers, we have also promot-ed animal welfare for dogs. The farmers used to abuse their dogs. No more. Now they take them to the vets. They rely on them to protect against wolves."

The Portuguese government produces a monthly valuation sheet on livestock and will compensate farmers whose sheep or cattle or goats have been killed by a wolf. The problem, says Francisco, is that some farmers cheat. They will claim that it was a wolf that killed their sheep, whereas it could easily have been their own negligence. So Grupo Lobo encourages the government to be cautious in its response to the submission of claims so as to prevent abuse of the system. In reality, the vast majority of sheep mortality results from natural causes or farmer negligence, not from wolves.

With millions of sheep in the country, and only a few wolves, the predation statistics are fairly obvious. Wolves, by and large, are benign.

Of the nearly 6,000 visitors each year to the Wolf Sanctuary, the children, Francisco says, are particularly amazed by the wolves. For 35 euros one can adopt a wolf, and many do. The money is critical to keeping the Sanctuary going, because it gets little government support, other than a basic tax exemption (which does not extend to the money generated from the sale of postcards). For conservation here money is everything: a base cost of 60,000 euros a year provides the veterinarian care, staff

salaries, upkeep, ecological restoration and 99 kilograms of fresh meat every week. Each of the 11 wolves eats three kilos of meat three times per week. Occasionally they will supplement their diet by eating vegetation. They also consume a lot of water which, fortunately, is plentiful in the valley where the Sanctuary is located. Local people have come to admire the Sanctuary, says Filipa, probably because Sanctuary staff utilize their services and buy coffee, food and other things. There are now signs posted everywhere pointing in the direction of the wolves.

The animal welfare "bug" seems to have caught on. In an adjoining village, a friend of Filipa's, Diogo Pimenta, has started an Association for the Protection of the Portuguese Burro, Burricadas. Portugal has one native breed indigenous to the country, the Miranda. While it slightly resembles the French Poitou towards whose genetic future the Miranda has been cross-bred, it also differs, in its bay coat, enormous lips, and overall equipoise (what some have called "corpulent and rustic"). A true symbol of the country, the Miranda has interbred for centuries with white African donkeys and black Catalonians, such that very few pure Mirandas are left. [2] Burricadas has eleven of these exquisite creatures. Diogo Pimenta and others are doing everything in their power to teach farmers that these magical creatures should not be oppressed, abused or killed, but rather adored. Also in the north of Portugal, in the Miranda Do Douro Parish and Plateau, a second organization is dedicated to protecting the breed from extinction, the Natural Reserve of Douro Internacional.

"Farmers have a long way to go in terms of real animal welfare consciousness in this country," says Diogo. But his smile and dedication are infectious and already one landowner has turned over the use of his meadows to the animals for grazing. Now all they need is money for the fence and veterinarian care.[3]

Prado has consumed his breakfast of chicken. After twenty minutes, he returns up the hill to the shade of his forest. His enclosure is large enough for him to escape detection. So far he lives alone, unwilling to abide the company of another male and lacking a suitable female.

There are nine males and two females at the Sanctuary. In the twenty years since it was established, with assistance from a dedicated Swiss philanthropist and the scientific vision and love of Professor Fonseca, 14 pups have been born. And, they continue to rescue wolves caught in the wild. "They normally survive the snares which have been set for prey such as wild boar, red and roe deer," says Francisco. "We find them in bad shape, but here they nearly always recover and will live ten, fifteen, even seventeen years. In the wild, rarely do they live to be ten. Six is more normal."

Zibru, named after a native bush, is every bit as wild as Prado. The slightest click of the camera, or a sudden motion, sends him darting away. But he comes back, walks confidently up to us, inside his large, forested enclosure, glares probingly with his intense green eyes, and then places his nose to our fingers, gathering the necessary information. Now, we are convinced he is OK about kissing and being scratched. He loves to have his back and sides (never his face) touched, even rubbed. We apply acupressure to his back. When we stop, he forces his back to our fingers, demanding more. He kisses us with licks thirty times in five minutes.

Ticks are rampant in Portugal, little black ones, and the wolves get them. "You can pick them off their back, even the top of their head, they know you're helping them," says Filipa.

Zibru has become a sort of ambassador at the Wolf Sanctuary because, unlike Prado in his nearby two-hectare enclosure, he is least likely to flee from onlookers. But he is wild. Not dangerous, just wild. Rarely does anyone other than staff ever enter his or any other enclosure. "You just don't do that," says Francisco. "Maybe two or three times a year someone gets to go in, for a short period of time. Assuming the wolf says its 'alright'. But you never know what will happen. We do not encourage socialization with humans. These are wild wolves. We intend for them to stay that way."

Indeed, they are the only wild, free-roaming Iberian captive wolves in the world. And this Sanctuary may one day become the only gene pool left to revivify a desperately declining species. Twenty-five percent have been lost in the last 20 years. Now, north of the Douro River, the 270-odd wolves seem to be in a somewhat stabilized situation, between the national parks and buffer area, with cross-over populations into Spain where their numbers are far greater. Each wolf is estimated to require about 100 square kilometers of territory. This habitat requirement is available in the north, but almost none is left south of the Douro.

We ask Francisco what he would like to see in the future for the wolf. He looks to a stable consortium of packs that could exceed 500 animals or more. They might have a chance at survival if those numbers could be achieved. At the Sanctuary, they hope to receive three more wolves. One has come from a zoo that closed down in Spain; another, from a zoo with an animal whose jaw is congenitally deformed. Their goal is to find fecund females. If the male and female like each other, they will breed after as a short a time as three weeks. Once they expand their base population from 11 to 15, and then perhaps add a few more, their next task will be to acquire more land for the increased number of wolves. As for reintroducing them into the wild, perhaps in the future, says Francisco. For now, their primary goal is to maintain a vital, robust gene pool and to allow several thousand visitors per year to get a glimpse of one of the rarest wolves in the world. This is an animal that symbolizes what Portugal should be, says Francisco, free and wild.

The European grey wolf was reintroduced from Italy into France, recently. But, as with the European brown bear, farmers across Western Europe are up in arms. They, too, harbor misconceptions about predators—mythologies or misconceptions that run deep. Without predators, from any ecological point of view, the entire system of nature begins to collapse. Lose the predators and numbers of rabbits, deer and wild boar (all nuisances to the farmers) will explode. But wolves particularly evoke a Little Red Riding Hood syndrome, a knee-jerk reaction of fear of the fairytale demon, that has led to the destruction of these magnificent canids from Ethiopia to Russia.

Now, in Portugal, there is the faint hope that the gorgeous Iberian wolf will survive, just as the lynx, in Spain, has also been enjoying a meager comeback.[4]

"I just love them," says Francisco. "My burst of emotions does not adequately convey the depth of my true feelings. As a scientist, I suppose I am somewhat reluctant to speak personally about them. But actually, that's what it is all about. I simply love them. I want to be like them."

And, as the man who has spent his entire life devoted to the Iberian Wolf, he may be the one person who can save this species from extinction.

THE MANY LOVES OF BRIGITTE BARDOT

LA MARE AUZOU, FRANCE

It is mid-morning in northwestern France and a light rain falls. Before us is an expanse of grassy meadows, surrounded by forest. In the distance is a magnificent chateau. A beautiful Norman farmhouse lies in front. The barking of dogs and a vista of strolling equines signals a pastoral oasis. This is the refuge, La Mare Auzou, founded by Brigitte Bardot. It is the hub of an organization that works not only in France, but throughout the world, to save animals and educate the public.

A veterinarian on staff of Bardot's foundation leans his head against an enormous palimino and for a few minutes the two old friends commune silently. Several dogs wander up to us for snacks and pets. Kittens scamper throughout the grass,

while others lay dozing in the late morning. The whole setting speaks to gentleness, patience and the astounding tenacity of one woman in particular.

By her late twenties, Brigitte Bardot had appeared in more than 30 feature films. She was and would continue to be a world-famous movie star with a huge heart. Deeply empathetic to suffering and indignant at humanity's brutality toward other creatures, in 1962 she publicly denounced the callousness of the French butchers and slaughterhouses. By 1977 she had stewarded a ban on the trade within France of fur from baby seals. In 1986, she started her Foundation. Three years later, she hosted a series on European television entitled "S.O.S. Animals." And by 1992, donor response to her ardent compassion enabled Ms. Bardot to acquire eight hectares in Normandy, which she christened Mare Auzou. "Oues" is an old French word for goose, and the protection of geese was one of the Foundation's many causes.

While this work continued in France, Brigitte Bardot and her colleagues were active throughout the European Union and elsewhere to alleviate the suffering of animals. She created the first elephant hospital in Northern Thailand where more than 600 pachyderms have been treated. In China, the Brigitte Bardot Foundation works to save the Hainanese gibbon within Bawangling Reserve; in Indonesian Kalaweit, Ms. Bardot is funding a gibbon rehabilitation program. In Chile, her involvment with the Silvestre Rehabilitation Center helps save injured wildlife and relocate them back to the wild. In Canada, Ms. Bardot has made headlines and stirred the hearts of tens-of-millions of people with her impassioned efforts to halt the killing of baby seals. In 2003, one million seals were slaughtered. The following spring the Brigitte Bardot Foundation formally asked President Chirac to demand a ban on importation to France of all products derived from seal hunting (skins, grease, oil, fur, clothing, etc.). She continues to collect over 350,000 signatures a year denouncing this barbarism. Chirac and the leaders of other European countries, including Belgium, have taken Bardot's pleas to heart and banned seal byproducts and condemned the hunting of "blanchons" (baby seals under 14 days of age).[1]

Reminders of all of these activities haphazardly adorn the crowded wall space in the four-story headquarters of FBB (Fondation Brigitte Bardot) in Paris. Around the corner is one of the great views in the city of the River Seine and Eiffel Tower.

The offices not only pour forth with pamphlets, flyers and numerous down-to-earth animal rights afficianados hard at work, but also rescued animals—everywhere. Dogs in little carpeted carriers, cats sleeping happily beside computers or flower pots, turtles, birds, guinea pigs, hamsters . . . one loses track. Every room is teeming with humans and their rescued companions who have found splendid sanctuary in the heart of Paris. It is a dream worthy of an opera by Monteverdi.

But this lovefest is also a very earnest thinktank where policy analyses of humanity's treatment of other species is carried on at the highest levels by a staff approaching 50 people. That research and advocacy for change beautifully complements the fact that Ms. Bardot and her compatriots are actually on the ground saving animals and maintaining sanctuaries. In Senegal, Tunisia, the Cameroon, Congo and South Africa, and in Bulgaria, Serbia, Montenegro and Romania, Ms. Bardot personally intercedes to spotlight cruel practices, whether with circuses and zoos, pet fashions, hunting or the transport and slaughter of animals. She also focuses on the need for pet sterilization programs. Her Foundation works to find alternatives to animal testing, to ban captivity of wild animals and the deplorable breeding conditions of animals destined to be killed.

FBB (Fondation Brigitte Bardot) recently took part in the Netherlands' meeting of the Convention on International Trade in Endangered Species of Wild Fauna and Flora (CITES) conferences; conveyed a demand to the new British Prime Minister, Sir Gordon Brown, to rally against animal vivisection and the use of primates in science; rescued 32 beagles from experimental testing in Croatia and got President Stjepan Mesic involved in freeing the dogs; secured the release of three "dancing bears" from captivity in Bulgaria; revealed cruelty in Chinese zoos where cows and chickens

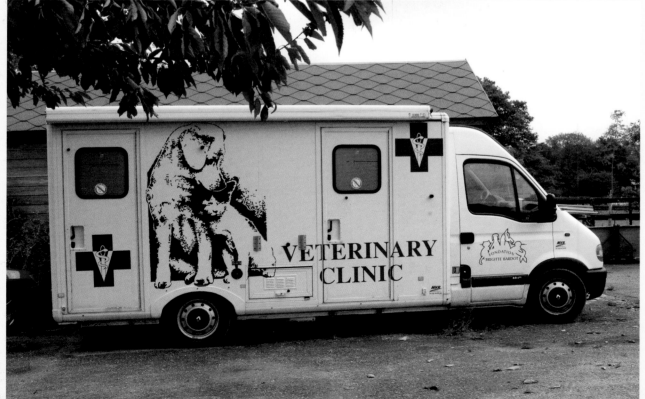

were being fed alive to caged tigers and lions while the audience laughed; petitioned President Bush to ban aerial hunting of Alaska gray wolves[2]; and agitated for an end to the French fast food poultry assembly line factories.

The FBB also works with the Eurogroup for Animal Welfare, the Fur Free Alliance, the Federation de Liaisons Anti-Corrida (to stop harming bulls in bullfighting arenas) and the GAWC (Global Anti-Whaling Campaign).

These activities require courage, inspiration and energy. And, they take a psychic and physical toll on Ms. Bardot and on her dedicated staff. It is difficult to appreciate what it is really like to work in the trenches of animal rights and to stare into the eyes of suffering. Even after the rescue of three bears in Bulgaria, FBB was trying to figure out how to save another 800 dancing bears in India, Pakistan and the Ukraine. The effort to help animals around the world puts one in a continual state of stress.[3]

Brigitte Bardot did not need to do anything. Her beauty, talent and success assured her of comfort, luxury, global fame and adulation. But her heart had opened to animals at an early age. And so, with a staff of 49 people, between Mare Auzou and their headquarters in Paris, FBB looks after approximately 500 animals, mostly dogs and cats, some horses, sheep, goats, cows and donkeys.

Mme. Calmels-Bock, the Vice President and financial guru of FBB came from a career at the Bourse (stock exchange). She is not a scientist but she knows French habits which are not necessarily geared to philanthropy like the U.S. and some other countries whose tax codes provide incentives for planned giving. The French traditionally have neither government incentives for, nor the cultural understanding of, such donations.

"It's changing," says Mme. Calmels-Bock, surrounded by about fifteen dogs and cats in her busy offices in Paris. In fact, FBB has now received well over 250 properties throughout France that have been either bequeathed or pledged. They work with a current annual budget of approximately five million euros. Mme. Calmels-Bock is a vegetarian who acknowledges that French cuisine is indeed an obstacle to cultural sympathy for animal rights. When FBB challenges the Canadians on seals, the Canadians come right back at them with the matter of the French taste for frog legs and goose liver pâté.

There are at least a dozen vegetarian and two vegan restaurants in Paris and fantastic vegetarian cooking throughout the country served in restaurants specializing in traditional cuisine. But, according to Mme. Calmels-Bock, in France it is thought that if you eat strictly vegetarian food, you must be nuts. Moreover, France is a country of hunters.

Mare Auzou, all 19.5 acres of it, is a kind of gorgeous, inspired epicenter of compassion with regional parks to all sides. As of 2003, 11.3% of France's total land-cover was protected with 259 Nature Reserves, Wilderness Areas and National Parks.[4] Twenty-four of those reserves are larger than a quarter million acres. This total conservation collective represents approximately 2% of all protected areas on the European Continent. Another 47 million acres are cultivated.[5] With a known 4,630 plant, 93 mammalian and 283 breeding bird species in the country, there remains a formidable volume of biodiversity in France, especially in relation to the rest of Europe, where the average for protection amounts to 8.4% in any one nation. More than its protected areas, France still maintains one of the highest rural components in all of

Europe—a measure, albeit partly subjective, that accounts for the number of full-time or part-time farmers, rural villages and pastoral traditions still deemed vital to French culture.

French artistic tradition is steeped in the countryside; as are festivals, architecture and the classification of forests and forest management that go to the heart of the "ancient regime."[6] Farmers in France probably have more clout than any single constituency in the country. That both supports and negates much of the animal rights platform. For all of France's rural traditions and protected areas, a high percentage of French biodiversity is at risk with 19% of the total species count listed as Threatened in 2000, up from 14% in 1996.[7] Elsewhere across Europe, endangered species statistics are far worse, with a total of 3,562 Threatened species reported as of 2007.[8]

Visiting Mare Auzou for a day provides an insight into these complications and a window on the souls of the precious creatures who dwell there, having been rescued by Ms. Bardot and her colleagues from oblivion. They are, like the citizenry of Farm Sanctuary, a diplomatic corps, if you will; emblematic of the rebirth currently inspiring people throughout the world. A staff of 15 caregivers and over 500 animals, including some 24 ponies, 21 sheep, 15 bovines, 250 cats and at least 200 dogs make the manor and three free-range parks within the 19.5 acres, home. These pastures are alive with thankful creatures who emanate a sense that this—this precious turf of peace and love—is the real France. This realization is made abundantly clear by Julinka , Isis, Cesar, Bichette and Magnolia, among others.

In many respects, the French are more advanced than most when it comes to appreciating the fine life the countryside can provide. What animal protection saints like Brigitte Bardot are striving to convey is that traditional lifestyles can embrace non-violence.

Here at Mare Auzou, it is easy to believe in that vision.

GUT AIDERBICHL: REMARKABLE OASES OF COMPASSION

AUSTRIA AND GERMANY

In the green countryside—a mere twenty minute drive from the historic city of Salzburg, birthplace of Wolfgang Amadeus Mozart and a vortex of great music and art—lies the enchanted and blessed sanctuary called Gut Aiderbichl. The name derives from Celtic and old German and means Good Hill of Fire. This paradise is the brainchild of an extraordinary man named Michael Aufhauser.

As one enters the property, one beholds an unbelievable, almost surreal panorama. Amidst a backdrop of forest lies a ring of exquisite traditional chalet-style farm buildings bedecked with flower boxes overflowing with color, in the center of which is a large meadow. Roaming freely in the meadow and on the many

paths that meander through the estate, there are cows, ponies, miniature horses, sheep, goats, chickens, geese, donkeys and others. And, mingling comfortably amid this assemblage of creation are human families and individuals many of whom are walking their dogs, others sitting at picnic tables or on benches eating, drinking or resting, obliged to share their food with the donkeys who visit and nudge them suggestively: 'feed me, or better still, let me just take what I like.' Inside the offices and sitting rooms that are above the stables and beneath high-tech haylofts, one finds antiques and oriental rugs upon which dogs play and roosters strut.

As we enter the property, passing the sign "Gut Aiderbichl—Ein Paradies für Tiere" (A Paradise for Animals), Michael laughs and says, "From here on, it's the world of animals!" But, happily, we know we share that status and are welcome in this special realm of peace and compassion. Michael points out a person massaging a handicapped cow, loosening her muscles as someone does each morning for the comfort of this three-legged resident. "Each cow tells you her life story," says Michael. "We purposely take all stress away from the animals, and they come closer to us and show a side of themselves I never realized they had."

"The rules inside Gut Aiderbichl are unique. There are no sticks or chains, and no bad words are permitted toward the animals. One hundred people work and forty-eight observation cameras always check that nobody ever mistreats an animal." These cameras also provide security and permit members to view online the activities on the estate 365 days a year.

Michael Aufhauser believes we only need to learn how to listen. His philosophy of "humanity" embraces everything that lives, for all need closeness, protection and "a chance." Here at Gut Aiderbichl, many fortunate creatures get a second chance and people have the opportunity to meet animals eye to eye and enjoy a unique communion.

Michael explains his remarkably successful approach, "I practice what is a kind of soft animal protection, but it works and it is based on my vision. Aiderbichl's first phase was building up here on the hills of Henndorf near Salzburg. The second, more important phase of the vision is the transformation I hope to bring about in the hearts and minds of people. This vision is for a good cause, and it profits the average person. It is accessible, it is understandable. Gut Aiderbichl stands for non-aggressiveness, for love. It's a mixture that goes from Buddhism to the positive part of Christianity to Judaism. In fact, it embraces what is good in all religions. 'Love life': that's my motto. And, because you love life, protect it."

Many people who previously embraced cruel practices have had a change of heart and recognized what was evil after coming to the Sanctuary. Michael Aufhauser believes viciousness, cruelty and intolerance are habits of mind that can be lifted in an instant with a change of heart. He has seen it time after time. And, he has faith in models of exemplary virtue: good acts, persons and relationships among species.

"Jane Goodall is so wonderful. When she came to Salzburg, she had lost her luggage. She had spent all day at the London airport. It was thirty-five degrees centi-

grade; hot. And, she was wearing a sweater and had five minutes before going on stage. She said not a word about lost luggage because she had more important things to talk about. The first thing she said was 'be courageously optimistic.' Then she said, 'we all can do something, so let's go ahead and do it.' In other words, offer optimism. Don't point out only the negative."

"Gut Aiderbichl is a platform for optimism. I am positive as a private person, always positive. I always say, 'count the blessings you have.' We have to be optimistic. We can't give up." And through persistent optimism, Michael's vision has expanded to three other Gut Aiderbichl locations in Austria and three in Germany. And, his approach to communion and peaceful relations among all creation evident at Gut Aiderbichl and in his films and writings, is expanding beyond the borders of Europe.

Despite the brutalities we witness in this world, Michael has faith in people. "We all have one thing in common: we want to be correct to our mothers, and we would love to look up to our fathers. We want peace. Basically, human beings are very good.

If a six-year-old girl finds a little bird that has a broken wing, she will take the bird gently in her hands and bring it to her father or mother and say 'let's help this bird.' That impulse is right in our soul. We have other aspects, of course. Children stomp their feet when they see a chicken walk by and enjoy seeing pigeons fly up in horror. It's up to elder, more experienced persons to pat their shoulders and say 'you've done great. You were so quiet when you approached that chicken. You did marvelously because you rescued that cow' like with the girl who received our Golden Heart for Animals prize for saving her cow. By giving her that, we said 'you did great'."

Michael told us that he experienced similar encouragement when he made his first rescue, saving five dogs and flying them to Frankfurt where he delivered them to a rescue agency. "The lady looked at me and her joy was limited because she had to think what she was going to do with the five dogs. If she had used the wrong words, and said 'You're revolting. Here you come from a luxury hotel with your five dogs thinking they need to be washed, vaccinated, everything. Drop them off and go back

to your lovely clean home—who do you think you are?' then she would have destroyed a future animal protector. What she showed was tolerance; she was grateful for that little thing I did, and she said 'you did great, thank you so much.' And, I went away with a feeling that she was great and admirable. And, I felt I did not do quite as well as I had thought. She induced me to think in a very intelligent way, and that's how I learned to grow and to have greater understanding."

"I can't avoid thinking what I'm doing is helping individuals. But if one looks at the larger picture, all we're doing is taking care of symptoms. You don't find results to the origin of the problem. This was the reason that I switched from animal protection and developed my own philosophy, a philosophy that is able to be adopted by many, many people and that finds the roots in how we treat weaker beings on this globe."

"We are not very kind to the weakest. We might spend our money to give them beautiful places to live, but we don't want to see the handicapped and we are happy when the old are in trailer parks or in senior citizen homes and, if they have dementia, then we are very happy not to see that on a daily basis. This we leave to others, assuming that we have the money to pay for it. We don't want to listen to old people because we think that they are too slow in their way of expression. I think personally that ninety percent of the people we declare mentally challenged are not, we just haven't learned to listen."

"I experienced that when I had Mongoloid children at Gut Aiderbichl. The guide that was supposed to tour with them had not shown up, and I became the guide. It was a nightmare for me for the first ten minutes because I had never been in contact with Mongoloid people. And, the children didn't fit into the program of the rest of my day, which was very structured and organized. And, all of a sudden I had children who would grab me, who would touch me, and it did take maybe twenty minutes and then I began, in their repetitions, to find out what they were saying, and after an hour I was able to see how well they thought of each other, of the animals and how kind they were. And after two hours I had a problem letting them go home because they were so marvelous. And, it showed me once more, if we would only take the time, these moments are a gift.

I then opened Aiderbichl to people that are living in hospice that have three more months to live. They know it. They have been given up by clinics, and they're waiting to die. When I brought these people up to Aiderbichl, I planted for each one an apple tree. We were spending the day together, and I was able to observe how they get close to animals. One lady was a hundred and one years old, and she held a chicken, and I have a photograph of that."

Michael describes how the centennarian held the chicken caressingly, spellbound, because until then she had only really considered chicken as something suited to a frying pan or between two slices of bread with mayonnaise. Now, she held the living, gentle creature and stroked the delicate feathers the way one might adore a kitten, hearing the soft breath, noticing every sensuous contour of the bird, its remarkable sensitivity to the slightest nuance of touch, eyes all enquiring and bright. A smooth perfumed scent, a fidgeting little body seeking out its pleasures . . .

Michael reflects deeply on this encounter, "I did feel and I'm very convinced that this is a very important experience for people that know they're leaving this earth: they would love to get close to animals. So we do this every so often. And, I lost my own fear of meeting the 'imperfect.' As a matter of fact, I shiver today when I see too much perfection.

Michael shows us further around the Sanctuary. "We have specialists for cows, goats, pigs, horses. We employ doctors but we also hire outside doctors. The reason why I came late this morning [he picked us up to drive us to the Sanctuary] was because three chickens were ill and my driver took them to Munich to the best bird clinic where they are being cared for, because that is the promise we make to the animals that come under our protection. There shall be no more fear, no more stress and the best medical care available."

"Altogether, here and in Bavaria, we have one thousand animals. We have four hundred horses. It has become huge. We are just opening a new stable this year for fifty more horses and we are opening a new place for animals that have been found in the forest and raised by humans and bottle-fed. They can't be released into the forest again, so we have built a totally fenced-in forest environment in which to release them. We are building a fox habitat of steel mesh. They can't get out and nobody can cut the enclosure open and that's one reason why we have twenty-four-hour security on all of our estates. I must say that my last jumping horses were poisoned as an act of revenge." So, all is not perfect in paradise, and Michael struggles to protect the animals in his care with the help of devoted and expert colleagues, while practicing compassion for and trying to understand the victimizers as well as their victims.

Michael introduces us to Basti, a wild baby pig who lost her mother. Hungry and thirsty, she made her way to a nearby castle where she was found. Michael received a call for help and welcomed her into the fold. Now, Basti is a very popular resident of Gut Aiderbichl. She is affectionate and endearing. It is Michael's hope that the fathers of children who meet and love this little orphan may think twice before killing a wild pig.

Here one finds a noble police horse whose story Michael tells: "This horse was going to be killed because he has arthritis. Now this young policeman, Stephan, approached us and said 'I want to help my horse because I gave my horse a promise to take care of him.' When he came to us, he had no money to have a horse. In our Christmas show we will use his example of love and devotion that we never let some-

99

body down and we must never break a promise. Here is a handsome man and his beautiful horse, and we distribute their photograph and tell their story to reach others. Now we are taking in many police horses. And, every time a horse comes to us it is kept like a private horse, which is very costly. For example, a horse that is twelve years old will cost us four hundred thousand dollars over the course of his lifetime. And, that's a very low estimate."

Here, an autistic boy hugged the little pony Schecky with such passion that he was given the privilege of a ride (not a regular occurrence at Gut Aiderbichl where pony rides are not permitted). After the boy, Eric, got off the pony, he reached out to express his gratitude and joy to his father, and said his first word in two years: "Papa."

We met Snoopy, a lovely beagle living at Gut Aiderbichl as a result of Michael Aufhauser's negotiations with a chemical company that does product testing on this intelligent and highly sensitive breed. The cooperation resulted in the company agreeing to sell all their beagles to Michael after their use. Though this insures their survival, it incurred the wrath of some animal protectionists. "Cooperating and dialoguing with animal farmers also brought criticism of me. But, I am not concerned about *my* image. We cannot afford egos. We all work for the cause here."

"We have to have people that say 'no compromise'. I understand and respect this, but it isn't my approach. The good thing about our organization is that we don't have to stick to any such rules. We go right to where animals are mistreated, we sit with farmers that have five million chickens in cages and explain our point of view. We have convinced many of them to change their way of keeping animals. We work together with companies to build compassionate stables, and the sales managers are part of our lobby. When farmers want battery cages, our lobbyists are there to persuade them to adopt compassionate alternatives for keeping chickens. In one place we were able to save one million chickens from being put into cages."

Michael is non-didactic in his films, television, newspaper articles and radio shows. Yet, his technique of friendly persuasion is not without purpose and successes. He describes the beautiful sanctuary magazine, "This is how we educate. There are always little sentences that remind readers that we're talking about life: our lives and those of poetic, magical animals. The magazine is a diary of how a day looks at Gut Aiderbichl."[1]

"My goal was that fifty-one percent of the average persons on the street, when you asked them about animals and animal laws, they would repeat the sentence 'animals are living, feeling beings.' If only we establish this sentence in more than fifty percent of the peoples' consciousness, the politicians will be inspired to establish further animal protection laws."

In fact, the constitution of the region of Salzburg is the only legal framework in Austria that mentions animals. Michael Aufhauser invited politicians from all parties to visit Gut Aiderbichl and meet the animals face to face then decide for themselves the value of this work. As a result, the Ministers of Salzburg voted unanimously to include a statement specifying respect for and protection of animals in their constitution.

Salzburg is noble for more than its extraordinary musical and literary history (the Benedictine monastery of Saint Peter's has the second oldest library in Europe). Salzburg is more delicious than its famous Mozart Kugeln (chocolate balls) and Salzburger Nockerln (a literal mountain of a dessert made of sugar and whipped egg whites). Salzburg is more lyrical than its continuing tradition of great musical festivals. For, Salzburg boasts one of the most progressive philosophies of and homes for human compassion and animal protection that we have encountered, in the person of Michael Aufhauser and in the sanctuary of Gut Aiderbichl.

A REFUGE
FOR BEARS:
ALERTIS, RHENEN

THE NETHERLANDS

When standing a few feet away from a thousand pound bear who is doing his own thing; unconfined, unbothered, fully attuned, gazing at himself in the reflections of creek water, rolling in the grass, frolicking with his mate in the mist of a waterfall, one is peering back into the essence of wilderness; and, one hopes, peering forward to the future.

In Holland, on a drizzly morning, we find ourselves with Koen Cuyten, Project Coordinator and Head of Welfare for Alertis, the Dutch Fund for Bear and Nature Conservation, inside the huge sanctuary he and his colleagues have created to save, rejuvenate and provide a good life for seven rescued brown bears. From the look of it, the bears are most certainly happy to be here. And the empirical behavioral data, which Koen and others have gathered, reinforce this impression.

The Alertis sanctuary is located twenty minutes outside of Utrecht in the town of Rhenen in Holland. Rescuing abused, confined, traumatized bears from Eastern Europe is no easy matter, Koen explains. A rapid response time is critical, and surmounting the various political, economic and cultural obstacles to secure the animals and transport them can sometimes seem overwhelming. Once the bears reach their new home, they must be medically assessed, stabilized, then gently released. The bears have no reason to trust their new captive situation, but the release area here represents true freedom.

This is known as the Bear Forest enclosure. Twenty thousand square meters (or roughly four acres) in size, it has native woodland, a waterfall and creek bed, with sandy banks and a forest understory. And, it harbors no threat to the bears. The sanctuary was lovingly created next to the Ouwehands Zoo, adjoining the largest tract of wild forest left in the Netherlands, about 20,000 acres of wild land. This provides enormous quantities of seed, bird life and endless wonders for bears to sniff. The sanctuary can accommodate up to 13 bears. At present, the seven bears who call it home are Dadon, Wolke, Tory, Bjorna, Niki, Mascha and Mackenzie. They are its fortunate residents.

With them, in the same large area, is a small group of free roaming wolves, whose presence helps to reestablish the authentic ecosystem in which bears and wolves would normally cohabit.

Few words have so many meanings as *bear* and few species evoke such awe and mystery. Ancestors of the brown bear (*Ursus arctos*) inhabited the European continent for possibly twenty million years. Among the known 231 mammalian carnivores, that trace their genetic roots to the great dispersion during the Oligocene period 40 million years ago (including cats, hyenas, weasels, mongoose, raccoons and dogs), bears are probably the most recent arrivals.

Today, globally, there exist between six and eight distinct species of brown bear. The number varies because of the conspicuous variations in Alaskan populations. There, in addition to black bear, there are three brown bears: the brown, the grizzly and the Kodiak. The behavior, diet and size of these bears may change according to whether they live in the interior, along mainland coastal regions, or on an island such as Kodiak or Admiralty.

The three evolutionary lines of bears have continued well into the present Holocene era. Two are in Asia, from where the black bear derives, and the third line gave rise to the famed *Ursus spelaus* that is best remembered from European cave paintings of the Paleolithic era and is now extinct. A second recent European bear species, *Ursavis elemensis*, that was the size of a miniature French poodle, also disappeared.[1]

Prior to the bear coming of age sexually, between the ages of four and seven, they are universally of one species: the Teddy Bear. And, the truth is that even at 1,000 pounds or more, a male during spring mating—for all of his formidable strength and character—is gentle, though few humans seem eager to accept that fact. Females seem to require numerous male partners prior to ovulation. Males are thus in great demand, and they know it. In a wintry den, between one to four cubs will be born and will remain dependent on their mothers for nearly 30 months.

Bears are largely vegetarian throughout the year. That said, they can also help themselves to moose or insects, when they tire of blueberries. Few mammals have such a capacity to enjoy so varied a diet, love life and global territory like the bear. It is their reputation and resulting relationship with humans that impedes this joy.

Ten wild populations of brown bear are known to exist in Europe with two slight-

ly varied mitochondrial DNA profiles.[2] Four of these groups comprise numbers of individuals exceeding 1,000, while four have fewer than 100 members. Another four are intermediate in population size while two other clusters are down to just a few individuals each.[3] Geographically, these estimated 50,000 wild brown bears are found mostly in Northeastern Europe: European Russia, Romania, Poland, Latvia, Estonia, Finland and Norway, as well as in Slovakia, the Dinaric-Eastern Alps, Austria, and surrounding countries, as far south as northwestern Greece. A few bears remain in Spain, the Pyrenees, France and Italy, though these individuals are at the highest risk; their futures totally uncertain. They might be gone as of the publication of this book. And if one subtracts the Russian population, the number declines dramatically to about 15,000 brown bears in Europe.

Despite hope that in some areas their populations may be stable, these animals are suffering from the usual human-induced problems. These include poaching, habitat degradation or loss, barriers in the guise of train tracks and highways, fire, improper food (e.g., from garbage dumps) and loss of genetic viability. But with brown bears there is an additional constraint on their ability to survive unfettered into the future: like any large creature, they pose an elemental level of discomfort for most people, and across Europe there are hundreds of millions of people within close proximity to the bears. There is little wilderness left in Europe and the history of bear translocations is, at best, a record of marginal successes and many losses.[4]

Recent good news includes the campaign to save the Carpathian brown bear in Romania by the NGO AVES, efforts by Austrian, Italian and Norwegian authorities to compensate farmers and ranchers for damage to livestock, and the excitement when a brown bear was seen recently crossing a pass into Switzerland for the first time in 80 years. Opinion polls suggest that 75% of all Europeans would welcome

brown bears back into the wild. This type of good news, however, fails to capture the actual problem people have with bears. They see films like *Grizzly Man*, which reconfirms their fundamental uneasiness about a species that can choose to kill people on rare occasions, usually in revenge or under extreme circumstances. Attacks upon humans by black bear are somewhat more frequent than by brown. That said, bears usually pose a threat to humans only in proportion to the extent that bears, like any carnivore, have been trapped, cornered or hurt, or their options for survival palpably frustrated.

Fortunately, bears have many human friends in Europe and Russia. One such individual, Professor Pazhetnov, has raised 70 bear cubs and successfully released them into protected Russian sanctuaries that had few, if any, remaining wild bears.[5]

Moreover, since 1982, the brown bear has been legally protected in Appendix II of the Bern Convention on the Conservation of European Wildlife and Natural Habitats signed by 40 member states throughout the European Community, and four non-member states. Three countries with bear populations have thus far not signed, and one of them is Georgia.[6]

In Holland, where no known bears in the wild remain, Koen and Alertis are working with colleagues in Georgia to change that situation. Alertis has managed to embrace compassion-in-action through the difficult conservation work involving captive management in a wild setting that adjoins some of the most densely populated human areas in Europe.

In 2000, a Natural Feeding Program was begun, says Koen, in which food items similar to bears' natural consumables were introduced. Lettuce "simulates broad leaved herbs" for example. "One of the main characteristics of the diet," Koen explains, "is the seasonal variation" both in the type of foods and the level of calories. "After the start of the new diet, hibernation became more solid and stereotypic behaviour decreased."[7]

Dealing with captive bears who have likely suffered terribly was never easy. Relations between wild bears, for all their unpredictability, and humans is much easier:

the bears are on higher ground, their ground. They have not ceded anything to the species that has become their nemesis. With captive bears, the complexities escalate. Koen recently co-supervised (with Drs. Margje Voeten and Jos Dekker) a comprehensive report on strategies and protocols to most humanely and progressively accommodate the needs of captive bears.[8]

The whole idea was, first, to save the bears; and second, to provide them with a wonderful home that would also allow for some human access without undue disturbance, for purposes of educating the public and giving ethologists the ability to discretely observe bear behavior in the semi-wild.

Established in 1993, this Dutch Bear Sanctuary followed upon efforts by the Greek and Turkish governments to halt the rampant abuse of bears as circus freaks and street side attractions. With its partner, Noah's Ark Centre for the Recovery of Endangered Species (NACRES) based in Georgia, Alertis was able to mobilize Dutch support to rescue three bears from a bankrupt zoo in Rustavi City. The animals were going to be euthanized because the city could not afford staff care or food. In April 2007, the bears arrived in Holland and were released into their new safe haven: "the first time that they could stand on grass, swim in a large pond, play with other bears, climb trees, and go into hibernation like other bears do. The first time," writes Koen, "that they could experience what it is like to be real bears."[9]

The Bear Sanctuary comes at a time when the Dutch are struggling to expand natural habitat in their small country, from approximately 1.66 million acres in 2007 to 1.8 million acres by 2018. That would put nearly 20% of the country back into a natural, or semi-natural condition and hopefully relieve the ecological pressures that have to date resulted in a situation in which 29% of all known in situ biodiversity is threatened with extinction across the Netherlands.[10]

That might even mean that these exquisite bears could someday soon be released into sufficiently buffered Dutch habitat, back to one of the most densely human populated countries in Europe. Wild bears and tulips, a poignancy Rembrandt would have understood.

PROTECTING THE LAST OLD FORESTS OF EUROPE

BIALOWIEZA NATIONAL PARK, POLAND

In the many chronicles of forest life, biologists and fanciers of nature have looked at trees in terms of their longevity, or height and breadth to express their amazement. Thomas Parkenham marvels at the Montezuma cypress (*Taxodium mucronatum*) in the town of Tule, Mexico whose girth, 190 feet, makes it—or the three contested trees of near identical DNA that comprise its tight circle of companionship—the widest tree in the world.[1] Trees are not the biggest living things athough they are unquestionably the tallest. A carpet of moss in Wisconsin spreading for many square miles, a coral reef or enormous stand of monoclonal aspens in alpine Colorado comprise larger "single" life forms. But humans stand in awe of the largest of the redwoods (*Sequoiadendron giganteum*). One named the General Sherman Tree in Sequoia National Park is 1,500 cubic meters. Its combined age and size constitute a humbling biological concept. However, considering that portion of the

standing tree which is actually dead, an adult blue whale proffers a greater amount of living tissue. Still, in terms of longevity, many species and individual trees have few peers. A Caspian sturgeon may live to be over 200 years old, but there are creosote bushes in the Mojave Desert that have enjoyed 12,000 birthdays, while *Gaylussacia brachycera* (related to bilberry), particularly one in Pennsylvania, is over 13,000 years old.[2]

Jonathan Roberts expresses his admiration for the ancient Sherwood Forest (hardly a forest at all, but, rather, a scattered, if legendary cluster of trees) and for the Black Wood of Rannoch, Scotland, those last remaining Caledonian pines of the ancient Highland forest, protected by private owners over the centuries. Roberts is reminded of the caveat that human beings are capable of felling every last tree in sight, if given a chance or motivation, and thus rallies to this small grove of hangers-on in the spirit of one man unabashedly enchanted by trees, championing this botanical underdog. His case study also underscores the importance of privately owned good habitat when the owners are instilled with a conservation ethic.[3]

In his intellectually provocative artistic study of trees, James Balog seeks to celebrate "outstanding individuals," assembling photographic slices into testimonial collages that make up a single tree from dozens of compass points. The resulting celebrations are stunning and unexpected. In an earlier book, Balog had similarly photographed individual animals, many representing endangered species, to provide stirring profiles of these beings as individuals with biographies. His portraits of trees claim a similar lyrical intensity and respect. "A great tree infuses empty space with memory and turns it into a place, creating a bridge between civilization and the wildest wilderness," he muses.[4]

Sylvan complexes of groves and forests and bushlands comprise the vast majority of life on earth and incite a peculiar mixture of superstition, horror, comfort and salvation among our own kind, while sustaining the fundamentals of terestrial biology. Such cultural semiotics as "knock on wood," "not seeing the forest for the trees," "tree-huggers," and "Tree of Life" are rooted in our imagination. Our memories of the forest go back to our hominid beginnings, which were arboreal, our visual rods and cones oriented to a thousand shades of green. We likely evolved out of the trees and learned to walk on curled hands with good reason to be nervous out in the open. Our memories are deep as were our childhood yearnings to construct and dwell within a tree house.

Historian and philosopher Simon Schama, reflecting on the Jews living in Poland during one of that country's many horrific political convulsions, calls them "martyrs' martyrs."[5] The term might equally apply to the great Polish primeval forest itself, Bialowieza, where many Jews lived, and which once covered much of Poland and a large portion of lowland Europe after the last of the Ice Ages ten thousand years ago. That forest, today, though vastly truncated, spans the border between northeastern Poland and central Belarus. For the last century it has been associated with its largest living mammal, the wisent or European bison, who is gaining a foothold after nearing the sacrificial altar of extinction.

The European bison is its own species, distinct from the Canadian wood and American prairie bisons. This shy creature, 15 of which we fleetingly glimpsed at the edge of a Bialowieza clearing at 5:30 on a misting morning, was first described by Aristotle (*bonasus* or Żubr in Polish) and later celebrated by the Renaissance scholar Mikolaj Hussowski, who composed a Latin paen to the beast in one thousand seventy lines of heroic verse. Later, locals of the region attempted to exterminate every last majestic animal and the forest, as well.[6] Such are humanity's contradictions.

Religion, reality and a strange, perdurable yearning for redemption dominates these magnificent depths of forest. Crosses here and there in the heart of the thousands of acres stand as testimony to the execution of hundreds, possibly thousands of Poles by the Nazis. And cemeteries—Jewish, Catholic and Eastern Orthodox—are found on all sides. One Jewish cemetery in particular, on the edge of the northern fringes of Bialowieza, adjoining the eastern corner of the village of Narewka, lies up a hill, unmarked. Here are several dozen stones engraved in Hebrew commemorating those who died of natural causes, prior to World War II. Never has there been a more peaceful setting for Jews in this part of Eastern Europe: a sanctuary for the dead.

Puszcza ("forest") Bialowieska is one of the sanctuaries in the world for both the dead and the living; a place that both scientifically and emotionally recognizes

115

the interdependency of these two facets of biology. For Bialowieza is a forest where deadwood—anathema to most forest management methodologies—is considered sacred and with good reason. Across most of Europe, and the world, foresters, city planners, gardeners and many park administrators, proudly and dutifully perceive in deadwood a universal nemesis—the fuel of wildfires, bark beetle infestations and other pariahs. In truth, deadwood contains at least 25% of all known forest biodiversity, and possibly much more. Without deadwood, the vast majority of species that are native to forests cannot exist. A forest without deadwood is not a true forest. Our colleague Tomasz Wesołowski, the 57-year- old Chairman of Avian Ecology at Wroclaw University, rejects the term "dead wood." Instead, he says, it is "ageless." Scientifically speaking, he is correct: the perpetual ecological flux of pristine forest ensures a continuity dating back, at least, 425 million years to the emergence of the most ancient plants. In what is today Ireland, for example, the Middle Silurian period saw macroscopic plant emergence with stems, spores, root hairs and sporangia. And, closer to Poland, in Czechia, *Cooksonia* fossil plants from that same period have been uncovered. In the Late Devonian, from Scotland to Belgium, the first seed-bearing Gymnosperm plants have been found from which the majority of bryophytes (non-flowering grasses, mosses, lichens and fungi), as well as forests and flowering plants evolved. By 385 million years ago, stumps called *Eospermatopteris* belonging to the most ancient group of trees, the cladoxylopsids, had come into being making for the earliest forests and forest ecosystems, of which Bialowieza is a living descendant.[7]

Because of this ageless legacy, it is not surprising that Poland named Bialowieza its first forest "Rezerwat" in 1921, its first of 23 National Parks in 1932, and in 1979, it was registered as a UNESCO World Heritage Site. By 1992, UNESCO extended the Heritage status to encompass both sides of the Polish/Belarussian side, making it one of only seven transboundary World Heritage sites in Europe, encompassing a total area of 1,250 square kilometers. A small portion of that on the Polish side is Strictly Protected and lies within the heart of the National Park.

The forest's botanical wealth is unequalled anywhere in Europe.[8] But it is not simply "primeval" forest: it is the way the forest is supposed to be and always was. This is simply one of the last windows on that past. One other in Europe exists and the senior statesman of Białowieza, Professor Czesław Okołów, has visited the place: a 400 hectare private estate owned by the Rothschild family, outside Vienna.[9] But there is nothing to compare in size, scope or ecodynamic complexity to this relict forest in Poland and Belarus, surviving from an atavistic past.

This was once Lithuanian forest, as it was Russian, Prussian, Austro-Hungarian and German. The tragic joke goes, one could spend his or her entire life in his Polish apartment, never leaving, only to be informed a century later that his passport had been stamped, confiscated, or burned by half-dozen nationalities. These turbulent transitions of geopolitics were inflicted upon not only Poland (which enjoyed only twenty years of independence in her entire history prior to modern liberation), but upon these innocent forests as well.

Such was the tumult that in times past "hour by hour" Bialowieza was being destroyed; her virgin forests milled, her animal life slaughtered. But on December 3rd, 1820, Tsar Alexander I issued an order, the first of its kind, turning all of the forest into a "strict reserve."[11]

"All around in solemn splendour stood/The glory of the Lithuanian wood!"[12] wrote Poland's famed Romantic poet, Adam Mickiewicz. Mickiewicz set down his epic in 1834, at a time when the Romantic Movement in Polish arts was enjoying a true renaissance. Painters like Jan Feliks Piwarski and Kazimierz Wojniakowski invited lyrical admiration for Poland's forest habitat.[13] In 1828, the German Baron J. Brincken, a forester from Warsaw, visited Bialowieza and published his memoirs[14] containing fanciful illustrations. A couple of years later, Polish artist Leonard Chodzko[15] was busy also drawing the creatures of this primeval region, including a great forest bison. Then turmoil again resumed in the form of arsen, massive felling of old trees and poaching. By 1846, there were rewards offered by local officials for assistance in exterminating wolves from the area.[16]

Death stalks the forest in positive ways, as well. Of a tree's total weight, typically 90% is dead.[17] The so-called coarse wood debris (CWD) of fallen trees is that portion accounting for the earlier mentioned 25% component, a figure deduced from the study of forests in North America.[18] But that is only the beginning. The great ecological enigmas of the forest concern the incalculable volumetric space inhabited by micro-organisms, fungi, bryophytes, insects, organic anomalies and the trillions of individuals known as saproxylic creatures who are dependent at some point, if not always, upon dead or dying trees. In just the hollows and cavities of decomposing logs, at least 100 species of Polish beetles thrive. Elsewhere across Europe in such deadwood exist beetle species from at least 29 known families, a remarkable abun-

117

dance of life.[19] In human terms, the word necrosis is considered synonymous with death. In dendrology, the science of trees and sylvan nomenclature, "side necroses" are the quintessence of life, the place where saproxylic insects spend their entire lives, inside, under, or between layers of bark, sapwood and heartwood. Consider a single ancient old tree that has fallen. Try to imagine its three-dimensionality, as if in the hands of a radiologist, taking into account every rotting curvature both on the unknowable insides, and decomposing exteriors. That microlandscape comprises vast stretches of terrain; magnitudes of topography whose dimensions encompass unknown, exponential powers-of-ten in terms of distances measured in angstroms or cubic millimeters; an endless array of habitats scarcely visible to the naked eye, essential curvaciousness supporting creatures which make forests and the life of the terrestrial world possible. It is a sensuous cornucopeia between life and death.

Real-time imagery with ultrasound or PET scans, as applied to deadwood, could well unravel universes as yet unknown to science, not to mention untold scores of new species interacting at levels we rely upon, but typically ignore.

In the case of Bialowieza that biodiversity is astonishing: over 2,500 huge trees over 20 metres (one exceeding 56 metres) and tens-of-thousands of other trees and shrubs; over 13,000 *known* animal and insect species[20], 809 vascular plant species (though some scientists suggest that number exceeds 1,050), 165 moss, 74 liverwort, 156 aerophytic algae (those inhabiting bark and moss) and a remarkable explosion of fungi—more than 3,000 varieties, including 283 lichen species and 81 slime-moulds: the richest fungal vortex on the continent.[21] In a single outing during the early 1960s, a group of scientists found more than 60 undocumented organisms in the forest, six were altogether new to European science.

To put Bialowieza in its ecological context, a nation-wide survey on forest biodiversity across Poland in 2001, utilizing input from many of the leading agencies and scientific departments in the country, found a total of more than 50,000 species of which 31,000 were invertebrates. There were a maximum of 370 bird species and 98 mammals. Taking into account all kinds and degrees of forest (including primary, secondary, tertiary and other degraded forests) a total cover of 28% was discerned.

Sixty-five percent of all Polish biodiversity was found in these forests, which comprised 69 tree and shrub species, a third of which happen to be represented in Bialowieza.

Autumn is the best time to visit Bialowieza, if fungi are a consideration. September is when we chose to make our expedition. Professor Okołów, who walks in the lead, has seen Soviet occupation, Nazi tragedy and the frustrating ecological illiteracy of locals played out in the (admittedly difficult) rigors that life and the environment of northeastern Poland exact. He strolls easily with a dignity befitting the elder statesman he is, and he exercises that tenacious curiosity that is the hallmark of a great scientist. Along with Mrs. Karas (the Interim National Park Director) and a local park service forester, we examine a remote coniferous bog. The varieties of creatures great and small are miraculous, as are the odors, colors and forms. Countless tomes have been written on the extraordinary fungal potpourri that is Bialowieza.[22] Yet, in the middle of the afternoon, Mrs. Karas kneels down in perplexity: "I have never seen these!" she exclaims, showing her find to Professor Okołów. Despite more than 40 years of research in this forest, he, too, looks surprised and takes a tiny specimen, anxious to send it to a colleague. "It could very easily be a new species," he volunteers. "On the other hand, I am an entomologist. So when it comes to fungi, well, that's not my expertise." Of course, the entire forest is his home, and he knows it like few people on Earth. Later on, with Tomasz Wesołowski, we head into a deep copse in the Strictly Protected Area within the National Park. It is more of a stroll than a trek. Due to the welcome quantity of deadwood, Bialowieza is not unpassable like Alaskan or Amazonian backbush. Rather, it is a nearly park-like semi-open setting with quite manageable groundcover. Riparian sections take more of a toll on the intruder, however. There tall stinging nettles and a plethora of ticks guarantee torment. Only a few dozen scientists per year are allowed into this region, where monitoring has gone on since the 1930s, making this one of the most intensively and continuously studied forests anywhere in the world. Wesolowski, who is married to a taxonomist specializing in jumping spiders (there are many in Poland), is unabashedly in love with, and thus greatly concerned about, the nine species of woodpeckers that breed here[23], as

well as the ten other cavity nesters (or hole excavators) from among the 180 known breeding bird species in Bialowieza.[24] Without such old forest—with its 24 dominant tree species, including enormous Scots pine, Norway spruce[25], spruce bog and pine, oak-lime-hornbeam, marshy alder carr and ash, birch and willow, along with various other mixed broadleaved and conifer tree species—such birds would not survive.[26] Between 20% to 40% of the breeding birds in Bialowieza make their homes in the holes of deadwood, at least half of them using unclaimed woodpecker cavities. Even the blackbird, which can nest and breed among bushes, seems to prefer these holes.

There are no endemic birds in Europe. But over 250 of the migrant and immigrant birds spend some or all of their lives in northeastern Poland's forest, the "last reference point for temperate forests in all of Europe," says Tomasz. He reminds us that 6,000 years ago, the entire continent was like Bialowieza. The problem now, says Tomasz, is that without other forest refuges within close proximity, these birds will vanish. "Migratory connectivity" is key in conservation biology, especially so in regions of Europe where migratory birds are forever heading between the northern boreal forests and the Persian Gulf or Africa, stopping in Europe for breeding and feeding, or simply to rest.

For 35 years Tomasz has been monitoring seven plots within Bialowieza, making his research the most sustained of its kind anywhere in the world. In this, he is like a "Biruté Galdikas" of primeval forests with a lifetime of observing the birds that inhabit them. His data is by now indisputable. It indicates that if the surrounding buffer areas ("forest management zones") continue to be depleted because Poland, like much of Europe, has a policy of removing all deadwood that occupies more than 5% of the ground-cover, then this sanctuary of Bialowieza will disappear, her creatures silenced. And, with that descending gloom, so too will disappear the falling leaves of autumn which grace us all around in golden, orange and hundred-storied hues of sunswept green raining down from the red oak, horsechestnut, white poplar, single-leaf ash, mock orange, sycamore, hop tree, hawthorn and amelanchier.[27] The wind turns fierce as a rain mounts, and more leaves fly past us: silver birch, small-leaved lime, Norway maple, sallow, downy birch, common elm and rowan.[28] The forest haunts the soul with a life that teems in compounded varieties beyond what we can possibly fathom. The "fine-grained mosaic boreal/temperate meeting points," which Tomasz has been studying, harbor a vast diversity of microhabitats. Densities of populations are diminutive; numbers of individuals are also small. What is huge is the overall diversity of species and genera, and that's what makes Bialowieza so remarkable. It is also the reason buffer zones and refugia (surrounding oases outside the immediate forest) are so critical. If the Polish economic drivers and political winds deem untouched habitat of diminishing importance, then they shall have doomed all the resident primeval, wondrous creatures to certain death.

Tomasz' research shows that 53% of all the species of birds they have studied have fewer than three pairs per hectare. And, the really tiny species, like the marsh tit, have a metabolic output that is enormous. They are "income" breeders (as opposed to "capital" breeders), which means they have meager energy latitudes. They must find food quickly or die. Their breeding itself consumes them. If the habitat is usurped to any extent, they will slip inexorably into energy-deficit mode and perish. Bialowieza's birds, and the insects they depend upon, rely upon the trees and shrubs and vascular plants. The low densities imply the low productivity of the forest, which can support

but few individuals. Yet, again the equation: low densities translate to high diversity. Hence the uniqueness and the fragility of cool temperate forests—Bialowieza in particular. There is nothing quite like it in the world.[29]

A conference Tomasz convened among avian cavity experts from around the world, he says, is about to be enlightened as to the current peril to Bialowieza. Polish politics will kill the forest because the Ministry of Environment, which sits above the Forestry Department, is driven by the economics of forest extraction and, says Tomasz, their documented graft in the 26,000 or so member consortium that comprises that forest enterprise run as a private corporation. It is a "good ole' boy's club" masquerading as rational resource use in the public's interest. But this historic paradigm is incompatible with conservation, says Tomasz. In old growth forest, or tropical or deadwood-laden forest, there is no such thing as sustainable harvesting. Selective cutting invariably results in incremental forest demise. Close your eyes then open them again and something is missing. A few more logs have been taken, another patch of clearing has emerged, more sunlight gets in, less moisture accumulates, the patches grow larger and larger, day by day. And it is even worse, he says, on the Belarus side.[30]

Satelittle imagery confirms the alarming pattern of patchy and degraded forest across this part of Eastern Europe. Few sanctuaries remain.

"The habitat fragmentation is so bad," says Tomasz, "that the total amount of protected area in all of Poland is no more than one percent, or approximately half the size of Yellowstone National Park. Bialowieza is not the country's largest park, but it is certainly its oldest and most important. Lose Bialowieza, and you lose an entire suite of deep lineages, the critical component of biological evolution in Europe."

To underscore the incremental threats to this remarkable sanctuary, the day-by-day nearly imperceptible deletions, we drive along dirt roads outside the National Park Protected Area, but still within the Forest zones, where pile after pile of both young and old trees have been cut and await removal. These roads follow the old Russian "versts," a measure equivalent to 1066.78 meters that demarcate the maps and constitute collectively the network of roads hewn through the forest.[31] In the town of Hajnowka on the western border of the forest, the symbol for the community and its Chamber of Commerce logo, is a circle, the upper half consisting of forest, the lower half a chainsaw. Tomasz tells us that that's how the majority of locals think of these trees: as nothing more than money. According to one senior researcher in the government, few locals in the greater Hajnowka-Bialowieza-Narewka area appreciate the fact that the National Park has put them on the map; that hotels and nearly 100 guides are making money from the nearly 50,000 eco-tourists who come here every year to enjoy a living forest. "They don't care. They hate authority, they hate outsiders, and they want it their way," says an unnamed source. Park authorities have to live in these towns and the last thing they want is to make more enemies. Of course, it is also unfair to generalize. Many residents deeply appreciate the park's presence and status, although not enough of them, apparently, to fulfill the wish of Polish ecologists like Tomasz who have called upon the Ministry of the Environment to make

122

all of the surrounding forests part of the Strictly Protected Area. The Ministry's response has persistently been, "No, the locals don't want it."

Tomasz and a growing number of unhappy researchers and European conservationists are now appealing to the European Union courts, under the Natura 2000 Agreement to which Poland is a signatory. He hopes the treaty will force Poland's environmental authorities to increase the nation's number of endangered species and habitat protections, or risk heavy fines and the loss of subsidies from the EU.[32] The appeals include tougher safeguards against continued logging on the edges of Bialowieza ("edge effects" include the loss of the forest's flagship species, including woodpeckers, thousands of other individual birds, and untold multitudes of insects, amphibians, reptiles, mammals and vascular plants). And, a second battle looms: the planned road by Polish authorities that would cut right through two other hugely important ecological zones in the northeast: Biebrza National Park, Poland's largest, a true paradise for birds[33] and the Raspuda River Valley.[34]

What is particularly tricky and distinctive about Bialowieza is the fact that there are a huge number of represented groups of organisms present, but very few individuals of any one species. The reasons are complex and ecologically brutal: it is not the number of available tree cavities for birds, but the availability of food. Among the large mammals, there are approximately 1,200 roe deer, red deer and wild boar inhabiting the National Park. Each individual needs at least a kilometer or two of territory. This much is known. There can be territorial overlap, but food availability is everything.

The countless back-country roads Tomasz drives form a labyrinth of confusion, both on and off the many maps to the area. Visitors to the National Park will at once discover the complexities of the park's various boundaries: No Entry points and the

ever-present and perilous proximity to the no-man's-land, which is the border with Belarus, a country on less than amicable terms with Poland. Those near political hostilities have not favored scientific collaboration. Nor has the veritable hot-wire erected by the Belarussians (reminiscent of the Berlin Wall) been particularly friendly to the larger mammals inhabiting the forest, particularly the over 750 European bison that straddle the two nations.

The story of this bison is key to understanding the remarkable promise and success of this last great deciduous/coniferous southern fringe of Europe's boreal forests from time immemorial.

Among the forest's 44 resident mammals, including five wolf packs, red deer, roe deer, lynx, small wild boar, wild cat, otter, raccoon-dog, elk and the exquisitely pragmatic rodent the beaver—one monarch stands out from all the others: the European bison or wisent (*Bison bonasus*). This emperor occupies a unique niche in Bialowieza. As Zbigniew Krasinski elaborates, the taxonomy is historically lucid, while more recent breeds and cross-breeds make for plentiful confusion.[35]

The genus is *Bison*, both in Europe and North America for hundreds-of-thousands of years. Of that genus, there are two species: the European (*Bison bonasus*) and American (*Bison bison*). Both species have, in turn, diverged into four sub-species: the European lowland bison, found in Bialowieza, and the now heavily-hybridized mountain bison (*Bison b. caucasicus*) of the Caucasus. In North America, a similar divergence occurred between the prairie bison (*Bison b. bison*) and the Canadian wood bison (*Bison b. athabascae*).

These great chimeras of dawn and dusk once inhabited most of Continental Europe. But, from the time of the Ice Age and before, hunters pursued them. Their cousin, the last wild ox, was slaughtered in 1627. Some 60 to 75 million bison were killed in the U. S. As ecologist Christian Kempf points out, "step by step, their increasing rarity drove them into the exclusive hands of the royal hunters." It was this fiefdom of privilege that ironically saved the forests themselves from obliteration.[36] In 1923, an international nature congress in Paris under the inspired aegis of John Sztolcman, concluded that the species was going extinct but proffered the method to save it, as the separate, but genetically-related American bison had also been saved. There were five distinct bison left in Poland at that time.[37] But until 1956, when captive-bred bison were released back into Bialowieza, there were none living in the wilds of the National Park. During World War I, all had been killed, as had a sub-species in the Caucasus, *Bison bonasus caucasus*.

Today, thanks to the efforts of many scientists and public and government support, particularly the many years of passionate dedication of Mr. and Mrs. Krasinska of the Mammal Research Institute in Poland, the number of bison across Europe is approaching 3,500, half of whom dwell in the wild.

While this provides for optimism, all remaining herds descend from 12 individuals, leaving the future genetic viability of the species vulnerable without continued initiatives to preserve remaining habitat and enlarge protected area networks.[38]

Here at Biaolowieza, human interventionist breeding work takes place in a large fenced area far from public access. Subsequent translocations back into the National Park and the adjoining forest preserves have resulted in a population approaching 400 animals on the Polish side and an estimated 350 on the Belarussian side. These

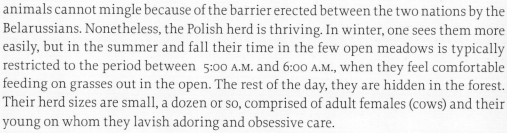

animals cannot mingle because of the barrier erected between the two nations by the Belarussians. Nonetheless, the Polish herd is thriving. In winter, one sees them more easily, but in the summer and fall their time in the few open meadows is typically restricted to the period between 5:00 A.M. and 6:00 A.M., when they feel comfortable feeding on grasses out in the open. The rest of the day, they are hidden in the forest. Their herd sizes are small, a dozen or so, comprised of adult females (cows) and their young on whom they lavish adoring and obsessive care.

The adult males are more solitary, though two or three may graze together. Strictly herbivorous, their diets vary according to the season. But in the winter, they are assisted by park authorities who leave them hay as well as white beets at the adjoining lovely chalets in the middle of the few multi-acre clearings. But for most of the year, the bison feed on the bark of four primary trees: "oaks, hornbeams, ash and aspen".[39] This consumption is not alone sufficient to fill the bison's 100 litre rumen, or stomach chamber. They consume another 15 or more tasty species of food. Between half and two-thirds of their day is spent eating and digesting.[40] The animals may weigh nearly 1,000 kilos or over a ton. With their predators now largely gone—wolves will rarely attack them and no brown bear has been seen in these forests since Poland's Independence in 1918—they are truly in charge. The mothers go off alone to give birth during the months of May, June or July, returning with the newborn a few days thereafter.[41]

For over 30 years Mr. Eshe Dackiewicz has been in charge of breeding the wisent at Bialowieski Park. He leads us in his jeep through the dawn hour in search of a wild herd. It is not easy to find them in the late summer, early fall. They are skittish and prefer privacy. The map shows three clearings in over 600 square kilometers of forest. On the third try, after traveling 40 kilometers over mud, there they are, quietly meandering. In this enormous creature, nature has tested her theory of non-violence: the larger the mammal, the gentler. This is so with mountain gorillas, hippos, elephants and blue whales, among many others. In fish species, the whale shark is comparable. The theory is tested when we come nose to nose with a 2,000 pound male at the breeding center. There Eshe and his staff of 25 are presently working with 42 bison in

a large captive habitat area within the heart of the forest. The bison wants to play.

The final day in the forest is one of memorable weather changes and remarkable sightings: song thrush, buzzard, lesser spotted eagle, red squirrels, admiral butterflies, dung beetles, hazel grouse, nuthatch, raven, marsh tits drinking upside down on lime trees, great spotted, black and three-toed woodpeckers—the flagships of this forest—and numerous frogs (*Rana temporaria*) hopping across ground cover dominated by wood sorrel. For two weeks during their riotous mating the male frogs will turn bright blue. Of all the creatures, it is the black woodpecker that leaves the most enchanting call. When he or she perches, the cry is like that of the loon: lonely, haunted, audible for miles. In flight, however, the call more resembles the high-energy acoustics of a chaffinch (the most abundant bird in these forests) or a warbler.

Whether this woodpecker will survive, as Tomasz and his students have been endeavoring to ensure, is not just a question of ecology but of human history, culture and virtue. It will take courage and not a little passion, on the part of the Polish people, to preserve that which has managed to survive Ice Ages, conflagrations and World Wars. In the end, it will require the love and dedication of scientists, officials and the public alike to keep Bialowieza and the surrounding forests intact, as the sacred sanctuaries nature intended. Says Tomasz, "We have a forest which is priceless, unique; a single last piece of this kind in the world. If we destroy it, we are fools on all accounts: economic, moral and spiritual."[42] Once it's gone, there is no way to buy it back.

FOR THE LOVE OF WILDLIFE: MARIETA VAN DER MERWE AND FAMILY

HARNAS, NAMIBIA

A 200-mile road, much of it dust-sprawling gravel, leads from Namibia's capital, Windhoek, due east toward the Trans-Kalahari Highway and Western Botswana. It is an expanse of indescribable freedom, at first glance, rimmed by desiccated blue uplifts.

Petite black-backed jackals cautiously skirt the edges in search of roadkill from this path that gives the appearance to the unwary of a pastoral calm. More confi-

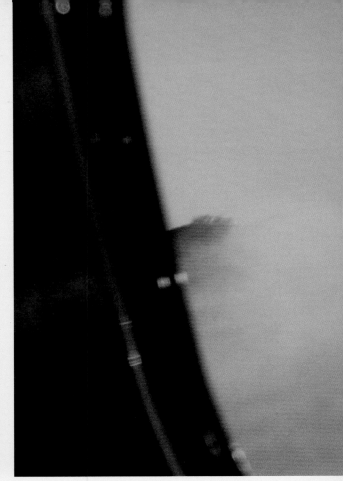

dent chacma baboons patrol this fast, two-lane thoroughfare, and guinea fowl in healthy numbers skittishly make the roadside home.

Namibia's fewer than two million people and 800,000 square kilometers translate into a theoretically sparse human ecological footprint. This impression is enhanced by the numerous wild mountain and Namib desert tracts throughout the country and an extensive network of conservation areas and parks fostering plentiful natural heritage, including a new wave of Transfrontier parks throughout east and southern Africa.[1] Namibia is famed for its wildlife: from the Etosha National Park in the north to its lush Caprivi Strip woodlands containing four parks, the second oldest rift (the 300-million-year-old Fish River Canyon) in all Africa, the important Tsaobis Leopard Nature Park and the newly established Three Nations Namib Desert Transfrontier Park. Elephants and lions, cheetahs and leopards, white and black rhino, buffalo, hippopotamus, giraffe and two species of zebra (Burchell's and Hartmann's mountain zebra) can all be seen, with serious luck. A dozen large antelope species and seven smaller ones roam the country, in addition to spotted hyaena, the two forms of jackal (black-backed and side-striped), the rare African wild dog, warthogs, and two primates—the vervet monkey and baboon. In the desert are wild horses, probably the only ones in all Africa.

Most of the 630 known bird species present in Namibia are not endemic (fewer than a half-dozen are), but most of them do breed in the country.

This plethora of biodiversity intimates itself en route to Gobabis, a town of approximately 12,000 inhabitants that emerges at the very edge of the great Kalahari. Herero people and Kung Bushmen, dialects of English, Afrikaans, Mbandieru, Kung-Tsukwe, all interact in a free-flow arrangement that settles the nerves as a great calm descends over the cypress and palm estates, expansive ranching enterprises to all

sides. A sign makes clear that this is "Cattle Country". It is also the Black Nossob River lands, almost a mile high.

The town was founded in 1856 by Friederich Eggert, a leader of the Rhenish Missionary Society, whose incarnation today is Evangelical Lutheranism with an ecological message at its heart. In a powerful, indepth statement issued in 1993 at a convention in Missouri, this branch of the church declared that humans are the "creation's caregivers" and acknowledged the terrible destruction to the natural environment that was occurring. The Biblical injunction to "love the earth as God loves us" assumed real urgency and a "call to justice."[2]

The huge Gobabis region, with its far-reaching savannah scrublands of camelthorn, acacia, paper bark and quiver trees, is dominated by some 800 farms. This collective human presence cannot easily live up to the Biblical urgings of Evangelical Lutheranism, however hard many might try. Indeed, like most of Namibia, and Africa in general, poverty and ignorance has led to massive encroachment upon most biodiversity. In fact, as one ecologist put it, this is a country that kills to stay alive. There are deadly traps everywhere you look; every three feet along every animal pathway. The steel claws trap indiscriminately, and rural people will eat or sell whatever they succeed at killing. This is just the way it is.

In the mid-1970s, Nick and Marieta Van der Merwe, third generation farmers in this district, started behaving in a manner new to the region: rather than killing wildlife, they rescued the animals. Considering that a lion and an African wild dog each consume 22 pounds of meat every day, a leopard 18 pounds, a cheetah and hyena each over 15 pounds, lynx-like caracal and jackals 10 pounds per animal; and that a baboon will consume enormous amounts of fruit, grasses, and other palatable proteins, these facts posed a perplexing challenge from the beginning of the family's

commitment to a wildlife orphanage. They did not know these details when they saved a gorgeous vervet monkey from a neglectful owner for five rand (the equivalent of a couple of U.S. dollars) and a piece of bread.

Additional costs soon erupted with each new heartbreak needing mending: a full suite of complex medical care facilities, fences, vigilance, staff, money. The Van der Merwes were cattle ranchers, not millionaires. Marieta, however, could not help herself. And soon, across tens-of-thousands of square miles, it became known that this former Namibian policewoman turned animal rights zealot would never say no to an animal in need.

Arriving at Marieta's sanctuary at sunset, honey badger, hardebeest, eland, warthogs and kudu showed their moon-reflecting eyes through the acacia groves. Already, the deep undulating calls of the lions were haunting the thousands of acres of Harnas Wildlife Refuge. Harnas is Zulu for "shield" or protection, and that is precisely what Marieta and her family and staff have accomplished. A true sanctuary in a warzone.

We wander in the night, absorbing the clicking of bats and the call of the giant eagle owl (*Bubo lacteus*). We hear the wiedehopf, or hoopoe, and the last high-energy song of familiar chat, fork-tailed drongo and common waxbill. The stars are naked and unabashed, and music is emanating from the bar at the lodge which serves the eco-tourist guests who come from near and far to support this remarkable dream of compassion in the desert.

The next morning we wander with Marieta through her sprawling hacienda-style complex that must serve the needs of animals and also provide some revenue stream by way of the few tourists who visit here. She leads us into her private quarters where large cats and a dozen other species greet her the way family dogs would in more familiar surroundings. All of these animals were once clinging to life as orphans, their legs mangled, or their mothers slaughtered—familiar stories throughout the world.

First there was the lion, Elsa; then Shabu, Savannah, Macho, Ushwayau, Terry and

then Goeters, a cheetah now 23 years old. Other cheetahs followed: Dumah ("chee-tah" in Swahili), Zita, Kiki, Avram and Nekita. And the leopards, Keanu and Pacha.

"Great hunters," Marieta says matter-of-factly. "A cheetah succeeds in catching her prey twenty to thirty percent of the time. A leopard: sixty percent success rate."

These cats are sometimes separated, sometimes not. They are dangerous, if in heat or holding down territory or startled. The stories flow, too many to assimilate. What is happening at the moment is what fully throttles us with awe. There is Marieta, rubbing the stomach of a lion, Zion, an adolescent.

The young cheetah, Pride, and a pipsqueak lion, Trust, dominate their tandem worlds.

Cleopatra, an infant cheetah, is one month old. At this age, she is almost impos-sible to distinguish from a California mountain lion of the same age. Cleopatra is

136

taken with an endemic tortoise that has found a home here, but stays clear of the larger crocodilian in a nearby pool.

The cats follow us everywhere. There are complications involved with moving large felines into huge fenced arenas, some several thousand acres. Angolina Jolie has supported Harnas and, according to Marieta, she was incredibly inspired and generous when it came to helping with one of the major fence projects.

We pass through a fenced area to cavort with the baboons—Kevin, Mimi, Caren, Smittie, Booboo, Violet.

And later, we were with Stinky, Anna and Monsieur Robert, each a native mongoose, craving affection. We find ourselves mobbed by 20 of them. Suddenly a bite by one jealous for our affections. It is superficial as puncture wounds go.

The wild dogs, however, are not so accessible. They have plenty of reasons to fear human beings, who have tried to exterminate them from all of Africa.

Cheetahs were being shot by farmers when Marieta and her husband first started taking them in from the Herrero, San and Damera people in the region. She and Nick would plead with the locals not to shoot them. They had their reasons or so they believed. Few people gave it a thought. But with respect to African wild dogs (*Lycaon pictus*), the painted dogs are one of the most critically endangered mammals in the world. Their lives would be cut short by worse than bullets: gin traps. Steel snares trapped them and while still alive, suffering from their wounds and dehydration, they would be devoured by ants. Marieta shows us photographs of some they rescued just in time. Now they are leery of getting too close to us.

When Marieta first started taking the wild dogs in, driving hundreds of kilometers without asking questions whenever the phone rang to alert her to another crisis, she provided rehabilitation to seven adults all similarly trapped. Then four more pups were rescued, the last survivors of a massacre in the Otjiwarongo District, near Bushmanland. Marieta nursed them back to life. Today, Harnas has the only free-roaming captive African wild dog population in the world. A vast terrain enables them, for

the most part, to survive as they would in their wild habitat, which includes all of Namibia. Most of these dogs will be released into a metapopulation, a large, well-managed biologically robust tribe of canines on a 24,000 acre reserve which Harnas is intent upon acquiring.

Already, the medical infrastructure is in place: translocation facilities, bio-medical baseline data, disease screening, genetic work-ups, parasitology and reproductive physiology research, data on behaviorial ecology of the animals, and much more.

We watch a young pup playing with the pack. Gorgeous, fast and nervous; with sharp teeth, penetrating eyes and glances that are fleeting and controlled—their joy is evident, unleashed by the heart of one woman.

Marieta's story has been told brilliantly by Chris Mercer.[3] It is a great epic. To hear Marieta downplay the saga, while frolicking with her playmates (cheetahs, lions and the wild dogs, Leska, Calbe, Anja, Anita, Aninja and Boer) is astonishing.

We see the meat being readied to be tossed to all the big carnivores. And we are hesitant to ask from where she gets it. Noting our discomfort, she simply declares: "Everyday somebody, usually a member of our staff, of which there are usually about thirty, must cut up old horses and donkeys that have been slaughtered. But I come from the one-bullet school. Domestic animals must be slaughtered properly. This meat is what keeps these native carnivores alive. Every August we buy seal meat from the coast, some seven tons of it, to feed these cats."

That is the reality. While some of her charges are herbivores, most are not. And, the staff—many from Germany, Canada or England who pay for the privilege of un-

derstudying with Marieta—seem to cotton to her philosophy. She cannot alter millions of years of African wildlife diet, nor would she ever imagine doing so. What she can do, and what she has been doing all her life, is spread hope and manifest love in a way that matters most to her: saving individuals and thereby, incrementally, staving off extinctions across this ancient land.

She tells us how before she and Nick knew it, back in the 1970s, they were living with 300 animals. One vervet came during a war between Namibia and Swapu. Soldiers returning from Angola with captured animals found they were not allowed to carry the animals into Namibia. So they would either kill and eat, or abandon them. That is when the newly formed Nature Conservation agency of Namibia called upon Marieta and her husband to see if they would take some of the orphans. "We couldn't say 'No'."

One vervet in particular was screaming in panic. Marieta comforted her with a glass of whiskey and the technique has worked ever since with monkeys, she says. "Particularly J&B."

"My husband, Nick, died at the age of forty-five in five days after being bitten by an ant that carried a rare fever." Nick had earlier crash landed a small aircraft on the property and nearly burned to death. If anyone could be deemed a survivor, it was Nick. But that ant was something else.

Baby leopards, lions, cheetahs and, at one point, more than eighty baboons were living in their house.

"Eighty baboons?"

"Yes," she giggles girlishly. "Oh and six wild dogs, also."

One of those baboons has three legs, from a fire in a garbage dump where, famished, it had been searching for food. Another baboon had been shot through the hand by "trophy hunters." Two of his fingers are gone.

She described how four of those wild dogs before us had been caught in the horrible gin traps, then chained to some trees. Other dogs came to help them, only to be caught themselves in yet more traps. She drove 500 kilometers to rescue them. There were bone fragments all over the place.

We come upon a perfect, gentle-appearing leopard. He had been shot through the leg at the time Marieta saved him. The man she took the cat from was about to shoot the animal: a despiser of great cats. The man's wife would not permit it and hastened to get Marieta there as quickly as possible.

The Harnas Wildlife Foundation hopes to acquire another large sanctuary close to the Windhoek airport, a place where rescued animals can be rehabilitated with easier access to good and secure medical supplies, prior to relocation back into the larger Harnas sanctuary 100 kilometers east of Gobabis.

It is a job that never ends and her weary smile acknowledges that. There are indeed hunters and despoilers of wildlife everywhere around them. The continent is imploding. People are hungry and greed cares not for innocence.

Marieta hates trophy hunting. "How can you put a head on the wall?" she asks. Adding, "We must be one happy family. These species must be saved."[4]

It has been said that "conservation biology is a crisis discipline" and that "decisions must be made in the face of considerable uncertainty,"[5] but, herein, one family in Namibia has shown how life can be treasured and adored unconditionally.

HOWARD BUFFETT AND THE WORLD OF THE CHEETAH

JUBATUS, SOUTH AFRICA

Howard and Devon Buffett inhabit many worlds across Africa, but Jubatus Cheetah Reserve, about three hours North of Johannesburg, just off the N1 at Bela Bela at the base of the Waterburg Mountains, is—along with Decatour, Illinois—their primary home.

The cheetah is in trouble. Fewer than 15,000 survive with only 200 in the wild in South Africa. A species known to have existed throughout much of the world for five-and-a-half million years, the cheetah's future is likely to be cut short because of human ignorance, the destruction of the animal outright and/or its habitat. The largest number (perhaps 2,500 at best) still inhabit parts of Namibia, but thirteen African countries have lost all of their cheetahs, while seventeen African nations

still host the remaining 12,500. South Africa, which boasts of dozens of parks and private wildlife reserves, represents a stark palette of differentiated sanctuaries, with wildlife corridors punctuated by 45 million people and their farms, cities, townships, roads and ecological challenges.

Yet, amid this tumult of habitat fragmentation, Jubatus, the brainchild of Howard Buffett and his wife Devon, represents a 12,400 acre microcosm of good will, informed and tenacious vision, and—when we visited—all of two cheetahs, Peter and Howie, who were brought there for a number of critical scientific and practical reasons.

Howie's mother had died under tragic circumstances. Howie had been captively bred and taught how to hunt. Within ten days he had learned. Peter, the larger, six-year-old cheetah, was a skilled survivor. He had killed as large an antelope as the kudu, as well as a zebra foal. To feed this nascent core group of two cheetahs and refurbish a tired landscape with native species, some twenty zebras and well over seventy blesboks were brought onto the property. Impala and other smaller antelopes were already here.

Howard and Devon had been working for months to obtain permits for three more cheetahs. Within a few years they hope to see cubs raised here, to open up the quadrants to enable these majestic cats to hunt on larger blocks of 10,000, 12,000, 14,000 acres each.

Jubatus is in the northern quadrant bordering upon southeastern Botswana, a region known simply as Bushveld Basin in the Highveld. Nearly 450 kilometers across, at its southern boundary, which encompasses South Africa's capital, Pretoria, and roughly 375 kilometers to Tom Burke at the northern edge, the region contains at

least 53 nature reserves, sanctuaries, game lodges, resorts, national parks, ecological research centers, wilderness areas, nature trails, zoological gardens, wildlife breeding centers, ecoparks, game ranches and game farms. Multiply that density by South Africa's 27 other enormous regions and the proliferation of commitments to nature and eco-tourism make this country stand out as one of the premiere conservation zones on Earth.[1]

Directly to the West, over a long low-lying mountain range is the Marakele National Park of nearly 240,000 acres that encompass the Waterberg Ridge, savannah dominated by acacia trees, abundant greater and lesser antelopes, as well as rhino. Nextdoor to Jubatus is the De Wildt Cheetah Research Centre. Ann and Godfrey van Dyk were persuaded by Dr. D. J. Brand of the National Zoological Gardens that cheetahs could breed in captivity, a concept rejected by most scientists in the 1960s. Fencing off a portion of their farm, the effort was initiated and has since resulted in the birth of more than 600 cheetah cubs, including king or striped cheetahs. The animals have been translocated throughout the country.

Sadly, fewer than 200 wild cheetahs remain. Each death is a tragedy for a species with fewer and fewer options, as humans usurp their long standing dominion. Connectivity for these various private and public initiatives is a critical survival issue for *Acinonyx jubatus* and was a motivation for Howard and Devon Buffet's 5,000 hectare sanctuary. The attempt to understand what the cheetahs need to survive and how metapopulations (self-sustaining aggregates of distinct but related groups) can function in an ever deteriorating ecological landscape are being investigated. With less than 15,000 cheetahs in the world, understanding these primeval creatures has become a major priority for those with the heart and sense to care. Surprisingly little is

known about this animal, which has been semi-domesticated at least since the time of the Egyptian pharaohs.

Howard knows Africa from inside out. But his commitments, and those of his wife Devon, go far beyond Jubatus and far beyond Africa. He is focused on agriculture, ending hunger, alleviating poverty and suffering. As a farmer himself, he knows down to the penny what a bushel of corn or a bag of soybeans costs in Nebraska, plus the so-called tech surcharge by the multinationals that control most production of staples in the United States. One of his countless projects is his Foundation's support of a genetically-modified sweet potato with iron enrichment for Africa, which Howard believes is likely to save millions of lives. Those lives, in turn, he reckons, will save the lives of animals like the cheetah.

In his presentation at a United Nations Office on Drugs and Crime Forum in Vienna in October of 2006, Howard shared some of his photographs of victims of poverty and human cruelty: the sole survivor of a massacred family, sitting in the church where some 500 people were slaughtered during the 1994 genocide in Rwanda; a Chinese woman, begging on the street with her two ragamuffin children tethered to her side to prevent them from being abducted and sold into slavery; a little girl in Niger who died of starvation three days after Howard took the photograph; a sobbing Armenian child with no apparent hope (Howard's caption read: "she is likely to become a statistic, something that will ultimately mean very little to anyone in the world"); a Bangladeshi boy foraging for his livelihood through a garbage pit; a one-legged street urchin in Bucharest who lives in a sewer, a member of "the forgotten generation"; an AIDS orphan in Malawi and two Senegalese children chained, enslaved, their lives an unbelievable horror. Howard risked his life to get these images: From Mali to the Mexican border, where hopeful illegal immigrants risk "rape, death or enslavement" to gain access to the land of the free; from the Democratic Republic of the Congo to Chad, Guatamala, Peru and Rwanda, Howard Buffet's commitment to alleviating oppression and suffering is staggering.

Howard writes, "My education on the subject did not come from school. My learning took place along homeless-lined railroad tracks in Bangladesh and the arid soils of Mali. It came from sitting around fires in Namibia with Himba women and visiting homes in Armenia, listening to stories of lives which had deteriorated from poor to terrible. I learned that systems fail people and that words like "democracy" do not feed children. Much of what I believed about the human race, how humane or how cruel we can be, has been verified in acute ways."[2]

With the commitment from Howard and his Foundation, two cheetahs on 5,000 remote hectares of South Africa are being saved as is a broad biodiversity base within the refuge. Howard perseveres with a great sense of humor and a great common sense of the poignancy and urgency inherent to the human condition. His wealth has not obscured his purpose, diminished his ardor or deterred him from his causes.

He spends about four months a year throughout Africa, but considers Jubatus his home when he is not farming corn and soybeans in Illinois. He started taking photographs of wildlife and of the human condition in his 30s. Two decades later, his books and funding commitments demonstrate that he has what it takes to turn the tide and engender significant potential for change.

Certainly, the two cheetahs that we visited – Howie and Peter—are grateful to

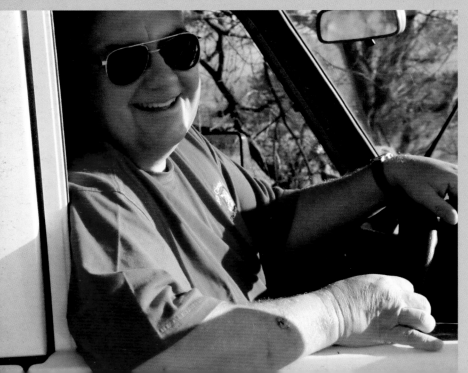

Howard and Devon Buffett. So are all of the other hundreds of other species that inhabit the sanctuary the Buffets have created.

It took seven years to get to this stage and they have overseen every detail, from a 30-ton bridge that can withstand occasional floods, to a vast network of electrified fences to ensure the integrity of four distinct blocks for scientific study. Chris, Jubatus' manager, is a local Robert De Niro look-alike who knows each and every species. Howard does too but is less concerned about Latin nomenclature. But when asked about some little white balls seen on the side of a dirt road, as we drive in search of temporarily-hiding giraffes, he instantly declares: hyena. Though not yet sure how many hyenas and jackals inhabit the nearly 22 square miles of native bush, he knows their scat.

Suddenly, a male ostrich displays his displeasure at our approach. The female is there, and the male is not about to let her down. He runs 35 miles per hour around the meadow in which Howard parked the Jeep. In the course of circling us twice, the male stops to take momentary dirt baths, spread his enormous wings and repeatedly grunt a sound neither Howard nor we have ever heard. Howard mimics it with remarkable precision.

We find a male giraffe who wanders alone and skittish, and Howard worries over the whereabouts of three others. Chris reassures him that they are out there, somewhere. We pass four zebra, white blesbok and blue wildebeest. Yellow-beaked hornbills, three white rhinos (a father, mother and one-year-old), countless quail, bee-eaters, warthogs and hundreds of other ungulates grace our path as we traverse the network of dirt fire roads that Howard constructed. This is a man who loves his farm equipment and who has a particular passion for and knowledge of irrigation systems, particularly the pivots. Water, he says, is the future of the world and we better get it right.

Finally we return to the site of Peter and Howie's kill—a blesbok or non-native antelope peculiar to this region. The two huge cheetahs feast. Howie is gorging on the intestines while Peter, not ten feet away from us, stares lazily. For now, after 5.5 million years, they are in paradise.

We discuss with Howard what it would take to engender a corridor for these remarkable felines, and he concurs that that would be a great thing for South Africa, but a challenge to get all the stakeholders to agree to it and work out all the GIS data that might support a geographical infrastructure for the cheetahs' uncurtailed movement. Howard currently is funding the metapopulation study which would be needed scientifically to achieve this cooperation. The study will provide much more data on any inbreeding depression; the amount of territory needed by cheetahs; the number of kills and amount eaten; prey species specifics; forest types and numerous other as yet uncertain characteristics regarding the life of cheetahs.

Next door to the main compound is a large immaculate scientific laboratory for in vitro data, conferences and educational outreach. But much has yet to be done.

Howard and Devon Buffett have established a complex sanctuary in a country where habitat fragmentation, real estate prices and abuse of wildlife is everywhere on the rise. Knowing local customs, finding trackers, working with officials, strenuously going through the hoops required for obtaining permits to have cheetahs, are monumental and ongoing tasks.

Our final evening sees us driving along a narrow dusty road behind Howie and Peter who saunter with elegant confidence for well over an hour, peeing on certain trees, generally exploring their world. Howie, particularly, on this tenth day of freedom in his life seems remarkably at home. They will live 20 to 25 years and grow to nearly 100 kilograms. Howard walks with the two cheetahs routinely, but he has to watch his back. Peter lost a canine a few years ago, which may have saved Howard's life the week before we arrived, because Peter became slightly rambunctious and bit down on Howard's arm. The puncture marks are healing, but had that canine been in place, it would have penetrated the artery and there is no telling the consequences.

Sunset at Jubatus in the bush is remarkable, following meandering cheetahs who amble at about three kilometers per hour. Their measured saunter is stressfree. This is their world.

Over dinner with Devon and Howard, conversation roams from genetically modified corn and soybeans, to the plight of intellectual property rights in Africa; the supercharged intelligence of Howard's friends Bill and Melinda Gates and his own dad, Warren; the fate of the earth, the nature of non-violence and a vigorous airing of views on the subject of meat eating versus vegetarianism. Joining us this night is a couple who hope to import a few tigers from China into South Africa, teach them the ways of being a tiger in the wild, then release them back into fenced protected reserves in China.[3] There are no answers. Howard speaks his mind, particularly on issues of multinational controls over indigenous agriculture. Having served on boards of four of the largest multinationals in the U.S., he has strong opinions. But he also has a terrific sense of humor, and his wife Devon loves to tease him.

Is it right, Howard asks me, to have spent something like nine million dollars on a couple of cheetahs, compared with what that money might do elsewhere? If it's

what your heart asks you to do, then it is right. Compassion isn't reserved for humans alone, in the great web of creation, we tell him.

Though he is putting more and more of his money into fighting hunger, poverty and disease throughout Africa, as well as trying to assist in rationally mitigating the sorrows along America's border with Mexico, for now he is intent on getting past considerable bureaucratic hassles to obtain those permits for a few more cheetahs, here in South Africa. And, as Devon points out, if they had not purchased their 5,000 hectares at a price of approximately 2,400 rand per hectare (US$350 at the time), this remnant of wild Africa would have gone the way of their corporate neighbor on one side, an 18-hole golf course with over 300 stands (lots) of less than a hectare each; and, condominiums to all sides.

They saved their bit of the wild and their satisfaction is palpable. But even more impressive is that glimpse, next morning, of sunrise over Jubatus, as Howard and Chris go radio-tracking to see where Peter and Howie ended up sleeping. We move into a rocky promontory overlooking the vast western expanse.

"Over there," Howard whispers. "They're still sleeping. Shhh!"

And we move on.

THE ORIGINAL GARDEN OF EDEN

SOCOTRA, YEMEN

The animal market in Yemen's capital, Sana'a, is like markets from Bangkok to Bamako. It is early February, a Friday afternoon, and the market is closing down. But there are still all the remnant life forms in their dark and moldering cages: two Africa Scops owls (*Otus senegalensis*), as well as a little owl (*Athene noctua*); a civet cat with no room to even turn around; falcons, doves and parakeets. Countless herbivorous animals, goats, cows, calves, horses and sheep—all of them tethered without the slightest ability to move. Hatchets, cleavers, blood and guts flow beneath butcher hooks. We purchase several of the birds to release. But the larger animals are beyond our help at this moment.

It was in just such a souk in Sana'a that one of the last wild Arabian leopards in Yemen, named Arnold, was discovered back in the mid-1980s, a period when all wild cats and wolves were being killed. Farmers thought them guilty of killing goats and chickens. They weren't mistaken for the prey species of these carnivores were hunted down by locals. The big animals were starving.

It is a sober introduction to an otherwise breathtaking country; a profile that comports with Yemen's difficult demography. Her population of 21 million is destined to exceed 71 million by 2050. Current life expectancy for men is 59, for women 63. Seventy-four percent of the nation is rural with a per capita income of US$820 or $2.27 a day. Contraceptive use of so-called modern methods among married women is only 13%. All of this leads to environmental decay. 220,800 acres of precious forest were lost in the last decade. Fifty-five percent of the people are without adequate sanitation. There are 20 known Threatened and Endangered taxa of animals and 52 known plant taxa that are in trouble.[1]

The towns of Aden and Al Mukalla are scarcely suggestive of what's out there, 535 kilometers further south. In Aden, a fish market is haunted by the glare of eyeballs beseeching passers-by beneath the cliffs near the last Sultan's old palace. A few miles away is a hidden wetland that is critically important to thousands of migratory birds, protected by three local rangers. These young, bearded sentinels take obvious pride in their showcase, wading through knee-deep water with us out towards the center of the marsh, where several hundred lesser flamingos (*Phoenicopterus minor*) feed eagerly in the brackish pools. There are at least two globally threatened migrants, five regionally threatened birds and another nine high-flying itinerants who venture to these postage stamp-sized wetlands. The populations here in Aden comprise 1% or more of these birds' total number worldwide.[2] A bright male Ruppell's weaver (*Ploceus galbula*) shows himself in the waning light. Far across the embayment, where the Hiswa sewage flow originates, there is a congeries of heavy industry. And there, in that port, the American military vessel USS Cole was targeted by terrorists in October 2000.

Far to the South, beyond all the socio-economic problems of mainland Yemen, at the alluring juncture of the Gulf of Aden and Indian Ocean, to the East of Somalia's Horn of Africa, or southeast from Oman, the pristine Yemeni archipelago surfaces from the mist; a region long obscured in mythology and history. It has been called the primeval Galapagos of the Indian Ocean. And it is a candidate for World Heritage status, a place of "Outstanding Universal Value"—the island of Socotra.

For years we had dreamt of sleeping out on a cliff high up in the legendary Hamaderoh escarpment, where the famed Egyptian vultures breed, and succulent bottle-trees endemic to this furthest-most wilderness stand cosseted in the perennially flamboyant weather.

Socotra herself, named Dioscorida in ancient times, a place of giant lizards and crocodiles, was described by a mysterious Greek mariner sometime in the first century in an account entitled "Periplus of the Erythraean Sea."[3]

Tantalizing mystery has always enshrouded the six islands that comprise the Archipelago, which include in addition to the largest island, Socotra, the second largest, Abd al Kuri, Ka'l Firawn, Darsa, Samha and Sabuniya. On Socotra, which covers a formidable mountainous and desert area of 3,625 square kilometers (133 kms latitudinally by 43 kms longitudinally; the others comprising just short of 192 square kilometers), every single plant is irrepressibly an individualist. Specialists more accustomed to referencing taxa, here personalize each flower, bush and tree, endowing them with scientific traits more akin to poetic attributions. Bruno Mies, a geobotanist from the University of Dusseldorf, who has made several expeditions to the islands, writes "Almost every individual can be distinguished by its unique morphology. The trunks can be deeply dissected, pyramidal or columnar like a candle. The branches sometimes intertwine like lovers. One is tempted to give a name to each specimen."[4]

The island to which we have journeyed is legendary for its wildlife, including a giant hooded cobra inhabiting the central Haggeher Mountains, and several gigantic species of snails, silverfish, antlions (highly efficient ant predators also known as doodlebugs), the blood dragon gecko (*Haemodracon riebeckii*), and most notably, the caudex species of succulent plants, such as the cucumber tree, desert rose and cinnabar or dragon's blood tree.

New discoveries are made daily. In the last 120 years, expeditions to the island have unveiled a veritable ecological renaissance of Socotran zoology. These include Balfour in 1888[5], Forbes in 1903[6], the Oxford University expedition in 1956, which nonsensically described Socotran mountain people as belonging to the "stone age,"[7] plus the impressive Anthony G. Miller and Miranda Morris' comprehensive botani-

cal work[8] and the recent stunning and unparalleled overview by Catherine Cheung and Lyndon DeVantier[9].

Countless other species and types of species have recently been discovered, from unknown lichens[10] and earwigs[11] to the amazing dead sailor's eye, a green alga resembling an alien metallic sphere, which sits placidly in wait on the ocean floor—but for what?[12] A red alga, cave dwelling crickets, a new fresh-water land crab species, new polychaete tube worms and four new bird species also have been identified.[13]

Socotra's semi-arid tropics and botanical uniqueness invite every possible ecological superlative. The island is a living font of biodiversification, most notably among its bottle trees: *Dorstenia gigas gypsophila*, *Dendrosicyos socotrana*, *Adenium socotranum* and *obesum* and the most famous of all, *Dracaena cinnabari* or dragon's blood. This latter bottle tree belongs to an ecosystem that is today largely confined to this one spectacular island. It is only thinly represented in a few other remote parts of Arabia, with the exception of less than 200 individuals on the Canary Islands and a few more living on Cape Verde and the Madeira Islands[14]. All are caudiciformes (caudex meaning succulent), plants which are vegetative forms well-adapted to arid conditions. Typically, as on Socotra, the caudex, or base of the perennial trees and shrubs from which new buds originate, are the preeminent water storage and transport areas of the plant, as opposed to the crowns, which are small, and often attenuated. The first glimpse of these caudex forests is overwhelming: A magical kingdom like few places on the planet.

Because of her terrestrial varieties and uniquely quarrelsome weather for much of the year, including cyclones and hurricane-force gales on some parts of the island persisting for months, this archipelago at the northern-most reaches of the Indian Ocean, skimming the Gulf of Aden and Arabian Sea, sows seeds worldwide. Of the approximately 825 known plant species (some argue there are over 900), 307 are endemic[15] and 50 are listed as Threatened by the IUCN.[16] Botantists rank Socotra as one of the most important plant regions on Earth. The island is within one of the 35 hotspots and is included in the World Wildlife Fund's Global 200 Ecoregions. For a relatively small island, this seems extraordinary. But, in just one small portion of Socotra, the north, where our expedition was headed, 201 of those endemics were found.

Like New Zealand, Socotra's only native mammals are bats, four known species or subspecies: the insectivorous lesser mouse-tailed, the African horseshoe, the very rare trident and the desert pipistrelle.[17] In addition, a single Madagascar shrew population has been observed on Socotra. But the historical absence of any other known mammals adds fuel to the notion that the more recent wild and domesticated asses, the camels, the multitudinous goats and other introduced species are actually providing an ecological service. It might be in the form of co-evolutionary pressure upon plant communities, particularly those where there is some evidence of over-grazing; but also the contribution of feces to the soil, plus bacteria and parasites yet to be discovered.

The island's bird life is extensive, with 178 known species recorded here and at least seven endemics, including an island cisticola (*Cisticola haesitatus*), sparrow (*Passer insularis*), warbler (*Cisticola incanus*), sunbird (*Nectarinia balfouri*), starling (*Onychognathus frater*), and rarest of all—the Socotra bunting (*Emberiza socotrana*). This latter bird, as well as the island cisticola, was deemed Vulnerable by the IUCN as of 2000. In addition, there are either ten or eleven sub-species endemic to Socotra, including the Socotra cormorant (*Phalacrocorax nigrogularis*). With 22 Globally-Important Bird Areas on the islands, Socotra is one of the most critical areas on Earth, not just for the few endemics, but for the huge seabird colonies that include nearly 120,000 desert wheatear and the largest breeding group of red-billed tropicbirds in the entire Middle East.[18] In August of 2000, the first ever discovered breeding site of Jouanin's petrel was announced. Nadim Taleb of the Yemen Environmental Protection Authority and Socotra Conservation and Development Programme, found 50 of the birds near their nests on a cliff on Socotra. This news was greeted as "an astounding discovery for the ornithological world."[19]

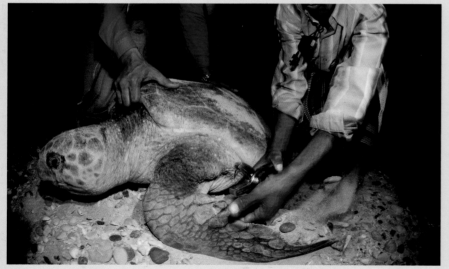

As described by Cheung and DeVantier,[20] who have comprehensively amassed and organized the wealth of biological and cultural data from Socotra, two freshwater carp, the only known primary freshwater species ever noted on Socotra and first detected in the early 1880s, have not been seen since. Presently, at least 44 other species of freshwater vertebrates are found on the island. Marine juveniles have long populated interior bodies of water, making their way inland from numerous estuaries and riparian outflows, such as the major wetland region of the northwest at the village of Qalansiyah.

The Red Sea leading from the Mediterranean to the Indian Ocean via the Gulf of Aden is particularly rich in wildlife and within minutes of any dive in any of the many identifiable littoral biotopes of these islands, hard and soft corals (270 species combined), crustacea (300 species), mollusks (500 species), algae (a known 260 species) and vast colorful assemblages of fish (a known 680 species in Socotran waters) seduce the eye.[21] There are huge seagrass beds and high kelp productivity. The water is arrestingly clean, as is the air. This island chain, which has been cut off biogeographically for 70 million years from the African mainland, supports abundant

green, loggerhead and hawksbill turtles nesting on many shores of the Archipelago. These creatures were the impetus for an extraordinary outpouring of Socotran conservationist sentiments in recent years, resulting in an official delegation from Socotra to protest the Ministry of Transport's plans to destroy a nesting beach with a new road. The Republic of Yemen's President, His Eminence Ali Abdallah Saleh, stepped in and supported the locals. The road was diverted.

Of the 30 known reptilian species on Socotra, 90% are endemic, including a legless burrowing creature and hissing chameleons whom locals fear will steal their voice if they are hapless enough to hear its strident sound.

This superabundance of taxa coincides with one of the oldest known island sites of continuous human habitation in the world. Today, the population hovers somewhere around 44,000 people whose lineage pre-dates the Arabic language by millennia, though Arabic is spoken in the Socotran capital of Hadibo, where any expedition into the island's interior typically originates. In the mountains, Socotran is spoken, and it is celebrated for being one of the most beautiful, if unpronounceable, languages on earth.

Along the dusty main roads of Hadibo we gathered our supplies one winter morning in preparation for our expedition into the limestone plateaux and granitic spires of the central mountain range, the Haggeher or Hagher or Skand, as this more than 1,600-meter-high wall of outcrops, encompassing hundreds of square miles, is called.

Hadibo has had a serious make-over even during the last ten years, a result of the scientific interest shown in the island and the inevitability of eco-tourism, particularly amongst Italians, French and Germans. The days of rampant lice infestations, TB, malaria, dysentery and outbreaks of cholera, referred to as recently as the mid-1990s, are largely over. While well water systems attract some mosquitoes, they are by no means swarming. And though wind and tidal surges keep the islands inaccessible for some parts of the year, February presents an enchanted stillness, weather as fine as the planet has conceived. The beaches, which spread for hundreds of miles, are empty.

Even vegetarians like us were pleased with the local or near local produce. Fresh grapes, lettuce, papaya, onions, potatoes, beans, watermelon, banana, dates, lemon, green pepper, red tamarind, nuts, and peaches, pomegranate, millet and cucumbers are all available. Four huge home-grown tomatoes cost US$1. Local honey is now available, thanks to a French Government project, and local bakers are superb. They also have various hot sauces on the island and good chocolate.

We were informed upon our arrival two days after the end of the protracted winter monsoon that there had been more rain in the previous two months than had ever been accumulated during any such period of the last 30 years. Such conditions enabled Socotra to be on her best behavior, although we were to discover the infernal heat that descends on the still interior mountain valleys beneath a particularly burning sun.

We met first with our liaison from the local United Nations-supported Socotra Conservation and Development Programme whose commitment to a "Conservation and Sustainable Use of Biodiversity" project has delineated those regions throughout the Archipelago that are to be set aside forever more as National Parks, Nature Sanctuaries and Resource Use Reserves. This "terrestrial zoning plan" has the advantage of thousands of years of native conservationist acumen. Because of the island's fantastic isolation, this regal confederacy of locals has long had its affairs in order. Like certain tribals in the Amazon, Australasia, and South India, Socotrans are intrinsically supreme ecologists. This is not to underestimate the considerable challenges facing them in the future, particularly with respect to industrial development, road construction, intensive agriculture, the control of grazing animals, the distribution and protection of fresh water, electrification (at present electricity is available from 4:00 to 11:00 P.M. each night) and ecotourism infrastructure.

Moreover, plant hunters from throughout Yemen have discovered Socotra and are now going after some 199 medicinal herbs found nowhere else. These herbs, known as al-jazeera, are touted in marketplaces throughout Sana'a as cure-alls, which they are not. Offered as dental herbs, laxatives, aphrodisiacs, fertility drugs—the list of medicinal magic goes on.[22] Thus far, Yemen authorities have been ineffective at curbing the extirpation of native plants by over-zealous entrepreneurs.

Road damage is one of the biggest issues at present for Socotra conservation. The Yemen Transit Authority would like to put roads everywhere, we are told, and they are very good at it. Indeed, the paved roads throughout Socotra are powerful lures after one has spent time in a vehicle on the traditional goat and camel trails, which are the most improbable "roads" in the world. Nonetheless, the problem for Socotra is that a modern road destroys unique habitat almost anywhere one is laid on the

island. There weren't any marginally-important areas on Socotra until the few paved roads demonstrated their biological edge effects. But the fact remains: every square inch of this island is absolutely precious.

There are some 300 villages on Socotra, so with each passing day, the network of interconnectivity increases and will necessarily improve. The populous thus desperately needs an ecological master plan, and Socotrans are struggling with that fact. A law exists for dividing the island such that approximately half will be utilized strictly for conservation, the other half for development; a 50/50 demarcation superimposed onto the parks, sanctuaries and resource-use terrestrial zoning grid.

Presently, far more than 50% of Socotra can be characterized as largely pristine. Much of it is unexplored. In fact, the Socotra Conservation Zoning Plan, as it was officially decreed, shows 75% of the island as National Park, with an additional 12 terrestrial and 27 marine Nature Sanctuaries gazetted. The coastal zone and almost all of the other five islands in the archipelago are protected. This is among the most untrammeled and officially enshrined conservation areas on Earth. Only one other large island that we know of, Rakiura or Stewart Island in New Zealand, has such a large conservation block, proportionate to the island as a whole.

At the EPA/SC, Amina Mohommed, who works in the Education Awareness section, goes out to the 53 schools on the island and makes presentations about conservation. Her colleagues, Ali Mohammed and Inas Enes, advise the schools, create educational posters and spread the message of ecology. The office is vibrating with the excitement of what is happening here. With World Heritage status pending (as

165

of the winter of 2007) these are heady times. More importantly, the outside world is coming to understand what has transpired in this remote place for centuries: native conservation.

Everywhere on the island you can feel it: a shared sense that Socotra is unique, sacred and inviolable.

Just outside of town, a nursery started in 1996 by its owner Adebe Abdullah Hadeed and his wife and son has now collected and/or propagated 41 endemic plants. Hadeed is trying to ascertain the aging process and longevity of Socotra's most famous, indeed mythic, endemic—the cinnabar—of which he has now grown over 15,000 seedlings. It is believed these trees live to be 500 years old, but no one knows for certain and data suggests the tree is declining in its number of individuals. Causes for this might be goat and camel overgrazing (or gurtling), global warming or some unknown combination of factors. Hadeed and staff relocate the seedlings after a few years when they are ready for replanting throughout the island. His zeal for conservation is contagious.

Later, we visited with a family whose quarters for at least five generations have been a privately owned cave well within the boundaries of one of the island's first National Parks, Ayhaft or "the place where one could easily get lost." Salim Abdullah and his five children—Ahmed, Abdullah, Fatima, Suad and Asma, as well as a cousin, Mohammed Ahmed—were gracious enough to introduce us to their esteemed way of life. Here is indisputable proof that a cluster of humanity can survive with dignity in the 21st century, exerting one of the lightest ecological footprints imaginable.

Proceeding into the mountains by foot, our goal was to climb one of the highest peaks in the region known as Skand or "Skent," as it is now officially called, within the central National Park. Its sheer walls are not only home to an impressive suite of endemic plants, but also the largest number of Egyptian vultures, Souedou in Socotri (*Neophron percnopterus)*, in the world. These graceful birds long ago took to this island with a calm, gentle affection. In town one bird per house seems the ratio. They wait for scraps and compete only with goats and smaller birds. On the sheer cliffs, their freedom is a fabulous dream lived out every day.

Above the Dekopkop pools of the Hamhil Protected Area, the sheerest peak looms nearly 800 vertical feet high. At 5:00 A.M. we began our ascent, first scrambling, then rock climbing up the sheer walls. Two endemic Socotran sparrows greeted us in the early morning light, as did the first of several high-flying vultures.

Half-a-day later, in the skillful company of Ahmed Abdullah Omer, a 22-year-old Socotran guide who was working on his B.A. in English literature at Riyad University when not greeting the occasional visitor on his home island, we reached Ghiridif, the island's third highest peak. This spot afforded the best view of the neighboring summit of Mashaniq (ca. 1519m). Skand, the highest of the three at more than 1,600 meters, remained hidden. A young vulture greeted us at our sublime vantage and stayed five feet away, preening herself. Without fear or implied wants, she offered companionship in the high clear air.

On the descent, we sought to record everything. Well over 100 plant species, including the rare *gigas* clinging to the steep granite ravines of the Dine'han Valley; as well as several indigenous skinks, birds, even the one endemic dragonfly, Grant's bluet (*Azuragrion granti*) who waited to show himself until the very end.

Mountain herders followed us down through the open stunted forests, boulder fields and ravines. A newly delivered calf soon joined our group. Children came with their father, who lay down on the rocks so that we could try to remove some minute fly larvae that were sticking to his cornea. We doused the eye in water, but failed, entirely, to rid him of his plague. He smiled cheerfully and carried on, barefoot, down the mountain with us.

All around us was an array of plants of utter enchantment. In so isolated a mountain area, so untouched and generous in their colors and variety, they each called upon a deeply rooted tier of the human psyche in ways that defy easy scientific or philosophical description. Take, for example, the lichen. A lichenologist might matter-of-factly read off the species, but here, amid granite spires and gigantic walls ten, twenty, fifty stories high, sculptured by rain and wind, the soul shudders before such beauty and hesitates to call it anything. No poetic analogy suffices here, where nature's own language has so silently perfected an entire island.

The species diversity here is significant in countless ways, and science helps us to focus this scintillating detail, for no less a reason than the seriousness and urgency with which we all need to conserve precious beauty in a world where so much is vanishing through our thoughtlessness. Here, in the space of half-a-day, we passed through edenic gardens, one after another. Science has names for most particulars, of course: croton shrubland, semi-evergreen woodland, montane mosaica of shrub, woodland and grassland, woody-based herbal eco-systems, et cetera. These were em-

blematic of the gardens of Socotra, populated by universes that greet the enquiring heart: not only the mesmerizing *Dracaena cinnabari* and *Adenium obesum* and *socotranum*, with their ebullient pink flowers just coming out after all the rain, but members of the myrrh, mulberry, frankincense, mint, carrot/parsley, cashew, grape, amaryllis, amaranthus, begonia and iris families; Persian violets, euphorbias, ficus, composites, legumes, acacia—a list neither tiresome nor exhaustible. It is as if all of the great families, clans, tribes, and dynasties of the world were gathered in one place, since time immemorial, to profess the meaning of deep lineage. This interconnectivity of life is Socotra's gift to our memory.

On our quiet wondrous return, other biodiversity emerged with equally pressing calls for their protection: the wild Socotran ass, possibly the last living relative of *Equus asinus somaliensis*, the only remaining wild donkeys in the world, verging on extinction. We saw two in the wild, and others that had unhappily been co-opted for human traction. Moreover, the Socotran cow, running across the landscape, includes a dwarf variety related to an Omani breed and is extraordinarily rare. In the distance,

we see a wild herd of camels with a newborn, and the frisky roaming goats (oze in Socotri, khanama in Arabic) whose numbers approach 20,000. Like the bottle plants and the Socotrans themselves, every goat is a unique and precious being. These little souls, inhabiting beautiful little bodies seemingly colored by children whose uninhibited imagination is pure and good, belong to this place.

Different Socotran tribes maintain traditional grazing grounds. Each region tends to be marked off by small stone walls. The grazing is planned with respect to calendrical timings, rights and duties that befall ownership. The whole collective corresponds with near precision to a conservationist ethic that is pervasive amongst these marvelous stewards of biodiversity, the Socotri people.

Back in Hadibo, beneath a full moon, there were goats still loitering in search of desserts. We wandered the quiet streets with them, long after the intoxicating calls of the muezzin, and fed our left-over food to these becalmed and spirited animals (*Capra aegagrus hircus.*)

As with all such great sanctuaries, we were homesick from the moment we even started thinking about our intended departure and are forever grateful to our hosts, who have so well and successfully endeavored to keep their native home true to life.

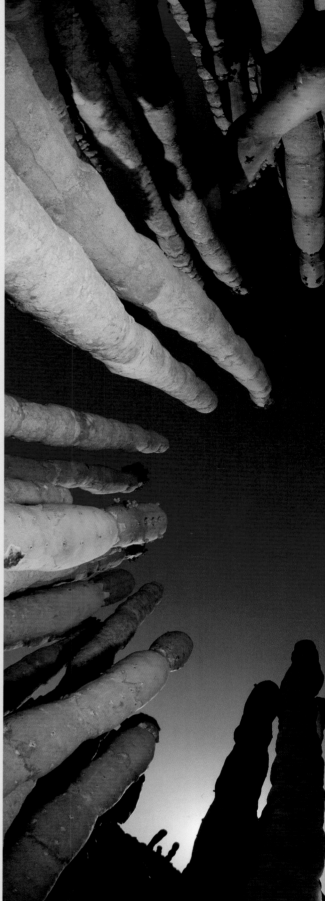

THE BIRTH OF AN ORYX: AL AREEN WILDLIFE SANCTUARY

THE KINGDOM OF BAHRAIN

In one of the world's oldest known literary adventures, the Babylonian epic Gilgamesh, circa 2000 B.C., the royal protagonist Gilgamesh, King of Uruk, searches for the God Ut-Napishtim, who is said to know the secret of immortality. This quest takes Gilgamesh and his friend Enkidu (a wild man reared among gazelles) to Dilmun, reputedly the original paradise (a rival claim with Yemen's Socotra), and the subsequent Cradle of Civilization. Dilmun was located in what is today's Kingdom of Bahrain, an archipelago comprising 33 islands and just over 710 square kilometers off the eastern coast of Saudi Arabia in the Gulf of Salwa. Its

capital is Manama, and the country is populated by just under 750,000 people.[1] Dilmun was also historically referred to as "the land of the living." After the great flood, the God Ut-Napishtim went to live there forever.

Pottery fragments and round seals reveal some glimpse into the atavistic ethos that was Dilmun's environmental legacy: equines, bulls, sweet water, the blazing sun and abundant signs of resurrection colorfully dispersed across the paradise isles where all animals lived harmoniously together, and man was devoid of sin. By the period of Moses and Homer, ca. 800 B.C. the copper industry that probably sustained the Dilmun renaissance had shifted, and this great capital of humanity and nature began to vanish from the historical record.

Today, this small country hosts over 300 bird species, 18 mammals (there are 92 on the Saudi mainland), 250 plant species, a rich, though largely undocumented insect and arachnid world, several reptiles and amphibians (only one venomous snake, the sand snake, said to be terribly shy), and gorgeous yellow-bellied geckos that locals see in nearly every home in the country. The marine biota is also rich, with several hundred resident dugongs, and numerous species of dolphins and whales that are seen off Bahraini waters.

In the last decade, conservation biology has taken hold of the country's consciousness, in good part due to His Majesty Sheik Hama bin Isa Al Khalifa, King of Bahrain, as well as the long-time efforts of local ecologist and wildlife photographer, Dr. Mike Hill.[2] Three protected areas in Bahrain—The Al-Areen Wildlife Reserve 20 kilometers southwest of Manama in the university community of Az Zallaq, the northeastern inshore coastal mangroves of Ras Sanad (Tubli Bay)[3] and the six small Hawar Islands off the southeast coast—have now provided the nation a basis for scientific research, future breeding, translocations, outreach and advocacy.

With pollution, traffic, water purification and global warming issues now bearing down upon the country,[4] Dr. Hill himself is quite outspoken as to the future. He writes, "Time is short and we must move with some urgency if we are to save Bahrain's natural heritage."[5] He, more than anyone, knows how exquisite that array of ancient and migratory wildlife is, and his coffee table book, *Wildlife Of Bahrain*, the sumptuous result of 20 devoted years of field research, chronicles just how much unsurpassed beauty still exists in this country.

The Bahraini leadership has long excelled at second guessing global currents and needs. Habitat protection was legislated as early as 1921, followed by subsequent Environmental Protection and Wildlife laws.[6]

On an early Sunday morning, the Vice President and General Director of the Public Commission for the Protection of Marine Resources, Environment and Wildlife, Dr. Ismaeil M Al Madani, and his staff were kind enough to meet us and provide access to all of Al-Areen, half of which is totally off limits to the general public. There were 71,702 visitors in 2006, or more than 10% of the nation's population. That would be the equivalent of 30 million visitors to Yosemite or Yellowstone, a figure ten times the actual visitations, which occur in the U.S. Of course, Al Areen is a mere half-hour drive by freeway from the center of the capital.

Dr. Madani is careful to note that all is not perfect here in the realm of Dilmun. There is much work to be done. Al Areen's mission is the reestablishment of pan-Arabic wildlife, the breeding both in captive and free-roaming conditions of regionally

native species. To that end, over 25 species of plants, including such flagships as the *Acacia Arabia*, *Proscopis Juliflora*, *Zizyphus spina-christi*, date palm and bottlebrush have been planted. The sanctuary of Al-Areen was created in situ in 1975, so that there was some pre-existing native flora and fauna, a natural seed source. Today, it is home to numerous species threatened in the Gulf. As we walked and drove throughout the compact eight acre reserve, Reem gazelle, Nubian ibex, sable antelope, beisa oryx, the incredibly rare scimitar-horned oryx, wild goat, Barbary sheep, Asiatic onager, defassa waterbuck, addax and lesser kudu, all grazed leisurely, whilst abundant birdlife followed suit.

Our radio alerted us to the fact that an amazing event was occurring out in the forest. Quietly we approached. There, amid some fifteen other Arabian oryx was a newborn. The herd gently nudged the baby to its feet, surrounding it and then moving slowly away. It was a little girl, the 98th to be born at Al Areen. She will grow up to lead the herd because that's what they do: the females dominate and take charge. Apparently they are better at it than males. Her water will come mostly from morning dew, and she will spend her many years nibbling on the delicious native plant species, like desert hyacinth, alqa and sabat, and she will never know fear.[7] Her long life is guaranteed, among scientists and vets and conservationists who adore her, and a public that has been re-attuned to the marvels of wildlife here in the world. A world which is, after all, a living paradise, just as Gilgamesh believed.

THE PRECIOUS SANDS OF AL MAHA: THE DUBAI DESERT CONSERVATION RESERVE

UNITED ARAB EMIRATES

Looking at the view from a satellite 400 miles above the 83,600 square kilometers that comprise the seven United Arab Emirates[1] or from kneeling at sunrise in a sand dune wedged between the neighboring giants of Saudi Arabia to the West and Oman to the East, Dubai's rugged outback might appear little changed since the Emirates united as one nation in 1971. The ever so discrete cream-coloured

courser, the crested lark and grey francolins continue to step delicately across the earth, exploring the relentless desert for seeds at dawn and at dusk, while a faint breeze is discernible among the dune and panic grass beneath a forest of ghaf with its high protein-bearing edible leaves.

It is 5:45 A.M. and a scudding mist engulfs the horizons, hanging heavily on the moist sand. We wait with South African Greg Simkins, the chief biologist for the Al Maha ecological reserve, as the strange wintry fog begins to rise, and a herd of rare Arabian oryx (*Oryx leucoryx*), Al Maha in Arabic, move along the rippled ridgeline. The dozens of large ungulates stop, peer back at us, then move on.

These large antelopes, related to several species in Africa, may be the source of the unicorn legend and we see it now: when in profile, their two graceful horns merge as one. With white hollow hair and black skin, their physiology wards off UV radiation, and their core temperature can reach 40 degrees celcius without apparent maleffects on the animal. As one of the UAE's leading biologists, Marijcke Jongbloed, explains it, their kidneys recycle their urine and their hooves do not sink in the sea of sand dunes.[2]

Greg has been checking camera traps in four sites throughout the 225 square kilometers of the reserve, expanding the biodiversity databanks for different groups. He hopes to find another bat. Thus far, only one has ever turned up at Al Maha and it was mummified. But life abounds here, with over 62 bird species in the immediate vicinity and at least 40 resident avians discovered thus far; 21 reptile and a dozen mammal species. Shrubs include a known 26 varieties, in addition to four grass and

six tree species. Some of these species are incredibly charismatic. For example, there is the Critically Endangered Scimitar-horned oryx, the sand and mountain gazelles, the Ethiopian hedgehog, Ruepell's fox, the yellow-spotted/blue headed agama, spiny-tailed lizard, desert monitor, Arabian toad-headed agama, several species of colorful gecko, the jirds, gerbils and jerboas, not to mention three highly poisonous snakes, the Arabian horned, Sind and Burton's saw-scaled viper.

Such diversity might seem absolutely spare compared, say, with tropical, even temperate forest areas (and it is). But when one considers that vast areas of the Arabian Peninsula have been labeled "The Empty Quarter" it becomes quickly clear at Al Maha that such designations are inappropriate. Step almost anywhere, wait for a few minutes, and a creature of exquisite beauty and global importance will show him or herself.

The Emirate Sheikhs always admired such wildlife (with an absolutely obsessive love of falcons and camels, of course) and traditional desert Islam has forever encompassed conservation measures that were deemed to be basic by the Bedouin, such as the responsible maintenance of waterholes for wildlife.

At the dawn of oil exploration in the region in the mid-20th century, there was not one paved road, hospital or school here; nor were there electricity, plumbing, telephones or harbors. But, there were plenty of waterholes. When the British left in 1971, no one could have anticipated the rapidity of growth that soon would transform a traditional nomad's world—steeped in poetry and gentle courtesies among the dunes—into one of the fastest growing, high-tech phenomena on the planet. The onrush of tens-of-billions of dollars each year threatened the simplicity of a life in the desert that had not changed for millennia.

Today, many are beginning to lament the metropolitan encroachment upon the desert, and wildlife is fast disappearing. With over 4.7 million human inhabitants and feverish consumerism outstripping demographic predictions of even a few years ago, the U.A.E. has been hard-pressed to target some of its enormous oil and gas and international trade surpluses for conservation. The Dubai Desert Conservation Reserve (DDCR), which surrounds the eco-tourist resort and preserve of Al Maha, is one unprecedented example.

Tony Williams, Managing Director and ecological architect of the highly successful endeavor, explains that the Ruling Family members have a personal love of conservation and have worked hard to enshrine those passions within a constitutional framework that can ensure the highest quality of international protection.

There is a huge amount to protect. Bird migrations from Europe to Africa cross the Emirates with many of the avifauna utilizing some of the 200 islands that belong to the U.A.E. Over 500 marine species traverse or inhabit its waters, including some 25% of all known Cetacea species (whales and dolphins.) And the U.A.E. hosts a large population of the highly vulnerable dugongs as well as five rare turtle species. In addition, significant genetic work and breeding of rare species, as well as general survey work and increasing animal rights perspectives, have galvanized a grass-roots pledge on behalf of conservation and alternative energy.[3] Biological work is being

done in colleges and institutes, manifesting superb international alliances that can only continue to enrich the opportunities at hand to save such species as the Arabian leopard, to build up viable metapopulations and improve the network of connected protected areas.

Even the local camels have been the subject of intensive study that might yield invaluable data for treating prostate cancer.[4]

When Tony was tasked with examining the prospects of creating some kind of ecological preserve in the first place, his research was rewarded 12 days after being submitted to the Ruling Family with a green light.

"That's fast," we remark over tea with him.

But Tony admits to little surprise. He knows how committed the Ruling Family is to conservation. The initial eco-reserve was to stretch for 27 square kilometers.

Eighteen months later, the legislation was formalized that would protect it forever. Then the DDCR concept that would engender corridors and buffers with the adjacent Hajar Mountain Range stretching east and south into Oman was conceived. By *Ruler's Decree Number 3 of 2002*, the 225 square kilometer preserve, the largest in the Gulf (5% of the entire Dubai Emirate) had materialized. Millions of dollars later, Al Maha, with a protective fence and strong science orientation, opened to the public. Translocations of species began, and today, Al Maha proffers one of the most exceptional high-end eco-tourism success stories in the world.

The positive note comes at a time when many might write off huge oil-producing regions that seem bent upon total economic exploitation as having little regard for the environment. Nothing could be further from the truth in the Emirates. But, Al Maha's success is particularly attributable to the sheer clarity of vision with respect to the environment shared by the founding fathers of Dubai, Sheikh Rashid bin Saeed Al Maktoum and his sons. And, by a Conservation Board at DDCR, says Tony, whose membership comprises many top people in industry and local government, all of whom share an ecological conviction. This luxurious oasis allows no cell phones, no loud music, and no small children, except a few times a year for special educational forays oriented to the young.

In reality, however, Al Maha is about the youth in all of us, and a sentiment much out of favor in the modern world: listen to the crickets, savor a sunset and disturb no living creature.

Tony and his two key scientific staff members, Greg Simkins and Ryan Ingram, are conservationists and educators. What Tony is trying to do, he says, is create "the commercial ability to support the conservation areas, which we establish." It's a model that a trillion dollar eco-tourist business worldwide is focused upon, but Al Maha has probably succeeded better than any other comparable venue. Part of that success is the unusual access by freeway to downtown Dubai—a mere 45 minutes through the desert. The chaos of a shimmering skyline, with the newly built tallest building in the world and an indoor ski area, not to mention a cacophony of shopping malls and five star hotels, confronts the poet, dreamer, and ecologist who has just been out communing with an ancestral Arabian wilderness. That unnerving juxtaposition of ancient and modern is both an ally and a foe of sensitive conservation. But Tony, Greg, Ryan and their many Al Maha colleagues and friends, and the leaders of Dubai, have managed to do what no one thought possible: balance seemingly incomprehensible odds and make it profitable for all concerned: the wildlife, the investors and those of the public who are lucky enough to visit this great sanctuary in the desert.

The balance is achieved by managing Al Maha as the equivalent of a national park. Other high-end luxury lodges, such as the Awhanee Hotel in Yosemite Valley, cater to similar instincts, but Al Maha with its average 80% occupancy, does so with the intent to be an absolutely exclusive getaway. At an all-in fee of US$1,200 per day (as of 2007) and a tight limit on the total number of guests, the impact on habitat is limited. The discreet resort takes up less than 1% of the 27 square kilometers within the 225 square kilometers and visitors are restricted to non-scientific and non-sensitive research zones. This environmental impact assessment approach contrasts markedly with the trends in the U.A.E. as a whole. By 2010 it is estimated that desert safari activities (usually four-wheel driving trips up dunes) will engage up to 800,000 visitors a year in Dubai, "irrevocably damaging the environment."[5]

A totally different, progressive sensitivity inheres at Al Maha, where Tony Williams has laid down a conservation ethic that not only comports with that of the Royal Family, but with the highest standards of conservation biology anywhere in the world. The sanctuary's very mascot, the Arabian oryx, was brought back here from the brink of extinction in the early 1960s when it was discovered that the remaining populations had been decimated by hunters throughout their range. In fact, "only a handful of antelopes remained," writes Jongbloed.[6]

Today, biodiversity is thriving here. The sanctuary saw over 6,000 native species planted, three full-time conservation officers hired and surveys initiated. As Greg, Ryan and we navigate for hours throughout the dunes and gravel outflows, from morning until late night, over the course of three days, the checklists expand with amazing discoveries. Sometime after midnight, in the cool air a skink and then a gerbil race toward us, stop in the downcast glare of our headlamps, pretend to hide and reveal their magnificence. To kneel among some of the great dune ecosystems on the planet beside these shy adaptive geniuses, is altogether humbling. We would not want to be anywhere else, among any other company.

Later on, conferring with some of the key biology sources for the area,[7] the revelation of a living desert hits us from childhood dreams.

As for the oryx, there are now an estimated 5,000 living in their former ranges that include Oman, the U.A.E., Saudi Arabia, Bahrain, Qatar, Syria and Jordan.[8]

VEGETARIAN ECOLOGY IN RAJASTHAN

THE CITY OF PUSHKAR, INDIA

The small city of Pushkar with its approximately 30,000 residents nestled in the sandy hills of India's northwestern Thar Desert in the state of Rajasthan, about 380 kilometers southwest of New Delhi, is home to an ethic that remains unique in the world: mandatory vegetarianism. In addition, no alcohol is permitted. The more than 1.5 million tourists who venture to this oasis in the desert every year will find that police periodically check hotels and restaurants to ensure that only vegetarian food is being served. No fish, no meat, no animal by-products whatsoever. What is particularly salient about this vision is the fact it works.

In most conservation circles today, the vegetarian "question" hinges upon discussion of evolutionary protein needs in primates, as well the relatively recent waves of burgeoning, impoverished human populations that are within, or near to high biodiversity areas. With "protein" being the pivot point upon which strategies

are formulated, the conclusions are predictable: a shift from inefficient, hugely destructive hunting for bushmeat to an alternative "way ahead" which is "a shift to efficient husbandry of domesticated animals."[1] This theory, pragmatic to a point, completely undermines the worth of farm animals as beings to be protected and cherished, let alone any pantheistic ethic, such as is manifested in Pushkar.

Pushkar's absolute insistence upon non-violence would, at first glance, seem to be at home within India, where Mahatma Gandhi himself proclaimed the worship of cows as fundamental to Hindu tradition. Yet, despite an admirable body of animal rights legislation, India remains (as is the case in nearly all other countries) inconsistent in its treatment of animals. Violations of Indian laws pertaining to animals are rampant. But Pushkar is different, and that difference presents a sobering, soul-relieving truth. We *are* capable of non-violence. Our species does have what it takes to be mature, kind and good. A visit to the city, which is considered the supreme pilgrimage site on Earth by Hindus (*Param Tirathstan*), is a requisite and much beloved tradition in the country. Moreover, Muslims, Jains and Buddhists also have sacred temples here.

Rajasthan is the home of nearly one million Bishnois, a sub-sect of Hinduism. They actually worship an ecological saint, the 15th century Guru Jambhoji, who outlined 29 critical conservationist principles. The Bishnoi are strict vegetarians and stewards of desert ecology. They maintain anti-poaching vigilance, harvest dew drops during times of drought and keep their animals from overgrazing. They have a strong connection with blackbuck and chinkara (native ungulates) and in order to save wood, will bury, rather than cremate, their dead.[2] When, in 1730, troops of the local Maharaja came to cut wood, 363 Bishnoi clung to their sacred khejri trees and were martyred. In 1988 the Government of India named them the first environmental heroes of the country. It was during the 1970s that the Himalayan Chipko or tree-hugging movement derived its techniques and logic from the Bishnoi.

Pushkar itself is something of an international environmental celebrity. Its citizens proffer food types that come out of the Indian heartland. Such staples as kair berries, sangari (the Bishnoi fruit, resembling a bean), numerous types of rice, bread,

legumes, potatoes, spinach and dairy that is produced non-violently are all intrinsic to the cuisine of the area. That a city can profit by non-violence is an economic masterpiece that could be replicated everywhere.

Pushkar's history is rich with divine tradition, beginning with the blossoming of a lotus, dropped by the Creator in Indian mythology. Pushkar is the home to the one and only temple in the world dedicated to Lord Brahma. His temple is in the city's heart. When the Creator, Lord Brahma, sought a bride, the rain god Indra found Him a milkmaid who was subsequently purified by being flushed through a bovine's womb. Why this method of purification, no one is certain. But her "second birth" corresponded with the arrival of two additional Gods: Vishnu, the preserver of life; and Shiva, the destroyer who purifies, also known as the Lord of the Dance. The milkmaid's marriage to Brahma foreshadowed the naming of the Hindu's noble caste of Brahmans and the sacred cow, icon of purity, innocence and fertility, whose life was deemed inextricably connected to that of humans. In Pushkar, unlike the rest of India, cows are truly worshipped, as India's ancient religious texts prescribe.[3]

Here not just cows are revered, but all animals including the monkeys, dogs, sheep, goats, cats, birds and people. Pushkar's history of desert environmentalism, animal rights and spirituality merge to create a viable 21st century city.

Eco-tourists are the lifeblood of Pushkar. While many visitors journey here to enjoy the popular chaos of the Camel Mela (fair) each early November, the majority of tourists come to be blessed in the sacred lake that forms, along with Brahma's temple, the core religious nexus of the city. Pilgrims take ritual dips at any of the 52 ghats, slipping into the water to do pujas or prayer ceremonies repeatedly through-

out the day and linger along the water's edge in communion with other animals. A great temple complex that includes not only Brahma's but also the Savitri, Varah, Mahadeva, Ramavaikunth, Warah, Apteshwar and the Old Rangji Temples attracts multitudes.

But it is Brahma—with his 23 names all confirming his creative supremacy—who is the main pulse and flow of this eternal sanctuary.[4] In May, when the heat exceeds 100 degrees by early morning, the animals that populate the streets and booming business district take obvious pleasure in the company of their cousins, the humans. While so much tourism has prompted considerations with respect to Pushkar's environmental, even "psychological,"[5] carrying capacity, it is clear that the unburdening of the human heart occurs in this sacred city, where one can rest easily at night knowing that every living creature is free to evolve in his and her own way, without hindrance or harm.

We had each lost a loved one this year—Jane: my brother, Bruce; Michael: my father, William. When a Brahman priest led us through the ceremony of remembrance and prayer at the central ghat beside the lake, it was done in the company of hundreds of birds, monkeys and cows; to the ringing of prayer bells, the swirl of incense and the appropriate dabs of body paint and rice. Sprinkling lotus flowers into the lake while repeating age-old prayers, we experienced gratitude and humility.

Spiritual vortex, economic template, this city of Pushkar with its sustainable urban plan; this global capital of vegetarianism takes the science of conservation and non-violent activism to its zenith, challenging the human world, now 50% urban, to do the same.

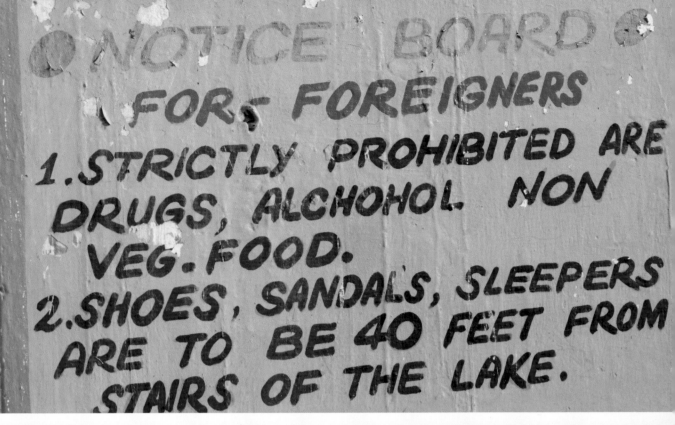

NOTICE BOARD
FOR FOREIGNERS
1. STRICTLY PROHIBITED ARE DRUGS, ALCHOHOL. NON VEG. FOOD.
2. SHOES, SANDALS, SLEEPERS ARE TO BE 40 FEET FROM STAIRS OF THE LAKE.

A TRIBE THAT WORSHIPS FLOWERS & BUFFALO

THE NILGIRIS, SOUTHERN INDIA

"The devotion to something afar
From the sphere of our sorrow.
This, I think, is the true gospel of the love of flowers"[1]

In his "Rule for a Young Student in Painting" Leonardo Da Vinci wrote, "The organ of sight is one of the quickest, and takes in at a single glance an infinite variety of forms; notwithstanding which, it cannot perfectly comprehend more than one object at a time."[2] Taking that into the realm of ethics, Immanuel Kant suggested that "This feeling (called the moral sense) is the pure product and effect of reason."[3] In India, indigenous peoples and their spirituality have achieved the perfect blend of such aesthetics and morality.

India has at least 96 national parks, 501 sanctuaries and some of the most ancient ethical systems of protection and non-violence in human history. At one time, the country was home to approximately "ten percent each of the world's mammalian, insect and fish species, and over 8% of reptile forms."[4]

Mahatma Gandhi observed that a society's treatment of other creatures is a sure indication of their clarity of thinking and capacity for kindness. While her formidable cadre of saints, scientists and explorers has long acknowledged India's remarkable biodiversity, conservationists have witnessed a continuous degradation of habitat, an epidemic of poaching, burgeoning population (1.2 billion heading towards 2 billion) and other serious systemic problems that impede enactment of practical, economic and spiritual programs to save biodiversity.

On paper, Indian protection seems impressive: 22% of her forests or 156,934 square kilometers are said to be safeguarded.[5] More than 60% of that is dense, though mostly modified, forest. But, this suggests spurious conclusions. For example, the Forest Survey of India in 2003 estimated that "23.68%" of the nation enjoyed forest cover, but that actually translated to only 3.04% of "tree cover." And despite all those national

parks and sanctuaries, only 4.74% of the nation is actually in a protected area.[6]

Moreover, the legally defined protection mechanisms in place for that meager percentage are steadily being eroded. In May of 2006, the Wildlife Institute of India, the primary organization focused on saving the tiger from extinction in 29 tiger preserves, reported that in 16 of those preserves 50% of all tigers had been poached in the previous four years.[7] And it's not just tigers that are being lost. In the south of India, national parks are especially under siege from poachers and forest encroachment. "It is estimated that more than 24,281 hectares (60,000 acres) of reserve forest lands have been infringed in totality over the last decade," writes Stephen David.[8]

At the poorest end of India's socio-economic spectrum, hundreds-of-millions of people barely survive. Their ecological footprint, as it's called, is admirably modest, but this is little cause for celebration among the poor, many of whom are truly desperate. Indian legislation has long grappled with, and been magnanimously egalitarian, in its efforts to reach out to this unfortunate majority. It was upon this very platform

that Gandhi built his non-violent revolution for Independence. Woven into the legalities of this largest of all democracies is an inadequate system for checks and balances for conservation. For example, the Tree Patta Scheme, introduced many years ago in several regions, allows each poor family with no land of their own to collect an acre's worth of any biomass, other than entire trees or Threatened and Endangered species. The toll of hundreds of millions of people each day gathering firewood and other forest commodities is staggering. By 1993, India was losing more of her remaining forest each year (3% or 15,000 square kilometers) than any country, including Brazil.[9]

Notwithstanding this challenging context, India yields a picture of remarkable legal precedents, inspired individuals and communities working to save local environments. One such indigenous group is the Todas, an ancient people and one of the last vegetarian tribes on Earth that today comprises fewer than 1,500 individuals. For thousands of years the Toda have inhabited India's oldest mountain range, the Nilgiris or Blue Mountains in the south. Since 1986, this region has formed part of the core area, along with the Western Ghats, of India's first and only UNESCO Biosphere Reserve, covering parts of the three states of Tamil Nadu, Kerala and Karnataka.

With our colleagues Dr. Tarun Chhabra and Rami Singh co-founders of the Edhkwehlynawd Botanical Refuge (EBR; Edhkwehlynawd is the Toda, or Ahl, word for "place from which a beautiful view is to be seen"), we trekked into distant parts of the eastern portion of the UNESCO Nilgiri Biosphere Reserve (NBR.) This was during the end of the second or "Fall Monsoon." We went in search of rare species and any new distribution data for certain vascular plants, particularly orchids, *Impatiens*

and *Strobilanthes*, all of which were flowering. Joining us were several members of the Forestry Department.

The NBR occupies a total of 5,520 square kilometers, combining numerous parks, sanctuaries and reserves into one "cluster".[10] Forest types are rich and diverse: tropical, moist, riparian dense scrub/jungle, dry, deciduous, montane, semi-evergreen and the endemic shola, a uniquely beautiful mosaic of "stunted evergreen montane," the trees never higher than about 20 meters, and deeply, mysteriously placed amid "moist hollows between folds of the extensive grassy hills" (as Dr. Chhabra describes it.)[11] The NBR hosts countless rare and endemic species, including 316 species of butterfly, some 3,700 plant species and 684 vertebrate species, including tigers, over 2,000 Asian elephants (the largest population in India), gaur, Nilgiri tahr and two Critically Endangered endemic primates, the Nilgiri langur and lion-tailed macaque.

Throughout the Western Ghats, the jungly, mountainous southwestern coast of India, are found over 300 bird species, including 18 endemics; 39 species of fish, 31 species of amphibians (including snake-like Caecilians) and 60 species of reptiles including rocky python and king cobra. Many of these are resident in the NBR, along with the largest population of marsh crocodiles in all of South India.[12]

Dr. Chhabra is himself a celebrated botanist and a practicing dentist. The magnificent flowers of the Nilgiris and the resident Todas whose language he speaks and whose livelihood he and Rami champion are his specialities. The botani-

cal wonderland we explore continues to reveal new and important information. More than a third of the 141 known genera endemic to India are resident to the Western Ghats and 11 are in Dr. Chhabra's backyard, the Nilgiris. Moreover, of the 2100 flowering plant species endemic to peninsular India, outside the Himalayas, 818 are also found in the Nilgiris, and 132 are endemic. Just in Silent Valley National Park within NBR, 23 rare or new species were found in recent years.[13] The NBR exists within one of 35 globally critical biodiversity areas, a region designated the "Western Ghats and Sri Lanka Hotspot," of which 15% has legal protected boundaries. It is also the core of what is described as one of the 17 "megadiverse" regions on the planet.[14] It is called a hotspot because of the high degree of vascular plant endemism found throughout the Nilgiris. This is an index that suggests other complementary phenomena in the form of biological richness, and simultaneous pressure borne upon this cornucopia by human demographics. This impact is tragically replicated across all of India, Asia and the rest of the world. But the hotspots are the nerve centers of high biodiversity on the planet. Lose those and we lose evolution.[15] No glib warning, rather a reality looming to all sides.

The Niligiri District has over 700,000 residents, and another 1.3 million people surround the Biological World Heritage site, injuring the ecological integrity of increasing portions of the reserve.[16] Poaching, the introduction of non-native species like pine, black wattle and eucalyptus for fire wood, the illegal transport of cattle and inadvertent introduction of diseases, manufacturing plants along watersheds churning out everything from Rayon and electroplating to film processing—all have negative impacts. Vijaya and Daniels describe "600 metric tonnes" of granulated pesticides, and "28,000 litres in the form of liquids" that are spread throughout the Nilgiris each year, primarily to control pests on the abundant croplands of millet, cotton, rice, coffee, tea and fruit orchards.[17]

For the Todas, who depend more than any other indigenous community on that ecological integrity, these environmental threats pose a world-shattering series of sea changes. The Toda's buffalo, upon which they rely, are the source of their worship and the milk of their livelihood.[18] These are river buffalo (*Bubalus bubalus*), one of eighteen such breeds in all of Asia. But this particular breed is unique, having genetically separated from the others between 1,800 to 2,700 years ago. Without the 80/20 percent grassland-shola mix, upon which buffalo survival depends, these creatures will go extinct. The Toda shepherd and protect them from tigers and from interbreeding with other cattle. These buffalo are truly the source of one of the oldest non-violent religions in the world. As it is, the breed is quite rare, endemic to Toda lands, and said to be in decline.[19]

As we trekked into Silent Valley, surrounded by the remarkable magic tinkling sounds of hundreds, perhaps thousands, of frogs (*Philautus wynaadensis*), Dr. Chhabra pointed out the countless species of flowers, which the Toda worship. The remarkable symbiosis between Toda culture and flowers reminds us of a lovely passage from Maeterlink: "All the flowers of the world, the successful efforts, the deep, inmost beauties, the joyful thoughts and wishes of the planet rose up to us, borne on a shaft of light that, in spite of its heavenly wonder, issued from our own earth."[20] Thus far, Dr. Chhabra, with his Toda friend Kwattawdr Kwehttn and others, has documented over 250 species or sub-species of plants utilized by the Toda. While UNESCO formally acknowledges approximately 200 medicinal plants within NBR, this number

is going to be pushed much higher by Dr. Chhabra and colleagues' discoveries. A thorough study of traditional Toda belief reveals the interdependency of culture and flowers as exists among few peoples on Earth. As Dr. Chhabra has written in various remarkable essays, the Todas look to specific flowers for insight as to when the monsoons will arrive and the dry summer end, and when the honey and wild fruit seasons have come.[21]

One of the most astonishing flowers in the Toda universe is the delicate carpet of lovely individual arkilpoof (*Gentiana pedicellata*). Dr. Chhabra writes, "The Toda name literally means 'the worry flower' and the flower indicates the anxiety levels of humans. It is believed that if a person with worries plucks this plant . . . it is very sensitive and closes faster if the degree of anxiety is pronounced. We have experimented with this over the years and found it to be very accurate—whenever a person with some nagging worry accompanied me, this flower would close in a flash!"[22]

Dr. Chhabra and his colleagues at the EBR Trust have already documented 35 *Impatiens* species within NBR, including 12 endemics. And they have identified the precise flowering cycles of Acanthaceae family rarities of the *Strobilanthes* genus. Among some of the more striking endemics, Dr. Chhabra and team have been closely watching *Impatiens clavicornu*, *I. denisonii* (which took EBR scientists three years to locate) and *I. nilagirica*. Their flowering, often atop black, wet granite slabs, is an incomprehensible beauty by mid-September (the time period of our expedition). Particularly

sensational is the orchid-like *Impatiens orchioides*, a higher altitude NBR endemic that simply defies description. Many have commented on the fact that a number of the species belonging to the Balsaminaceae family, like impatiens, both resemble and behave like orchids. Two endemic Nilgiri balsams, *I. campanulata* and *I. niamniamensis*, the latter commonly named "Congo cockatoo," are actually related to their African ancestors and are pollinated by birds. Amazingly, the flowers are bird-shaped.[23]

With over 17 flowering orchid species this time of year—particularly those of the *Habenaria* genus on one mountain range after another, spreading up to and beyond the Toda Otherword—this is a region of great beauty and inexpressibly spiritual calm known as *Amunawdr* that showers visitors with near hallucinogenic visions and color.[24] This place may well offer the most generous cosmography of flowering plants in any single refuge on Earth. Part of that is explained by the Todas, as attributable to their goddess *Taihhki(r)shy* who is apparently quite focused on specific flowers that must be exclusively used by the Toda for their religious ceremonies. And, since ancient times, "under no circumstance is substitution permissible."[25]

The rain poured intermittently. On the second and third nights we slept in a Forest Department hut surrounded by an eight-foot pit on all sides, to inhibit the possibility of elephants stomping us, as such accidents are prone to happen here. Tigers prey upon Toda buffalo, numerous wild boars surround us in the mists and are easily spooked, A year ago, while scouting this expedition along impassible dirt roads on the outskirts of Mukurthi National Park, Rami Singh pointed out a huge mudslide right above us, the result of an elephant tragically slipping during the monsoon and sliding hundreds of feet to her death while taking out huge amounts of forest with her.

On the morning of our fourth day, the tinkling frogs were symphonic and the rain was letting up. Sun pierced the muted sobriety of the mist-encinctured plateau over which we crossed and a riot of bird activity commenced. Asian fairy bluebirds, Nilgiri laughingthrush, black-and-orange flycatchers, crested goshawk and serpent eagles, Malabar pied hornbills—our birdlist grew rapidly.[26]

High atop one of the sheer ridges, we sat reveling in the play of swirling fog over the peaks, hoping for a glimpse of a tiger.

Despite the presence of carnivores, poisonous snakes, enormous avalanches, mudslides, deafening waterfalls and precipitous cliffs, this seems a gentle spot for reflection. It is made more so by the Todas themselves, a culture that knows no violence. As humans inhabiting a wilderness, these nomadic pastoralists sometimes sell their buffalo milk (milk of the creature they venerate and care for) at nearby markets. Building their spiral temples, dining as vegetarians surrounded by meat-eating cultures, the Todas present an extraordinary model of all that is best in human behavior: humanity itself as sanctuary.

The Nilgiri Biosphere Reserve is a paradise *because* this spectacularly beautiful Toda cuture has preserved it. They are scientists and metaphysicians. Their language, body of medicinal understanding and lifecycle insights, along with their absolute insistence on non-violence, persuade us to revise our view of human nature. Without such virtuous practices, conservation in this region might have had little chance of success.

One striking insight into the Todas comes from a British anthropologist, W.E. Marshall, who published one of the first studies on these people in 1873, when the total Toda population was said to be 693. Wrote Marshall:

> The Todas have . . . no violent exercise . . . nothing in fact to point to natural turbulence of character . . . They wear no weapons of offence or defence. They do not even hunt, either for the sake of providing themselves with food, or for the pleasure of the chase. They do not attempt to till the ground . . . No exciting and glorious war, with plunder! The feathers of the chief, the titles of the hero! No women to be attacked, or prisoners to be enslaved or tortured! No food but a milk diet and grain, whilst the woods are full of game, and flocks and herds to be had for the taking! What is the meaning of all this? Have we come on the tracks of an aboriginal reign of conscience?"[27]

Whenever the Todas do have issues, the elders meet on an ordained promontory in the forest called *Asxwilyfem*—a word typical of the excruciatingly difficult Toda language—and they have what is called a *noyim*, a very quiet discussion leading to reconcillation. Years ago Michael was present at a noyim and can attest to the absolute gentleness of conversation. Weirdly absent was the slightest sense of a disagreement. It was almost as if the Todas were not humans, but flowers.[28]

WAT PHRA KEO: ECOLOGICAL AESTHETICS

BANGKOK, THAILAND

Urban sanctuaries, like Wat Phra Keo, the Grand Palace of Bangkok, are studies in human ambiguity. In the heart of a megacity of ten million plus people and located near a badly polluted river, close to the Chatuchak Market, notorious for harboring illegal trade in wildlife,[1] the Grand Palace affords its myriad visitors a magnificent respite from the hardships of big city life. In its most expressive, quiet corners, one can languish far from the crowds, off in some remote time and place amid undisturbed reveries of pure Buddhistic contemplation.

Thai culture has always been oriented artistically to inward thought and outward gentleness. From an ecological perspective the nation is deeply troubled; so much so that the most seminal work on the country's biodiversity is named *Thailand's Vanishing Flora and Fauna*.[2] Every year in the 19th century, an estimated 8,000 rhino horns were exported from Thailand. While there are nearly "409 protected areas, 27 marine national parks, 10 RAMSAR sites, 2 World Heritage sites

and 4 biosphere reserves" in the country, representing approximately 20% of terrestrial Thailand as protected,[3] the number of threatened species in every category is very high. Of the 302 known species of mammal, for example, at least 37 are in trouble. Rapid development in the country has long been viewed as one of the great international biodiversity emergencies, given that some 87,000 faunal species are thought to exist in the country (though no more than 18,073 have yet been described, including a spectacular "982 birds, 350 reptiles, 1376 amphibians, 720 freshwater fish, and 2,100 estuarine and marine fish").[4] As in China, here a vast collective of wildlife is at risk from development threats representing all the stereotypical runaway-economic downsides: "illegal hunting, crop and forest burning, livestock grazing, forest clearance/illegal logging, destructive fishing practices, disturbance caused by tourism and transportation, environmental pollution, forest fires, coral bleaching and wetland loss."[5]

As of 1987, no large wild mammal has survived outside a national park. But if even another 5% of Thailand were protected under stringent conservation management, as the Thai Government envisioned as part of its iniatives for the Convention on Biological Diversity, perhaps this unhappy situation might improve. For now, Thailand faces an extremely perilous ecological situation. Although the first national park, Khao Yai, was created in 1962, public conservation awareness did not evolve until the 1980s. By then, despite having one of the best family planning initiatives in Southeast Asia, the country's demographic profile had exploded from the 8 million inhabitants of 1900 to over 50 million. By 2000, population edged towards 65 million and climbing.[6] The implications for wildlife could not be more dire. As L. Bruce Kekule concludes his graphic overview of Thailand's biodiversity, "With continued pressure from humans, wildlife and forests have dropped to critical levels."[7]

Bos sauveli, the amazing kouprey first described in 1937, was an exquisite bovine, considered the most ancient of living cattle. But by the mid-1970s, it appears to have vanished along with Thailand's Javan rhino and probably the Sumatran rhino within Thai borders. Other large mammals, like the gaur and banteng are also Critically Endangered.[8] Interestingly, the aggression, greed and callous indifference that has resulted in a hammered biodiversity within Thailand is described in great detail throughout the epic enshrined at the Grand Palace.

Hence, from a deep conservationist perspective, Wat Phra Keo recognizes that our ability as a species to focus on wildness and to celebrate the beauty and sacredness of the natural world is key to our own survival—however wounded this capacity now is in this Buddhist nation.

Thai people light candles for every auspicious occasion. The more pressing our environmental worries and corresponding burdens, the more relevant those healing and celebratory qualities of the human psyche become, as we emerge chastened as a species in the 21st century. This is a form of idealism that is grounded in religion.

There is suffering in the world. Among Asia's many great spiritual traditions, Thai Buddhism has offered solace and many paths to compassion, purification and enlightenment. Wat Phra Keo, a square mile of traditional architecture, spiritual landscape painting and prayer, just east of the Chao Phraya River that spans central Bangkok, is home to the most sacred Buddha in Thailand. The Emerald Buddha is made of jade though it was believed to be of emerald when it was revealed by a lightning strike and is still called by that name. Nearly 80 million people visit this important

pilgrimage site annually, including 11 million international visitors who come for a unique communion. Wat Phra Keo is the most popular destination in the country, possibly making it the most visited religious "power spot" on Earth.

As a park, the majority of living creatures at Wat Phra Keo are confined to vases containing water lilies, insects and a host of microbes. Occasional birds reside in the scattered small garden areas. But the mural paintings that extend the length of several city blocks contain both mythic and real ecologies: creatures from both Hindu and Buddhist pantheons and geographies across Asia, including whole forests of the Himalayas. These gardens of the imagination are an inspiration.

The mural paintings dating to the late 18th century depict the Thai version of the remarkable 3,000 year old Hindu epic, the Ramayana. Written in 1782 by King Rama I, this account of the Ramayana tells of the eternal powers of *dharma*, the Hindu code of being. In it, human behavior and free will and the ideals of good governance; modesty, restraint and love are all subject to the overarching laws of nature. The landscape, with its infinitude of spirits, is viewed as a sacred source of the divine and far more powerful than human beings. This is the real nature, as Buddhism often speaks of it; the wellspring of our eternal salvation.

นายครูเรียน วัฒนวิจิตร ศิษย์พระอาจารย์
มหาธีระ ธเนศิวร์ จิตรกรรมฝาผนัง

The Ramayana told in this Thai epic is rife with heartbreak and fairy tale; an endless array of wild creatures and exploits meant to remind the reader of traditional values. The story of Ramakian begins at the base of Mount Krailart, which is inhabited by celestial beings. King Tosakan, with his 16,001 wives living in a land of peace, enters the forest for a week-long trek, only to return to a vanished city. Lives are ruined, wars waged, kidnappings and feuds played out. Hanuman, the Monkey deity, comes out of meditation to assist humanity. Others make noble sacrifices. While a massive fire rages across the earth, Tosakan races with his family to the summit of Mount Satana. And so on. Perhaps no greater creature ranges across the landscape of these murals than the Kinarees—half-human, half bird—also found in the legends of Japan, Borneo, India, Laos, Cambodia and China. According to Kosint Shitamara, a scholar of Kinarees, the Japanese refer to them as "Hagoromo" or "Coat of Feathers." In Thailand, they figure at the heart of the "Phra Suthon and Manohra" legend, a love story that moves from heaven to earth.

The mural is called Phra Rabiang and comprises 178 chambers.[9] With the exception of the 14th century 104-meter-long "Tapisserie de l'Apocalypse" beneath the Chateau d'Angers in the region of Anjou, no other known artwork spans such physical dimensions. Phra Rabiang encompasses all four sides of the temple housing the Emerald Buddha. Thousands of images delicately place humanity in the confines of the natural world, delineating an entire kingdom of creatures, forests, rivers and seas. Thai schools of art traditionally focused on such nature, particularly from the time of the great monk, scholar and painter, Khrua In Khong, the most eminent landscape painter of the Ayudhya period (1351-1767). His mural work imbibed a sensibility akin to the Chinese Sung Dynasty as well as the European Renaissance masters. Fine perspective, vanishing allures, the stormy skies and lushly clad mountains falling into meandering rivers all combined to provide a setting for the human presence. A humble presence, well integrated into nature.[10] Across the vast mural landscape of Phra Rabiang, nature has become the world we idolize, seducing the senses and reminding us of the time when Thailand, and indeed all of Southeast Asia, proffered such a vision.

This poignant meditation on our ephemerality and the beauty of other beings, this oasis in the heart of bustling Bangkok embodies the message of Buddhism. The story told at Wat Phra Keo depicts our dual nature and the spiritual challenge to manifest goodness and maturity by demonstating non-violence and protection.

We sit and watch a little girl sound asleep against her mother, who is kneeling, bowed before the main mall lined with censers. A blue, iridescent damselfly alights on a copper bowl aglow in the steamy morning sun. A breeze lifts the ephemeral creature up and away, over an array of beautifully-attired school children who approach. Removing their shoes, the children ascend stone steps to pay homage to the Emerald Buddha.

Nearby, in one of many enormous ceramic vases, minnows flirt in the shadows of the half-submerged lotus flowers; a bee searches for nectar and a small gold bug circumnavigates the rim of the vase, in search of its paradise. Here, at Wat Phra Keo, the world stands still with the perfect collaboration of all species present.

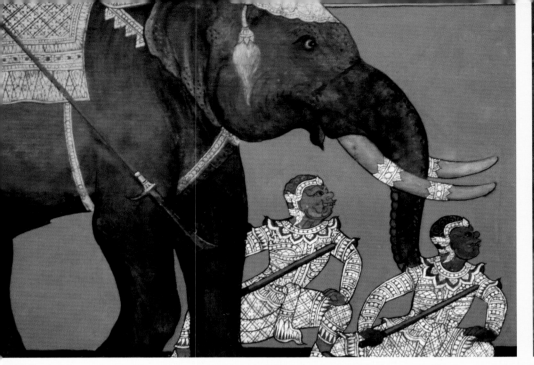

THE BUTTERFLIES OF KUALA LUMPUR

MALAYSIA

When biologist Alfred Wallace described discovering a rare butterfly, he spoke of his own heart beating "violently," of blood rushing to his head. "I felt much more like fainting, than I have done in apprehension of immediate death . . . so great was the excitement. . . ."[1]

Many have grappled with the unique beauty of butterflies, or Lepidoptera, who are possibly the most numerous of all insects. Living little more than three weeks as adults, after four transformative physiological phases, these glorious creatures inspire us by their exquisite beauty and ephemerality following their arduous metamorphoses.

"I do not know whether I was then a man dreaming I was a butterfly, or whether I am now a butterfly dreaming I am a man," wrote the Chinese mystic, Chuang Tzu.[2] But few have waxed so sympathetically as ethologist and author Myriam Baran, who writes of the butterfly, "These unique creatures have fascinated humans since the dawn of time. . . . Delicate and luminous, graceful and mercurial . . . it is a living

jewel that tempts human greed. Its fragile beauty has inspired poets, painters, and photographers. Its remarkable complexity has defied engineers and researchers, mocked military genius, and excited the curious."[3] In the Nazi concentration camps, pictures of butterflies drawn on walls were found in children's dorms. The children sought in these expressions some form of distant but imaginable salvation. Many of those artists survived and described their artistic prayers to the psychiatrists who assisted them.[4]

Of the 175,000 or so butterfly species that have thus far been discovered worldwide, over 1,000 inhabit Malaysia, the majority in East Malaysia (Borneo). In Peninsular Malaysia, this exquisite diversity has found a home in the center of the country's capital, Kuala Lumpur, at the Butterfly Park on Jalan Cenderawasih, where more than 6,000 individual butterflies, among 15,000 species of plants within a netted environment, reveal nearly 10% of all known regional species.

Like other gardens and parks across Kuala Lumpur, including the Bird Park next door, this butterfly sanctuary promotes a serious mission. If humankind is to spare the habitat critical to butterflies and moths, perhaps it can be assisted by becoming more familiar with butterflies themselves. A butterfly can sense a mate from 11 kilometers away, and most of the adult's body is given to two things: flight and sex. The colored wings that promote these two activities have provided some of the most astounding small paintings ever conceived. Butterfly behavior reveals an evolutionary stratagem of lovers' embraces that last, frequently, an entire day.

Tigers, zebras, birdwings, swallowtails, roses, helens, bluebottles, dragontails, saw-tooths and jezebels, albatross and orange tips, black crows, wood nymphs, evening browns, cyclops, fauns, leopards, blues, silverlines, banded demons, yeomans, lace-wings, jesters, admirals and wizards—such are some of the common names floating through the air in this steamy capital.[5]

Butterflies may save us one day with anti-rabies, anti-cancer and other drugs and healing balms we are only now beginning to divine. And they ask nothing of us; only that we respect them and not interfere.

Sometimes, when one least expects it, a butterfly chances onto a shoulder or into the palm of your hand. Or alights directly before you in a garden of dreams and seems to gaze into your eyes with a message spoken from life on earth.

At the Butterfly Sanctuary, thousands of visitors wander over bridges, around pools, throughout vernal tropics, with no agenda other than to marvel at beauty. The colors of nature are least subject to uniformity among butterflies. Unlike birds, these creatures will settle down inches from one's finger, preoccupied with matters of a leaf, a flower or a dew drop. They inspire us to reconsider the priorities upon which our world is focused. The antennae of a butterfly are sensors divining the unfathomable. We can get eye to eye with a butterfly, even see our own reflections there.

These intangible realities remind us that not everything need be understood. Mysteries still abound in nature. And our compassion and ecology of mind, in the face of the unknown, may signal our finest hour.

Rare & Endangered Birds' Aviaries
(Spesis Nadir & Terancam / 稀罕飞禽)

SINGAPORE'S HEART & SOUL: BUKIT TIMAH NATURE RESERVE

SINGAPORE

Along with the 32 square kilometer Tijuca National Park (Floresta de Tijuca) above Rio de Janeiro, Bukit Timah's 183 hectares of primary tropical rainforest in the heart of Singapore, protected since the 1880s, represent one of the truly unique urban ecosystems on the planet. This Nature Reserve is consistent with a country and a city whose verdant celebrity has evolved with deliberate finesse. Lee Kuan Yew, former Prime Minister, declared in 1995, "a blighted urban jungle of concrete destroys the human spirit."[1] With three nature reserves covering roughly 2,000 hectares in total and an additional 4,000 hectares spread out over "42 regional parks and 210 neighborhood parks,"[2] this city-state of 4.5 million people (a human density topping 18,652 persons per square mile, a US $130 billion GNP, or

nearly US $25,000 per capita income[3]) may deservedly be called a green capital.

Bukit Timah has more tree species than all of North America, 840 flowering plants, 100 species of ferns, more than 100 bird species, over 240 vertebrates and a plethora of insects. Whether a pig-tailed macaque (*Macaca nemestrina*), giant forest ants (*Camponotus gigas*) or the longest snake in the world, the reticulated python—along with 30 other significant reptiles, many native to the reserve—the interface between a city and the wild could not be more profound. Eleven kilometers from the heart of the city, Bukit Timah has no equivalent in all of Asia.[4]

As Veronique Sanson points out, Bukit Timah is also a "last refuge"[5] for many species that exist nowhere else, particularly some rare trees and ferns. This oasis has been unexploited since 1819, the year Singapore became a British trade center when Sir Stamford Raffles and William Farquhar arrived by boat to discover a green paradise. The years between then and 1965—when Singapore gained her independence—saw vast transformations that threatened to erase most native vegetation from the 626

square kilometer nation. Local cultivation of coconut, rice, pineapple, betel nut and other species, alongside one of the most formidable mercantile harbors in the world, suggested that Singapore would become an ecological sacrifice area. Bukit Timah reminds us what all of Singapore once was. So do many of the earliest images of the country.[6]

However there remain remnants of Singapore's green glory. From the Istana, Botanic, Chinese, Zoological and Mandai Orchid Gardens to such superb parks as Bras Basah, Jurong, Sentosa Island, Mount Faber, Emerald Hill, Fort Canning, and the MacRitchie Reservoir, the city still offers a vision of sensuous nature despite its many highrises. The School of Ornamental Horticulture at the city's Botanic Gardens, teaches a Garden City concept that has positioned Singapore to become a 21st century blueprint to ecologically counterbalance the world's urban maelstrom. This is also evidenced in all of the reserves (a huge amount for so small a city) and is even manifested along highways where angsana, golden rain, golden shower, coral and cabbage

trees have been planted in profusion, as well as the purple millettia and flame of the forest, jacaranda and frangipani.

Our friend Radha from Assam moved some years ago to Singapore. She conveyed her dismay upon learning that children are not allowed to climb trees in the city, an activity that much occupied her childhood in India. And it its true: there is a distinct sterility that can be read into the regulations of modernity and economic success in the Singapore model. The highway from the international airport and Changi Airport itself, seduce with seemingly perfect landscapes.[7] But with respect to nature, this city-state excels in ways best appreciated whilst trekking through the enormous forests of Bukit Timah, in the midst of repeated lightning storms and downpours throughout the day.

Amid keruing and seraya trees, we waited for the rain to cease. Running past us was a middle-aged man who jogged in running shorts to the summit of the Reserve, the highest mountain in the country: Bukit Timah Hill at 162.5 meters. Once there, he screamed and screamed at the top of his voice, a distinctive form, we imagine, of Singaporean stress reduction. He competed with the thunder. We chose to silently enjoy the storms and watch the bird silhouettes reemerge high in the canopies as the rain ceased and steam balls of roiling mist flooded the city, interspersed with voluptuous rainbows.

Descending through the dipterocarp forest on one of many trails, we looked for pangolin, flying foxes, lizards and lemurs, Brahminy kite, the wood scorpion and the lengthy lipan, the largest centipede in Asia, which is quite venomous and common here.

We happened upon an aquatic monitor lizard foraging for insects beneath a glen of *Shorea* genus tree species. For 20 minutes this large monitor raced back and forth across the forest floor, eventually coming right up to us and staring with the most appealing, unthreatening communion, of sorts.

Far down below the city could be heard, as rush hour traffic spilled out across the many freeways, two worlds co-existing.

A museum at the entrance to the National Park commends the work of such visionaries as Darwin and Wallace and points unabashedly to the destructive forces that had reduced so much of the native biodiversity throughout the Malay Peninsula. The educational displays are unstinting in their belief that sanctuaries such as this one can make all the difference, saving lives, whole geneaologies, while reminding today's generations that there is much work left to be done; lives to save; environmental promise to embrace, if only we can collectively exercise restraint and love that perdurable garden we have all been blessed with.

FORESTS OF ETERNITY: ULU TEMBURONG NATIONAL PARK

BRUNEI

The Temburong River has its unexpected moments: some 23 rapids flush our inflatable raft past jutting hardwoods that have tumbled from steep tropical slopes on either shore during the previous months of the winter rainy season. Access to the river requires an hour's ride in a speedboat through a maze of mangroves across Eastern Brunei, into the Malaysian waters of the South China Sea and then back into Brunei where the nerve-wracking route reaches Bangar, a small town 16 kilometers from the eastern-most village of Kampong Batang Duri. From there, we drive through the countryside, park the vehicles and trek by and through old long houses occupied by multigeneration families. We pass the children and grandparents resting in hammocks to fight the heat, then continue through backyards

past wild roosters until we reach the shore and board the flatbottom speedboat to greet the rapids.

Brunei's oil and liquefied natural gas wealth[1], coupled with a small population of under 400,000, has enabled the Malay-speaking monarchy, ruled by His Majesty Sultan Haji Hassanal Bolkiah Mu'izzaddin Waddaulah, to conserve a largely green, resplendent nation into the 21st century. With its ten forest and recreational green-belt reserves and one national park, Brunei's rainforest takes up more than 71% of the country's 2,228 square miles (5,765 sq.km, or 119,880 hectares). Moreover, 78% of the country is said to maintain its "natural vegetation" (as of 1984, 59% was primary forest, 22% secondary forest[2]) which is by far the highest such conservation achievement in all of Asia.[3] While that is a small area relatively speaking, it bodes of continued protection like few other places on Earth. With a projected population by the year 2050 of no more than 587,000[4] and strict legislation articulating longterm conservation goals (even the slightest disturbance of wildlife brings a US$10,000 fine and mandatory two year jail term) this country is unique. Ulu Temburong, the nation's one and only national park, is its glorious quintessence.

Since the park's creation in 1996, no more than 3,000 people per year have visited this 50,000 hectare, 400 square kilometer chunk of dazzling rainforest within the Bukit Patoi and Peradayan Forest Reserves. There are all of seven kilometers of trail in

the national park and off-trail movement is not permitted, except in limited and infrequent scientific research forays. A narrow, elevated causeway constructed of steel nearly 165 feet up permits views far into the adjoining states of Malayasian Sabah and Sarawak. This is the northern fringe of Borneo, just north of the Equator.

While the rest of Borneo is losing its forests faster than any other region of tropical rainforest on the planet, Brunei, which comprises less than 1% of Borneo, has accomplished what few other governments have imagined by creating a national sanctuary that is enormous relative to the size of the country. From the perspective of native biodiversity, that protective umbrella is critical. Research at the Kuala Belalong Rainforest Field Studies Centre has shown that a single tree in this national park can contain as many as 400 different species of beetle. It remains the least disturbed of all rainforest in any of the three "Heart of Borneo" Declaration signatories (Brunei, Malaysia and Indonesia).[5] Butterfly abundance is only partially documented, with an estimated 400 or more known species of the 20,000 that have been identified in all of Borneo. The largest and most celebrated Bruneian member of the Order Lepidoptera is Rajah Brooke's birdwing (*Trogonoptera brookiana*) but the rich diversity of butterflies (and dragonflies) confronting us at every check point, waltzing in profuse arrays above the water, the sand and up the slope towards the forest, suggests a staggering multiplicity.

This seems to be the case with amphibians of which 50 have thus far been documented, including two species with no limbs. And, there are a large number of reptiles, including the gorgeous Wagler's pit viper.

Mammalian diversity is also enormous with an estimated 221 terrestrial mammals in all of Borneo (including 92 species of bat). Since 1984, at least 90 species have been identified in Brunei's forests, including the spectacular proboscis monkey (*Nasalis larvatus*) in the Southwestern Belait District and along the Limbang River in the mangroves though not in Temburong.[6] Present in greater abundance than anywhere else in Borneo are leaf monkeys (*Presbytis hosei*) and the tailless Bornean gibbon (*Hylobates muelleri*), as well as the silvered langur (*Presbytis cristata*).

Avifauna is similarly rich, but lacking the biological inventories that have been conducted further south in Kalimantan. Rhinoceros hornbills (*Buceros rhinoceros*) are heard at regular intervals and swiftlets are prodigious along the river.

But it is the forest that provides the clearest indication that a wealthy oil-producing nation can make amends for its unwelcome contribution to global warming by setting aside, and keeping sacrosanct, a large proportion of its aboriginal canopy. Of course, it cannot ever come close to compensating in terms of the global "carbon sink" equivalency. The offset works neither biologically nor economically. In fact, when the Bolivian government received US$25 million in carbon credit cash in 2006 for keeping its 1,523,000 hectare Noel Kempff Mercado National Park protected (a World Heritage site), that meant $16.4 dollars per hectare, US$6.80 per acre, with no

appreciation horizon.[7] Numerous other financial aspects of the carbon sink computation vary from clime to clime, depending on soil nutrients, deadwood percentages and forest composition turnover rates.

Such "value" per acre of rainforest/soil components—if computed for Ulu Temburong according to the present voluntary markets and vastly underrated cost equivalents—would make the entire National Park worth a mere US$819,000 in carbon credits.[8] That is an indecent figure that does not merit serious discussion, particularly in the context of a Bruneian economy whose per capita income is over US$25,000, of which 60% is estimated to come from the sale of oil and gas abroad.[9]

One cannot overstate the importance of revising the dollar equivalence of living forests; of granting biodiversity the utmost gold standard when it comes to realistic value.

Moving into the canopy from the National Park guest quarters, we find that we are alone in this stellar, primeval terrain. It is a priceless experience. With a special permit to climb a steep jungly slope, recently laced with a rope to aid the few scientists who ever come here, we made our way through mixed dipterocarp dryland and lower montane forests, in and out of half-a-dozen lightning storms with pouring rain. Elsewhere across Asia these are precisely the sorts of huge trees (a family of 17 genera and as many as 680 tropical species of two-winged or ribbed fruits) that have fallen hostage to the timber industry, the most ubiquitous being the species of *Shorea*, *Dryobalanops* and *Parashorea*.[10] There are an estimated 1,900 to 2,000 tree species in Brunei Darussalam, many found here in Ulu Temburong, as well as nearly 3,451 flowering plants, and a richer mosaic of groundcovers than anywhere else in the country. The tallest trees in Brunei are found here, *Dryobalanops aromatica*, standing well over 50 meters.[11]

Over a hundred known plants are endemic to Brunei or 2.9% of all species thus far assessed in the country.

Leaping primates appear as distant silhouettes in the upper reaches of the 175-foot-tall trees. Birds are nearly impossible to see once inside the canopy amid the downpour. Thunder shakes whole hillsides which continue to rumble for long seconds.

When Ms. Nora Linda Abrahim returned home to Brunei from her studies at Sussex University in England, she made an appointment with the Forestry Department in search of a job. In her early 20s, she told the official, "I just love the forest. I love it. It's beautiful." She got the job and ten years later, bearing a modest grin, finds herself the Senior Forest Official in the country.

"We have one of the largest protected forest areas in this part of the world," she says, explaining how her department has succeeded in pushing forward legislation requiring that any tree cut within the legal timber estates must be no smaller than 60 centimeters diameter at breast height in order to allow the trees to mature. Nora works in the upper echelons of a Department employing over 420 people, with few women.

"Men find it strange to see a woman in the forests," she admits but goes on to add that she can think of nothing more wonderful to do and hopes and prays that she will be able to help ensure that these magnificent forests remain for all eternity.

Ulu Temburong, like all of Brunei, is only a microcosm on the world stage in terms of size. Added complications, to be sure, in terms of the global impact of the nation's wealth (what some cynics have labeled a "Shellfare" state) complicate the otherwise pristine picture. But in fact, people like Nora are undeniably in the forefront of conservation. Her commitment reflects that of the Sultan himself and speaks to a new era of reconciliation. Here is a sanctuary with a twist, but one that twists in the right direction.

THE EXTENDED FAMILY OF DR. BIRUTÉ GALDIKAS: TANJUNG PUTING NATIONAL PARK

KALIMANTAN, BORNEO, INDONESIA

We meet her in Jakarta and fly to Pangkalan Bun, near her village of Pasir Panjang, home to 700 or so people, located in south-central Kalimantan, also known as Borneo: 748,168 square kilometers or 288,869 square miles in size.

Many of the earliest works detailing the region, especially 19th century sagas by explorers like Alfred Wallace, describe Borneo in terms of fire ants and infernal heat, pit vipers, leeches, humidity and much more. One reads of lost worlds and huge romance—of danger, tribal warfare and the unknown. Our first impression conveys something altogether different, at least in the company of Dr. Biruté Galdikas. For she is gentle, strong and fearless in her chosen home. She is captivatingly real.[1]

Dr. Galdikas possesses an intuitive, nearly shamanic way in the world, hard-won by both innocence and experience. After over three decades in the field, she continues to earn accolades from every conservation quarter. Perhaps, as importantly, she has gained the trust and respect of the indigenous primates—orangutan and human—with whom she has chosen to spend her life. The outcome is her profound contribution to the creation and management of a national park and a scientific reserve with more such reserves and conservation areas in the making. This was all accomplished while she informed the world about the spirit, profundity and importance to the future of life on earth, of one of the forest's astonishing inhabitants: the orangutan.

Drawing global attention to the plight of these rare beings, Dr. Galikas has spent so much time among the orangutans that one might afford her the compliment of saying that she has nearly become an orangutan herself.

With her poetic strength, Dr. Galdikas embodies both the gracious warrior she has of necessity become and that National Geographic cover girl with movie star charisma that sky-rocketed her to fame in the mid-1970s. That beauty is a brilliant person, whose work was drenched in a language that few scientists of the day dared

256

to speak. It was a language shared by Dr. Galdikas, Dian Fossey and Jane Goodall—the language of "the Other," as Sy Montgomery wrote of it, citing Henry Beston's early New England classic work of nature meditation, *The Outermost Beach*, "caught with ourselves in the net of life and time, fellow prisoners of the splendor and travail of the earth."[2] We all are connected. This is especially discernible when in the presence of those primates closest to us, the orangutans. They are not as close genetically, it is believed, as the chimpanzee or bonobo, but they are the most similar to us. That is how Dr. Galdikas describes the uncanny resemblance.

One feels inspired to utter superlatives the minute one meets, not only the orangutans, but Dr. Galdikas. She lets you in, as the orangutans do. And, while the behavioral ecologists tell you time and again that orangutans are largely solitary, certainly the 300-pound adult males who may spend 50 years at peace amid the trees, rarely encountering or needing others, the sub-adult females are typically social, searching together for their fruit. Dr. Galdikas resembles her friends: sharing fruit, musing expressively in a free-flow that is part meditation, part secret slang, emerging like the most primordial of languages, the song of the forest.

Dr. Galdikas chose to live in the jungle observing orangutans with the goal of saving them. As ambassador from the orangutan world, she had to figure out levels of diplomacy that defy ordinary mortal machinations, so complex is the human landscape of Borneo. While navigating this geopolitical realm, she served as surrogate mother to great apes, human wife and mother, scientist, teacher, healer, poet and translator. The month before we join Dr. Galdikas at Camp Leakey, a major "Heart of

257

Borneo Decree" was initiated by the Indonesian, Malaysian and Bruneian governments. They are the three countries with stakes in Borneo—for better or worse. Brunei's impact is mostly positive. Having just arrived from there, we already dream that some of these orangutans might be translocated to the safety of protected forests far to the north of the island.

Dr. Galdikas mentions that she has heard of two sightings of solitary male orangutans wandering through Brunei. There have been no other known sightings. That means those males are, in biological terms "vagrants" who probably can't find what it takes to survive in Brunei. We think this a tragedy given the amount of protected area there. Dr. Galdikas knows what fruit is needed to survive, which species of trees and flowers, what the water color must be, the pH, the soil type, everything. She knows it after decades observing orangutans surviving in the forest.

There are about 7,000 orangutans on Sumatra, the enormous Indonesian island nearby. These orangutans have their own culture; possibly their own species. But long ago they were connected with Borneo before the islands separated, so they can mate with the three different groups comprising the approximately 50,000 remaining orangutans in Borneo. Throughout Kalimantan scientists classify them as *Pongo pygmaeus*. But there may be four subspecies.[3] Such taxonomic uncertainty has defied a consistent nomenclature ever since Wallace was there in the 1860s. His book detailing his journey shows a Dyak tribal ensemble stabbing an orangutan. Dr. Galdikas is married to Pak Bohap, a Dyak tribal elder. Together 28 years, they have two children. Pak Bohap's people no longer go after primates. But other Dyaks in the interior are opportunistic hunters, she tells us.

Wallace admired the Dyaks, noting that they are gentle and kind, notwithstanding traditional practices detrimental to the forest in a modern age. Wallace's account, first published in two volumes in the winter of 1869, departed in its characterization of Bornean tribal people from the "head hunting" spin of earlier writers such as Sir James Brooke. It focused upon a greater truth: "Against this one stain on their character [which in the case of the Sarawak Dyaks no longer exists] we have to set many good points. They are truthful and honest to a remarkable degree. From this cause it is very often impossible to get from them any definite information, or even an opinion....In a Dyak village the fruit trees have each their owner, and it has often happened to me, on asking an inhabitant to gather me some fruit, to be answered, 'I can't do that, for the owner of the tree is not here'; never seeming to contemplate the possibility of acting otherwise."[4]

Dr. Galdikas comes from a Gandhian tradition of non-violence and is one of the few conservation biologists we have met equally involved with spiritual ecology and animal rights. Every individual life counts for her.

We call her Dr. Biruté in the field and among her family and colleagues. Titles and hierarchy are fundamental to Indonesian cultural politics. They are a statement of earned merit and authority.

Dr. Biruté's work was championed by Louis Leakey, the great paleontologist, who also mentored Jane Goodall and the late Dian Fossey. Leakey knew that for evolutionary understanding to grow, committed long-term field work among critical primates was necessary. When Dr. Biruté first met Leakey at a lecture of his at UCLA, he mentioned to the crowd that he had just received a telegram from Fossey in which she

reported that gorillas were untying shoelaces. Today, that would not make news. In the late 1960s it did. Ethology (the comparative study of animal behavior) has come an enormous distance since then, largely due to the work of Dr. Leakey's three "angels." Says Dr. Biruté, "When Dr. Leakey said that, I knew I was hooked." She already identified closely with orangutans. Dr. Biruté first arrived in Borneo in 1971 with first husband, Rod Brindamour. They lived in a hut for three years.

Thirty-five years later, she is still in the trenches, selflessly working to save the species so like us from extinction.

Plans change before we even get into the field: something remarkable has happened. A huge 300-pound male has appeared in the trees across the street from Dr. Biruté's home. Her orphanage, scientific rehab center and labs are nearby. Clearly this

wild male has heard the calls of other male orangs and may sense that there are some 300 orphaned animals there. But, he is several blocks away, 40 feet up a tree and sunset is drawing near. He may stay there, but Dr. Biruté and her uniformed staff and three vets are panic-stricken. What if the orangutan leaps for the power lines thinking them ideal for hanging upon? Then, she tells us, the orangutan will be electrocuted. It has happened elsewhere.

He makes his "long call," and it booms throughout the neighborhood, repeated tone by tone, the notes getting lower and lower, until, tired, the call fades into silence.

Up in the trees, he is making a huge ruckus. He sounds exactly like King Kong on the move. Gigantic limbs of bamboo are snapping as he makes his bed for the night. There are 30 or more villagers on the road, motorcycles, cars, expectant human eyes on the lookout. This is a rare occurence. Many locals have never even seen a wild orangutan. The vets roll up their pants and wade through deep swamp to reach the base of the trees and try to use a blowgun to send a tranquilizer into the huge stranger, guessing its weight to get the dosage level right.

On the first attempt, the dart glances off him. Night falls. By the next morning they are successful and have gotten the male into a cage to check his vitals. The plan is to return him to the wild, far into a scientific reserve and beyond. We later learned that Dr. Biruté and her staff took him into the wilderness. The walk, during which he was carried in an animal carrier, took most of a day, and Biruté's malaria flared up. This acute event she takes in stride. At 61, she has contracted every disease known to these tropics.

Bornean orangutan populations, other than that of the 6,000 individuals in Tanjung Puting, are fragmented and in trouble. Human overpopulation, says Dr. Biruté, is the number one problem. Despite Indonesia's highly successful family planning program, the country now has over 240 million people and is growing. That is a far cry from the six million inhabitants of Alfred Wallace's time.

Tanjung Puting National Park, established under Dr. Biruté's co-management authority in 1988, comprises 400,000 hectares or nearly 960,000 acres. Forty percent of this is now degraded, which leaves 576,000 acres or more than two thousand square kilometers in pretty good shape.

Dr. Biruté's own home village is about 90 minutes by car and speedboat from the National Park. Her staff of 200 or more and their families work and live in her village, in the park and in various other surrounding locations, checkpoints and a half-dozen release camps. Her husband's home is on about 100 acres of good tropical peat swamp forest, symbolic of what all of Borneo was once about. Dr. Biruté is trying to arrange the purchase of as much land as possible to extend orangutan habitat protection. This goal includes 240,000 acres to the immediate east of the national park. Land in perfect, pristine condition, she says, which would give the orangutans another 25% of habitat. They're going to need it as illegal logging, zircon mining and palm oil plantations recklessly expand. In her village, she has paid up to US$13,000 per acre. Out in the peat swamps hundreds of miles into the interior, the cost, she says, will be about US$22 per acre. The entire 240,000 acres might cost US$5 million. If the goal of purchasing this land is achieved, it could be legally converted into permanent conservation protected area and provide employment for more Dyak people (who fish for their livelihood), by giving them the additional income for serving as enthusiastic park authorities. This would constitute a win-win for international conservation. It is a strategy that only Dr. Biruté's connections, sensitivity and long-term commitment can guarantee.

The local tribal people honor her, as do the police and the Indonesian Government. But it has not been an easy experience, more a rollercoaster ride navigating amid various turmoils of several political regimes, a kidnapping and beating, several death threats, defeats and triumphs. She is a survivor, and the 6,000 orangutans in the park are her living memorial. Biruté recalls seeing the cover of one of her mother's professional nursing journals, large red letters upon white reading "Burn Out." That sums up the ecological fatigue to which many in conservation work succumb. It is easy to understand why. In Dr. Biruté's case, for nearly four decades she has been in the middle of cross-fire: between illegal loggers and officials concerned with economic growth at all costs, near the center of battles between police, the military and five different Islamic political administrations, all of which inherited this strange persistent celebrity. She is a Canadian-born American of Lithuanian Roman Catholic descent. Always an enigma to the male Islamic rulers of the nation, here was a woman who adopted Indonesian citizenship and married Pak Bohap, the Dyak tribal chief and rice farmer known for his shamanic wisdom and goodness. For Dyak men, says Dr. Biruté, women's rights advocacy is ingrained in their animist, pantheistic religion. They worship trees, spirits, women and all of nature, known as *Alam Terang.* A dashing, charismatic figure, Pak Bohap has been an invaluable support for Dr. Biruté during their long marriage.

No other scientist alive today has devoted so many years (35 thus far) to observing a single other mammalian species. Hers is the longest field research study in history. "Unlike chimpanzees you don't have to get *through* the orangutanness," says Dr. Biruté. They relate to you as a recognizable relative. "They are like us—not the same, but so similar you can understand them and know that you are making sense to them. I wish I was smarter," she says repeatedly. Meaning, she would love to be able to figure it all out.

As we head up river through the swamps, we see where fires, fueled by global warming, have taken out thousands of acres. The sight leaves one shaken. Google Earth the area and see a striking mosaic of human interventions that make one sick with the realization of devastation in these remote and important regions with diversity approximating that of the Tropical Andes; even with 80% of original Borneo destroyed or in the process of degradation.

We watch a large freight vessel plowing in the other direction, carrying sand. Dr. Biruté tells us it will go to China to be used in the manufacture of triggers, nuclear components, ceramics and diamonds. Thousands of dollars worth of sand, the extraction of which takes out hundreds of trees that could take a thousand years to recover, if ever. Industrialists rob the soil and the trees simply fall over, collapsed. These are ancient trees that are the home of the orangutan.

Lamandau, the 4,000 acre reserve for which Dr. Biruté gained protection from resource extraction, was created in 1996 after a mere 18 months of persistent effort. She had gone to top officials to tell them she had personally witnessed illegal incursions by all sorts of small-time crooks going after various things: trees, animals, sand. She met the local governor and got his children on board; and she made repeated visits

to the Forestry Minister, got to know the wives of high-level officials, took endless meetings. In Indonesia, says Dr. Biruté, to get anything truly done requires 100% consensus. It would not be until the Forestry Minister's very last day in office that he signed the decree protecting the area for which Dr. Biruté had steadily lobbied. This would provide breathing space for the park, a true biological buffer comprising healthy black water peat swamp. Where the zircon mining has totally disrupted such ecosystems, the mangrove swamps are rust colored, filthy bodies of water thick with dirt, like the rivers downstream in Suriname polluted by bauxite mines. The black is what one wants to see: black water that brilliantly reflects moonlight and whose color is derived from all of the undissolved tannins.

"Mr. Bam Bang, the head of Tanjung Puting National Park, is the best in years," says Dr. Biruté with a quiet smile. "You have to be here, year after year, to appreciate the delicate politics that exist between the regents, the provincial leadership, the police, the military and those in Jakarta. And then you have the whole hierarchial dynamic inherent to the Dyak villages, and then there is Islam. It's complicated."

Quite remarkably, in spite of those complications, Dr. Biruté herself wrote the management plan for the National Park and, basically, got the park officially codified. Previously, it had been a Reserve area.

"How on earth did you pull that off?" we ask. She begins to answer, in the midst of the beginning of a very busy couple of days. "Well, initially when I started my field research I had no idea what I was hearing: a rhino; an elephant? No, a male orangutan, a Dyak tribesman told me. Three years in an old bark-roofed hut with my first husband, listening, watching. . . . There were five autos in Pangkalan Bun back then. I got the idea of hiring one of them, from the police, to get around more effectively. Suddenly, people thought of me as a policeman, or certainly a strong backer and ally of the police. That helped. And gave me credibility when I'd go up to somebody who had captured an orangutan and informed him that only the President of Indonesia could own an orangutan, according to law number such and such. People actually thought I was a spy for President Sukarto. You see, there was a village in the reserve—the area that would become the National Park. That village was not supposed to be there. It was me against the village, so to speak."

"Great odds," we throw in. Dr. Biruté just smiles. She knows the history. "The Colonial Dutch had overseen the last Sultan's gesture in 1936, when the Reserve was established to protect the last remaining rhinos in this part of Borneo. The village had to be moved and it was moved. Then the poachers and illegal loggers started moving back in, decade after decade. This is Borneo. And there was also resentment that perhaps the government was cheating the poor people, the little guy . . ."

Her cell phone jingles: another sudden change in plans. We are off to the police station where three young men stand behind bars, awkwardly greeting us with frightened smiles. They were the three that got caught. Another 27 got away. Outside the jailhouse, we count a dozen large hardwood trees, family Dipterocarp, genus *Shorea*, all felled illegally in the Reserve. The boys, at least two of them (the minor will be spared) could possibly get one to three years in jail for their offence. In Surabaya, those trees could fetch between US$2,000 to $3,000. These boys would have made US$150 to $200 each, or nearly two months wages, based upon the per capita income, which is, on average, US$1,000 a year in the region.

We leave the jail and head towards Dr. Biruté's local Orangutan Foundation International (OFI) offices. OFI is based in Los Angeles, a nonprofit organization with few staff in the States. Most are here, in the field, where she works with funding from donations and large long-term grants from the United States Agency for International Development (USAID) and other major donors. But her annual budget is a mere US$600,000. With that she has accomplished miracles: caring for the orangutans and supporting 200 Dyak staff members and their families providing for their medical needs, their lives and their futures. At the Orangutan Care Center, which she started in the early 1990s, and in various auxillary camps, 300 orangutan orphans are nursed to health.

The orphans cling to Dr. Biruté. She feeds them fruit: rambutan, durian and cempedak, an *Artocarpus* related to the jackfruit. Rambutan only flowers two months a year. Now is the time (late February), and they are gobbling it down. We try it and, frankly, it is horrible, coated in rubbery gel and spikes. It is definitely an acquired taste, unless you happen to be an orangutan. Dr. Biruté loves it. The cost of wild fruit like rambutan for her entire orphanage averages US$70,000 a year. In addition, the orphanage feeds supplements, which the orangutans relish. This attention to their dietary needs gives them a nutritious jump start as they try, with Dr. Biruté and team's help, to make a new life for themselves. So much of their diet comes in small, fragmented protein packages, says Dr. Biruté, and the orangutan spends much of the day—at least 60% of their waking hours—searching for food. Because they are not hoarders, but share everything, they seem to take great pleasure in extending this activity throughout their diurnal hours. By dusk, they are going about the business of making their beds up in the trees.

Babies remain dependent on their mothers until they are nearly nine years old. This is a remarkable duration for mentorship and parenting quite unlike that of any other primate, with the exception of humans. These babies have seen their parents abducted or killed before their eyes, often whilst clinging to them. How they maintain trust and faith in our kind is staggering testimony to their innocence and love and to Dr. Biruté's staff, whose love for them is abundant.

In the lab, Dr. Biruté's scientists engage in cutting-edge research, some still unpublished, on the impact and strain of malaria on orangutan populations. Dr. Biruté obtained her Ph.D. in biological anthropology at UCLA and is fluent in the language of primate physiology. By most estimates, she is one of the two or three leading primatologists in the world, but she doesn't parade her knowledge. In fact, she is anything but cavalier because, in true Socratic tradition, she knows how much she does not know. She photographs compulsively, takes notes and watches quietly. A few years ago, Dr. Biruté and some colleagues published a scientific study that proved that orangutans have culture. It was the patient, steady outgrowth of a few decades of field work.

Suddenly, Dr. Biruté declares: "Don't move!"

We are walking with a group of orangutans, some in our arms, some hand in hand, when she sees one of the orangutans peering intently at the ground before us. We don't see what the fuss is all about, but now Dr. Biruté does. A large colorful snake lies at Michael's feet. "I might have stepped right on it, possibly hurt it or been killed."

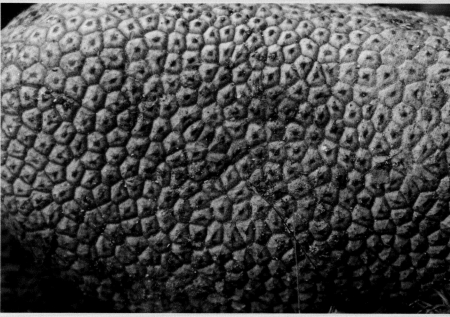

Perhaps that orangutan, whose senses are so infinitely more attuned than ours, just saved Michael's life.

We back away but not before taking a few digital images, although only part of the body of the reptile is now in view. Snakes are not at all aggressive in Borneo, she tells us. Later, we show the photograph to the police patrol that we join, during another emergency in search of a poaching ring, following the loggers' hastily built illegal tracks going over swamp into a virgin forest area they have been clandestinely clearing for months. The poachers clearly have their own spies up and down river and have gotten advance word of our three-boat patrol invasion. No one is there. Only the damage they have wreaked.

One of the forestry patrolmen recognizes the snake when he sees the photograph.

"Dangerous?" we ask.

"Absolutely," he replies.

During our return, crawling on all fours through rattan-relatives that shred clothes and skin, we now focus on the ground, on every vine and every log. The snakes are all around. "Not to worry," Dr. Biruté says. "We just don't want to get caught out in the dark." Of course, that's exactly what will happen for the next three nights.

We leave the port town of Kumai in Kumai Bay and head south in an open speedboat through the China Sea, then into the brackish black water of the Sekonyer River. We head up through the freshwater tropical peat swamp forest on the way to Rimba in the Sekonyer village. The people are mostly non-Dyak, Islamic coastal Melayu—the other huge tribe in Borneo. We reach a reintroduction site, what Dr. Biruté calls a "release camp." Here three orangutans, Toley, Jo and Janu, come to greet her. The camp is in the magnificent heart of Lamandau, the reserve Dr. Biruté saved from loggers and poachers. Every few miles we encounter another outpost en route to camp, with armed guards on the lookout for poachers and other criminals. These dedicated conservationists are employed by OFI and spend months at a time living in these elevated pole-houses above the mangrove swamp. There are few mosquitoes, to our surprise, but the heat and nearly 100% humidity are intense. The black water swamp, through which we frequently wade, irrespective of snakes, is cool comfort in such temperatures. We are two degrees south of the Equator. That is good news for Kalimantan in terms of global warming. The jungle here has elasticity—it is, in essence, prepared for heat. But not for the fire which recently swept through, leaving mile after mile of mangrove and nipa palm devastated. Still, had Dr. Biruté not accomplished her goal of protecting this region, the mangroves and nipa would have all been cut down for timber and sold, then replaced with plantations for palm oil and rubber tapping.

Jo and Janu come down from the trees to take our hands and sniff our fingers, getting to know us. A wild male makes his kiss-squeak sound.

Orangutans, when pregnant, take eight months or so to deliver. They are typically pregnant only once in every six years beginning at age eight, compared with gorillas whose fertility cycle loops in four years. Orangutans have few offspring and will never wean babies in less than seven years.

"For her first eight years the female shows no interest whatsoever in having sex with a male."

They are not omnivores, like chimpanzees, but herbivores. They eat fruit, vegetables and leaves and will devour supplemental foods. Other primate herbivores inhabit the forest. As we move along a tributary of the Sekonyer, two groups of proboscis monkeys (*Nasalis larvatus*) come near. Their unforgettable noses (the function of which is described as "unknown") and their restricted distribution (better characterized as Critically Endangered) together make them a unique biological player in the dynamic riparian environments of Borneo and a few nearby islands. They are large, weighing up to ten kilograms. The infants' faces are dark blue, which is unique among their kind. And their language diversity appears to be vast. The range of their distinctive calls is described by Payne and Francis as "including honks, groans, squeals, and loud roars."[5] Like the orangutan, they, too, are herbivores, feeding on shoots, leaves and fruits throughout the mangroves and mixed mangroves. We have left the screw and nipa palm areas of the swamp forest. These are bigger trees. Proboscis can swim but prefer to stay in trees. Given hunting pressures and their few remaining numbers (a couple of thousand), it is remarkable that they come even closer to us as we sit in

the boat. They must know Dr. Biruté, or smell her, because they are at ease next to our boat. This is a water course that she has been taking for 35 years. Other tourist boats, she tells us, rarely get so lucky when it comes to spotting these rare primates. And that's counting a mere 1,000 tourists a year, as of late, who make the journey to Camp Leakey. In the distance, we hear long-tailed (crab-eating) macaque (*Macaca fascicularis*) as well as Borneo gibbons (*Hylobates muelleri*).

That night, our lights reveal skimming short-nosed fruit bats (*Cynopterus brachyotis*) as we scan the area for giant wolf spiders and barking geckos. We're also on the lookout for the slow loris (*Nycticebus coucang*) and Western tarsier (*Tarsius bancanus*), neither of which we see. But Borneo's nightlife is rich with other mammals and reptiles. From leopards (one newly discovered) and Malaysian sun bears to the Asian elephant and rhino to a known 34 species of squirrels, 26 species of rats and mice (including a giant rat) and 92 species of bat (including eight pipistrelles and the lesser false vampire), not to mention her primates, Borneo overwhelms in the abundance of her biodiversity. There are 221 species of mammal alone. But you feel and see such biological abundance most impressively in terms of the insects flying past the small headlight on a boat at night, tens-of-millions, or is it billions, of individuals, coming into, and then veering from the light.

Touch anywhere and there is an insect, a spider, a snake, a bird, a dragonfly or butterfly, something. It is all alive.

And in the middle somewhere (we prefer to think of them neither at the apex nor the core) of evolutionary grace is the Primate Order. Six families live here in Borneo: Lorisidae (lorises); Tarsiidae (tarsiers); Cercopithecidae (monkeys); Hylobatidae (gibbons); and Hominidae (great apes and humans).[6] "We're the great unknown to them," Dr. Biruté says of our species in referring to all the others.

Who, but our kind would scrape the earth, slash and burn or dig for gold and zircon. One kilo of zircon is worth ten cents to the operator, no other royalties. All that remains is the long-term destruction of the forest. It's going on today, only an hour up river from Camp Leakey, which sits on the right flank of the Sekonyer River. Tourists come, says Dr. Biruté, and see only the magnificence. They leave unaware of what is happening all around the park.

In 2006, Dr. Biruté got word that 15% of the northern end of the National Park would be turned over to palm oil plantations. And, in 2007, with the "Heart of Borneo Decree," signed by the Sultan of Brunei and the Forestry heads of Malaysia and Indonesia, Dr. Biruté heard within days from a forest official that it was nothing more than paper pushing, conservation lip service all too familiar, and, if anything, it would provide additional motive, incentive and cover for so-called sustainable plantations and logging. One says "so-called" because according to most scientists who study tropical forests, there is no such thing as sustainable development in a tropical forest. Ultimately, the forest will be destroyed. That has been the lesson from other parts of the world, and that is Borneo's fate if "modernity" moves forward with a brute mentality.

At the same time, Borneo is in the spotlight in other ways. In 12 months, more than 50 new species were discovered here, including what is believed to be the most powerful leopard in the world, with body coloring resembling a python.

In addition to the continuing biological revelations, something deep in the spirit of the Indonesia that she has experienced summons a sense of hope in Dr. Biruté: "An interesting, strange idealism exists in Indonesians; a sense that unfairness is wrong. Strange and schizophrenic, their ancient Buddhist and Hindu ethics and a strain of pure, traditional Isalm all come together towards conservation. They respect certain things, and that never changes."

They respect Dr. Biruté and her husband. Government officials tell her, "You are an icon for our country." Ironic, given the tears she has shed in her struggle. But what matters to Dr. Biruté is the orangutan. They brought Dr. Biruté to Borneo. The politics she did not plan for nor expect, but her staying power has proved her indomitable. Now she has power, at least in the park, where there is a remarkable, healthy density of approximately 2.5 orangutans per square kilometer. A few years ago she came upon Akmad, the first wild born ex-captive orangutan, six kilometers from Camp Leakey, at peace in the wilderness. Dr. Biruté had not seen Akmad for five years. He had disappeared. When she first came to Borneo, she had rescued and hand reared him with a baby bottle and food supplements. As with more than 100 orangutans, Dr. Biruté was the surrogate mother. He slept with her and ate meals with her. That he survived all those years and then came back to Camp Leakey was incredible. Dr. Biruté brushes away a tear recounting all this. It was too much for her to bear, she says, to imagine a world without Akmad or Princess, Remaja, Rocky and Kuspasi, Peta, Unyuk, Gundul, Siswi, Siswoyo, Priscilla, Kusasi, Pola, Yayat, Adik, Sugito, and so many others that she rescued, raised, befriended, loved.

"You see, 1,000 orangutans were killed in the year 2006," Dr. Biruté tells us. Hunger, murder, kidnapping. She saw starving orangutans in Sabah, up north, walking into villages in desperation and going to the garbage dumps in search of anything to eat. Her research area within Tanjung Puting National Park, where countless sorts of monitoring and biological survey work goes on is limited to about 50 square kilometers, or 5,000 hectares, 12,000 acres. In that area her team has inventoried over 600 tree species. Nobody knows how many different tree species an orangutan needs to survive, but it is clearly quite a few, and throughout Borneo and Sumatra, where Dr. Biruté's research also takes her, the forests are being plundered, and all the animals with them.

"If this continues—the killing, the poaching, the starvation—the orangutan will go extinct. Add the wildfires, tsunamis, global warming and an Indonesian economy in turmoil….The message is loud and clear: these magical creatures need all the help they can get, and fast."

"Palm plantations clear cut the land. There is no replanting, just devastation. Tourists rarely see the lunar landscapes of Indonesia. And, they don't recognize it when they see orangutans in national parks who are bereft, abandoned or orphaned, maggot-infested, begging or dying. The huge cheek-padded males are killed off and there goes the whole biological fitness of the population."

Female orangutans are frequently killed for their young, the sorts that end up as orphans at the OFI orphanage, or in a cooking pot, the very unlucky ones. Muslims, she says, will kill them as pests, but Javanese will eat them. And she related several cases of eyewitnesses seeing the orangutans boiled and vomiting from the horror of it. "You see, they look just like us, especially when they are boiled."

So she travels the world, as time permits, trying to raise awareness and US$5 mil-

lion dollars to extend the park and ensure its future maintenance. Because the Dyak owners trust her, they will sell all that land to her, and by that collective mechanism Dr. Biruté and her team could complete the connectivity of the jungle all the way to the surrounding rivers to the East. "It is perfect orangutan tropical peat swamp forest," she reiterates. "Very little virgin forest like that is left in Borneo."

"They are the reciprocal promise," she says.

"What do you mean?" we ask clumsily.

Biruté pauses, then, "Our own mirror image. The highest ideal. The last surviving innocents from the original Garden of Eden."

And as we watch Borneo recede under the clouds, flying south over the Java Sea, we realize that Dr. Biruté, by saving these last innocents, is also saving the ideal of innocence, and the very Creation where it was born.

SACRED BIODIVERSITY ACROSS KYOTO, JAPAN

KYOTO, JAPAN

It is not quite spring in Japan, and the scientists are very nervous. It has become apparent that this will be the first winter in recorded Japanese history that it has not snowed in Tokyo. Interestingly, standing in an ancient rice field in the mountains above Lake Biwa and Kyoto, we are suddenly hit by a freezing wind, which brings with it a sudden snow flurry, but only for a few seconds. Then it is gone. An ominous feeling pervades our small team, one of whom comments on the fact he is seeing fungal species invading Japan from the tropics, while another cites the fact that Mount Fuji will soon be without snow at this rate. He worries about that not just as a scientist concerned that no water means no moss. But, he happens to live on its lower slopes, and his town depends, in part, on the spring runoff, so he is very, very concerned.

Lake Biwa is the largest freshwater lake in the country. It is also populated by nine endemic freshwater fish genera.[1] The Lake Biwa Museum, one of the great interactive museums of its kind, has gotten its message right: there have been recent extinctions here, including *Pungitius sinensis* (known as *Minami-tomiyo*) a fish last seen in a southern freshwater creek in Kyoto in the early 1950s.[2]

"The Japanese people are very concerned," Yasushi Hibi, the young Director of the Japan Program for Washington-based Conservation International (CI), explains. And, he offers one curious insight about the Japanese, citing a recent much-discussed television documentary in the country examining *koorogi* or crickets. Apparently, says Hibi, Japanese people use the left hemisphere of the brain to respond to the sound of crickets, whereas Europeans and Westerners use their right hemisphere. Most Japanese find the sound of crickets pleasing; for Westerners this is less so.

Many might gaze upon the Japanese stream toad, *nagare-hikigaeru* (*Bufo torrenticola*) with something less than outright affection. However, in Japan, such creatures evoke deeply-rooted and satisfying associations. And not just crickets and toads, but the delicate, infinitely minute pieces of life's puzzle such as moss, which may have the iconic value to Japanese that the bald eagle does to Americans, or the giant panda to the Chinese. While Europeans of the 7th century were burning peat moss and stuffing it into their stone huts for insulation, the Japanese were worshipping it in some of the most intricate and significant gardens in the world; gardens which remain to this day.[3]

Muso, a Zen priest (1275–1351) is credited as being the most influential champion of garden design in Japanese history, but the earliest known gardens, built around ponds, date to the late 6th century. But Muso's gardens—including Saiho-ji (ji means temple) built in 1339 during the Kamakura period at a time when Muso Soseki was living there in meditation—embody what is described as *kaiyu-shiki* or "pond-gardens for strolling around."[4] Today, Saiho-ji is known as Kokedera or "Moss Temple" (moss is *koke*). The pond, called Ogonchi, is composed of the Chinese characters for heart and mind. Much speculation has attempted to divine upon which rocks the monks sat and whether they propped themselves up on the bare rocks or used straw mats and pillows for comfort. They would not have sat on the moss, however, though the temptation is omnipresent. The reason is that Buddhism commends non-violence, non-intervention. To sit on the moss would be to harm it.

In ancient times some Japanese used moss for clothing. Artifacts discovered in an old warehouse in Nara Prefecture, owned by the Emperor, revealed certain apparel made of the moss species *Aerobryopsis sp.* This species is much less abundant in Japan these days, but centuries ago, it was much in use, according to Dr. Hiroyuki Akiyama, a bryologist with the Museum of Nature and Human Activities.

In this island nation, there has always been a tension between wild nature and modified nature (harmed wildness). Japanese traditions are supremely human because they have made an art form, almost a religion, out of modification, uncannily re-engineering much of the Japanese outback with a zeal for aesthetic domestication. The ambiguity is subtle because so much of Japanese nature religion, whether in Shinto or Buddhist tradition, holds in its heart the four seasons, the cycles of life and death and the fragility of this earth, plus all in which we take pleasure. Japanese aesthetics are heartbreaking because their vitality stems from this human intervention which couples austerity with a rich palette; eternity with the ephemeral. The

cherry blossoms will explode in beauty—then vanish. The good news is that trees well cared for will blossom every year.

Among the greatest of Japan's gardens are those born of the nature theology inherent in Zen Buddhism, both Rinzai and Soto schools. And while there is a defining rigor that sets these minimalist achievements apart from wilder-seeming gardens elsewhere in the world, in fact, the moss gardens showcase hundreds of species in coordinated interdependency. This aesthetic and biological fervor is not simply the outgrowth of human manipulation. Japanese wilderness gives birth to such moss gardens. But it was the humble Buddhist monk throughout history who recognized them and sought to re-create their beauty and significance within the human community.

Every visitor to Japanese gardens must have sensed the magic and spirituality inherent to this subtle yet bountiful approach to nature which may be among Japan's most important accomplishments as a nation and a people.

This nuanced cultivation extends to all of Japanese culture, especially in the tea ceremony (*cha-no-yu*). Paths laid with polished stepping stones wend their way to the

sacred tearooms (*chashitsu*). In a cup of tea, said one of its most prominent adherents early in the 20th century (Kakuzo Okakura, author of *The Book of Tea*, and an early curator at the Boston Museum of Fine Arts), the world's problems could and should be solved. And in the traditional teahouse, the fiercest of warriors took off their armor, laid aside their weapons, and meditated in peace.

We have come to Saiho-ji this morning with two of Japan's foremost bryologists, scientists devoted to the study of moss species. Dr Yoshitaka Ooishi is a young Ph.D. from the Laboratory of Landscape Architecture, Division of Forest and Biomaterials Science here in Kyoto, a global capital of aesthetics, spirituality and conservation. He is accompanied by his teacher, the famed Dr. Hiroyuki Akiyama. Dr. Akiyama is probably the foremost expert on Japanese moss, as well as the author of a comprehensive survey of moss species in Borneo. His ten trips thus far to Borneo have enabled him to record 670 species there including the 13 new species and two new moss genera he discovered.

Dr. Akiyama examines the moss at Saiho-ji with his Nikon 14x loop to ascertain precisely the shape of a leaf for purposes of identifying any new species. There are between 15,000 and 18,000 moss species worldwide. In Japan, about 1,700 species or nearly 10% of the global distribution. Akiyama has personally viewed more than half of those. In addition to his Bornean discoveries, five of the Japanese species were first found by him: two *Trematodons* (*hakusanensis* and *brevicarpum*), two *Leucodons* (*yokogurensis* and *alpinus*) and one *Brachydontium* (*polycarpum*). He did his Ph.D. on the *Leucodon* genus.

Dr. Akiyama expected Saiho-ji to be the best of all the moss gardens, based upon his work here many years before. But today he is alarmed to witness areas of bare

ground. This was not so four years ago. Now he is perplexed and the germ of a new research project is fast materializing in his mind, as we follow him and Dr. Ooishi from one part of the garden to another.

"What is happening here?" we asked Dr. Akiyama.

He wasn't sure but in a city whose most recent claim to fame is its association with global warming—the Kyoto Protocol—all change seems to relate to the global patterns now skewing much biodiversity. Moss species are no exception. "From an ecological point of view," Dr. Akiyama continues, "mosses as ground cover in a forest are perfect: they store the water and thus provide a good defense against erosion. It's a tiny organism but can do so much. Moss absorbs water directly in the leaf, not in the root. Acid rain," he says, "is therefore a significant problem for moss. And global warming could be very serious. Moss in the wild constitutes a nursery for insects laying eggs. Birds also use the moss for their nests and put moss under those eggs, including the river crow, or *Kawagarasu* (*Corvus* genus). Dense coniferous forests are symbiotic with moss, which possess antibiotic qualities that work as anti-fungal agents to protect the seeds when they fall into the moss. Without that chemical property of moss, there would be few Japanese forests."

And, presumably, if moss is an indicator species sensitive to the ramifications of global warming, this will ratchet up the stakes and demand necessary research to understand what is happening. After so many centuries of perfect endurance and growth, how ironic it is that the world outside Kyoto should dictate the fate of these precious gems of biological and artistic heritage.

While Dr. Akiyama believed that tropical mushrooms were probably better in-dicators of climate change, given that mosses are perennials, changing much more

slowly than fungus, here at Saiho-ji the decline in resident moss species diversity appears to be occurring so rapidly that he is now deeply worried. Something is happening.

Later he suggests to us that what will be needed is a longterm biochemical study of six to ten years, utilizing a base population of the one dominant species most noticeably in decline here at the temple garden, *Leucobryum juniperoides*.

The dominance of *juniperoides*, comprising nearly 90% of the ground cover, is explained by the fact the monk/gardeners over time focused on this species for aesthetic and practical reasons. But, among the other 10% ground cover, there might well be additional species decimation occuring now. Japanese scientists were examining this decline even before the country was declared the 34th international hotspot; a nation, in other words, with a huge amount of species at risk, not just the mosses.[5]

While there is no real translation in Japanese for the word sanctuary, there are countless other words, concepts, philosophical and emotional traditions that invoke the notion. Japan's 28 national parks and many other designated areas of natural protection comprise nearly 17% of the country, almost double that of the United States. Six percent of that region is especially at risk according to the IUCN and CI. As of 2007, there were a known "32 Critically Endangered and Endangered species" throughout the country's 3,000 islands and 24 degrees of varying latitude, encompassing alpine, boreal and subtropical climes in a region of 370,000 square kilometers. Japan is roughly half the size of Borneo.[6]

Japan's 127.5 million residents are for the most part affluent, though—as in every country dependent on the global economy—there are foreboding economic signs in Japan. Just recently, Ubari in Hokkaido was the first municipality in the country to go bankrupt, underscoring the reality of a national debt which translates to six million yen per person, or about $US 55,000. Unlike countless other nations containing forests, there is little logging going on in Japan to pay that debt. Most of the heavy extraction was undertaken for reconstruction following World War II, with much of the coniferous forest utilized for sorely-needed housing. That forest was replaced by plantations often including species such as cedar that produce pollen to which many Japanese are allergic. It is this widespread allergy that accounts for the high use of face masks.

Other serious ecological afflictions threaten Japan's wetlands: non-native invasive species competing with native ones, more and more development and, most grievously, the outright destruction of critical habitat. An egregious and tragic example was the decimation of one of Asia's largest wetlands, Isahaya Bay, in exchange for an agricultural boondoggle during the 1990s.

In Japan, such critical habitat hosts a plethora of biodiversity that is at risk. According to CI, the country has approximately 5,600 plant species of which a third are endemic. There is high amphibian endemism (88%) amongst its 50 known species; and of the 94 known mammals, 49 are endemic.[7] In addition, Japan has nearly 370 bird species, 65 reptile species and 215 native freshwater fish species.

Dr. Akiyama reckons there are roughly 30 bryophyte experts in Japan. They still find rare or new species. But it is impossible to say whether a species has gone extinct. Mosses are more subtle than birds. There are some 45 known bog mosses in Japan, and today, since bog habitats are disappearing along with estuaries and wetlands, Dr. Akiyama fears it likely that the species in those bogs will go extinct. Another problem is that the Japanese like to collect moss for their bonsai plants. There is legisla-

ゴケ ヒノキゴケ オオホウゴケ ヒロハヒノキゴケ ホソバ シラガゴケ ゴケ アラハシラガゴケ

tion protecting only one bog moss species, *sphagnum*, and that is very hard to police.

Here, in the geographical and spiritual center of the country—long ago its capital and said to be home to 10,000 gardens—Kyoto's greenbelt reveals the profundity of Japanese ecological continuity. This is where science, spirituality and the divine details of nature meet, with mosses being the celebrated champions of that convergence—a luxurious backdrop for the beauty of fallen flowers on green undergrowth and the peaceful demonstration, in nature, of an eternal dream.

Like mushrooms and ferns and liverworts, mosses are seedless plants whose reproduction is driven by spores. Their sex organs, known as *archegonium* in the female and *antheridium* in the male, grow on separate plants during their gametophyte or sexual phase. These are the leafy cushions typically associated with moss gardens. Every single shoot in those gardens is capped with a sex organ. In the males, the minute flower petals are filled with sperm. In the rain, that sperm wiggles speedily away in hundreds-of-billions of microscopic aspirations. The notion of plopping one's body down upon this sincere riot of life is unseemly, which is why the very biology of moss is oriented toward sanctuary. It needs protection if fertilization is to succeed, thereby initiating the second sporophyte stage in moss. Every facet of reproduction is out there on the surface, transported by water, which gives these otherwise modest life forms their rather complex internal biology.

Mosses have another characteristic that is life-fostering, even during times of climatic adversity: they are colonizers or pioneer plants, volunteering in new environments. From lava flows to the sides of highways, they are often the first to initiate a healthy comeback, which provides eventual habitat for other species. In this way they prove fundamental to life on earth.[8]

At the Gio-ji Moss Temple, Dr. Akiyama notices copper moss (*Scopelophila cataractae*) present because of the copper roofing of the temples and high concentration of specific ions.[9] Gio-ji's gardens are dominated by two moss species: *Trachycystis microphylla* and the bushy *Polytrichum commune*, as well as the newly named *Pyrrhobryum dozyanum*. The intermingling trees are primarily *Acer palmatum*, "Sango-kaku" (coral bark Japanese maple) with its epiphytic white lichen, and a species known as *Lemnaphyllum microphyllum*.

As part of his Ph.D., the 28-year-old Yoshitaka Ooishi conducted a survey of the moss species at Goi-ji in 2005. He loves them, he says. He found some 50 species here. Gio-ji receives approximately 1,500 millimeters of rain per year and has rather high humidity. The monks remove leaves from the moss with soft brooms to maintain the moss's exposure to sunlight.

Of the three native fireflies in Japan, one lays its eggs in such moss. And butterflies also feed on it, particularly during the height of the rainy season in June and July.

Surrounding us are Fagus trees on the hills and the most famed *Cryptomeria japonica* (*sugi* or Japanese cedar) lower down. Sugi is the country's national tree, part of the global cypress family and thus related to the California redwood. Its bark provides the matrix for an epiphyte, white lichen belonging to the genus *Lepra*. The tortured-looking twisted vertical trees are known in the scientific literature as *Aphananthe aspera* or, commonly, in Japanese mukunoki.[10]

Together with Drs. Akiyama and Ooishi, we visit several of the great garden temples across Kyoto, including Ryoan-ji, Ginkaku-ji, Manshuin, Kingkaku-ji, and Sanzen-in in the exquisite village of Ohara high in the mountains above Kyoto. There the prolific *Leucobryum juniperoideum*, *Pyrrhobryum dozyanum*, *Polytrichum commune* and *Trachycystis microphylla* mosses are in their full glory. In fact, the mosses of Sanzen-in were in the best shape either scientist had yet seen, perhaps because the higher altitude made for more humidity.

Each of these gardens is a result of intense human deliberation, coalescing with nature. Finely-tuned gardening schedules are financed by each particular temple, rarely by public funding. Collectively, they are one sprawling sanctuary that would take a lifetime of pilgrimage, if one thought of walking quietly through them all.

At Ginkaku-ji, at the base of Mount Daimonji in the Higashiyama District, Shogun Ashikaga Yoshimasa (1449-1474) abdicated his throne in order to study the fine arts here. In this remarkable garden—watching the moon rise over his miniature Mount Fuji and the enormous Mount Tsukimachiayama in the far distance—he studied the way of tea.

There are nearly 60 species of moss at Ginkaku-ji beneath huge Japanese blue oaks (*Quercus glauca*) and the subtropical temperate plant, chinquapin (*Castanopsis cuspidata*) and the dominant broadleaf evergreen bush species, *Eurya japonica*, which flowers in winter and is related to the omnipresent *Camellia japonica*.

Yoshimasa could not put an end to the horrible Onin Civil War, which devastated much of Kyoto, but ultimately it was Yoshimasa's legacy of garden meditation that would prevail after all.

While most of the old forests above Lake Biwa have been cut down in the last century, the tea house and Silver Pavilion at Ginkaku-ji show off one of Japan's premier aboriginal woods, namely, *Chamaecyparis obtuse*.

At Ryoan-ji, the fifteen stones (impossible to see all in one glance) placed in a sand and moss garden of 248 square meters is surrounded by a rusticated wall. The garden was designed for the Tokudaiji family during the Kamakura period. The moss at Ryoan-ji is of two dominant forms including that which grows around the rocks: *Polytrichum commune* and the tree moss, *Pylaisiadelpha tenuirostris*.

This UNESCO World Heritage Site is one of the most famous gardens of meditation in all Japan. While many other people across the country may be watching video games or baseball, the hundreds-of-thousands of visitors each year to Ryoan-ji simply sit in silence above the sand meditating or attempting to understand its mysterious allure. Some interpretations have settled on the Peaceful Dragon motif; others, the Leaping Tiger. Hugely intellectual arguments about psychic ricochets between the rocks have engaged poets, philosophers and painters for centuries.

Manshuin and Kingkaku-ji each have their own distinctive characters. The Golden Pavilion dominates Kingkaku-ji, built for Ashikaga Yoshimitsu during Kyoto's renaissance, the Kamakura period of 1185–1336. Manshuin is in the "Kobori Enshu" style of garden with large amounts of white raked sand.[11]

This same Kyoto greenbelt extends in a mountain range for miles. These lush native forests produced the finest bamboo for electricity in the world. We have been to the Shinto shrine outside Kyoto devoted to the worship of Thomas Edison. He is viewed as a prophet who literally illuminated our species. Edison came to the village of Yawata in Kyoto Prefecture to obtain pieces of the woody bamboo filament to use in his incandescent light bulb after having sampled over 6,000 other materials from various countries.[12]

Today, these forests and gardens surround a busy downtown district whose dazzling nightlights owe their brilliance to Edison. And, like most of urban Japan, its labyrinthine density contains a mob of alleyways and mid-size highrises. But, the greenbelt perseveres. A Harvard professor prevailed upon a personal connection with the White House during World War II to spare this blessed city from a punitive mili-

284

tary response. As with Paris, Kyoto's history and inner treasures are unprecedented. But, what renders Kyoto's gardens unique are their vast biological connectivity and ecological aesthetic. They remind us, in a manner found nowhere else, of the inner sanctuary each of us harbors.

When Dr. Akiyama goes into museums, he laments that the young students with him never show much interest in moss. Kids like insects, he says. Adults like moss. We asked him what he tells children in order to spur their interest.

"I tell them that moss has very interesting characteristics. When other plants get dry they die. But mosses are so tiny, their leaves are unicellular in terms of thickness: the leaves dry but they can easily rejuvenate: Reincarnation."

This is a perfect metaphor for Buddhist Japan. Of course, if global warming should reverse the curtain of precipitation even in so northerly a climate as that of Japan, the mosses will be in trouble. Extended droughts could kill them.

The middle-aged professor smiles wistfully, aware of too many unknowns, expressing a hope that his seven-year old son, Kota, will—like himself—come to love and respect moss, no matter what happens.

THE PARADISE OF SAKTENG: BUDDHIST ETHICS AND CONSERVATION IN BHUTAN

Tandin Wangdi is a senior biodiversity conservation officer with the National Biodiversity Centre (NBC) in the hills of Serbithang above the Bhutanese capital, Thimphu. He carries himself with the quiet, all-observant sobriety of a highly trained scientist. Restrained and, we soon discover, extraordinarily modest, he smiles calmly at the prospect of some 130 kilometers, much of it uphill and at

high altitude: an expedition that will take our team through some of the least known, rarely visited parts of the eastern Himalayas.

Yamu Gallay, the younger head of our ten person support team, wears trekking knickers and is happy to carry any and all weight, doing whatever it takes to be of help. A sophisticated member of the newly emergent eco-tourism guiding community in Bhutan, Yamu loves his country and is an ardent scholar of Buddhist history, as well a budding ornithologist. Tandin, who knows almost every species he encounters, is equally tireless and glides serenely over the landscape from the very start. His eyes are trained on every orchid and bird, but particulary the fern species. He has already identified over 410 of them in his country, and his book on the ferns of Bhutan will be published soon in Edinburgh, where he completed a Masters degree.

There are a known 300 grass species and over 5,600 flowering plants in Bhutan (including 579 orchids), 1.9% of which are endemic. That number increases dramatically, it is reckoned, if the entire contiguous Eastern Himalayan ecosystem—encompassing parts of Sikkimese India, Tibetan China, Arunachal Pradesh in northeastern India and Myanmar—are included.

Our goal is to assess and help document one of Bhutan's most recently protected areas, created in April 2003. The country's ninth refuge, Sakteng Wildlife Sanctuary (SWS), is named for one of three primary villages in the reserve that abuts the border of the Indian state of Arunachal Pradesh. SWS is part of the 14,800 square kilometer Biological Conservation Complex in the country (35% of Bhutan's geographic area) that includes 12 corridors, four National Parks, a Strict Nature Reserve and three other wildlife sanctuaries. SWS is rarely visited. Local park wardens with two consulting scientists from the Wildlife Institute of India conducted the first biological survey of the park in June 2004. Their observations, sampled over the course of one week and 115 kilometers of trekking, revealed 18 species of mammal, 119 bird species, 203 plant species and 21 forest communities.[1] Our expedition would make a similar cir-

cuit over ten days, with some side journeys. The goal was to record as many species as possible and get to know the local nomadic people and the domestic animals with whom they share their lives.

The expedition was made possible by the generous logistical and political assistance of several people, most notably Dr. Ugyen Tshewang, then Director of Bhutan's National Biodiversity Centre (NBC) of which Tandin is one of 32 staff members.[2] Dr. Ugyen, the leading bovine specialist in Bhutan, had been on expeditions to Sakteng as early as 1988 to study the ecology of the yak (*Bos grunniens*) of which there were then an estimated 35,000 in the country, a number that has not much varied over the years. He obtained his Ph.D. in Australia specializing in equine fertility and contraception, went on to create NBC under the Ministry of Agriculture and spearheaded the country's three five-year Biodiversity Action Plans (BAP) under the international Convention on Biological Diversity (CBD). It was the second BAP that noted more than 770 bird and 165 mammal species in the country, plus a wealth of vascular plant species, expected to exceed 7,000 with future discoveries.[3] He also developed the nation's first gene bank and national herbarium.[4]

Recently, Dr. Ugyen accompanied Her Majesty Queen Ashi Dorji Wangmo Wangchuck into Sakteng. "She raced ahead of everyone like a mountain goat!" he said. We later discovered that Her Majesty also knew virtually every scientific name for the species she had seen in her country, and she has a special love for the Brokpa, the indigenous people of Sakteng and Merak, and their incredible surroundings about which she has written exquisitely in her book, *Treasures of the Thunder Dragon: A Portrait of Bhutan.*[5]

We had chosen the first two weeks of May to make this journey, knowing that the magnificent native Himalayan poppies would not yet be in flower but a large percentage of native Eastern Himalayan rhododendrons would be (46 known in all, of which four are endemic to Bhutan)[6]. Also, the waterfalls would be flowing at their

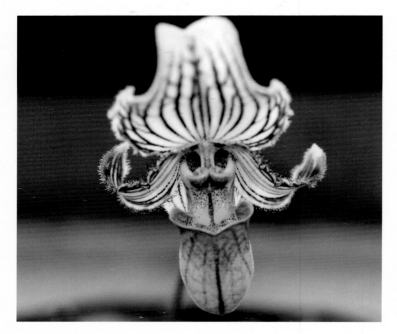

height (measured in cusecs, cubic meters of water flowing per second) and the snow depths easily manageable. Invertebrates would be out in profusion and, hopefully, a large array of avifauna and mammals.

Moreover, the Brokpa (Bonpo, pre-Buddhist animist) yak herders, who are the sole inhabitants of Jokhar, Merak, and Sakteng, would be moving their yaks into summer pasture. We hoped to interview many of them and gain insight into their way of life and the challenges facing them in the 21st century: challenges now confronting all of Bhutan.

The Brokpa, who trade freely over the border with fellow Brokpa in equally remote Arunachal within India, are probably the least assimilated culture in Bhutan. But such inaccessibility has not precluded the presence of at least a few Brokpa telephones, computers, satellite dishes, fabulous food, lovely architecture, schools, medical services and even talk, albeit ecologically suspect, of road access sometime in the future. This latter concept, touted by at least one aspiring politician, would likely hit head-on against existing legislation in Bhutan requiring thorough environmental impact assessments of engineering initiatives, particularly an implausible road into one of the last pristine wildlife sanctuaries on earth.[7]

We drove three long days from Thimphu over six high mountain passes, beginning the trek at a road-head 650 kilometers east of Thimphu. From the summit of the first of these passes, the Dochu-la, the distant expanse of peaks is revealed through a window in the morning storms: Khang Bum (6,434 meters), Gangchey Ta (6,794 m), Masang Gang (7,194 m), the Tshendaygang group (averaging 6,994 m), Teri Gang (7,094 m), Jejekangphu Gang (7,194 m), Table Mountain (7,094 m) and Gangar Punsum which, at more than 7,500 meters or 25,000 feet, is the highest mountain in Bhutan, and possibly the highest unclimbed mountain in the world. The last expedition to attempt it could not find it. The Bhutanese knew where it was, sort of. And as of several years ago, despite the loss of significant revenues to the country, mountaineering at heights above 6,000 meters has been forbidden on religious grounds. No other country in the world, with gloriously high mountains to climb and mountaineering

tariffs to be accumulated, has renounced such enterprises on ethical grounds. This restraint is consistent with many of Bhutan's other virtues.

Bhutan's one road from Paro, all the way east to the road-head that was the beginning of our expedition, passes near to, or through, several of the country's national parks and/or connective habitat (genetic corridors). The road is arduous. As recently as the early 1960s, there was no road. When the late U.S. Ambassador to India, John Kenneth Galbraith visited Bhutan in the 1960s, he walked or went by yak, and it took nine days to reach Thimphu. Since the early 1980s, a single airstrip, one of only two mile-long horizontal surfaces in the country, has enabled the nation's airline, Druk Air, to provide international service into the country.[8]

Coming off the 3,400 meter high pass above Bumthang in the center of the country, we find ourselves driving through sunny havens of *Abies densa*, the dominant fir forest that has been colonized by *Usnea*, Old Man's Beard, an opportunistic epiphyte seen in many forests of the world but not usually in company with bright blue *Primula denticulata* and *P. capitata*, as it is here. At a monastery in the Ura Valley, the Yakchoe Festival is in full force. A dozen artists perform the shacham (dance of the four stags) for hundreds of locals. The dance reflects a religious aversion to killing, and the message is made clear to a would-be hunter of yore.[9] The Buddhist ethic of interdependent biodiversity (*Tendrel Gi Choe*), of connected souls and an insistence on non-violence, looms like a third-eye over the entire country. Deities of the landscape are everyday affairs for rural Bhutanese.[10] Non-violence is a mixed affair in Bhutan, as it is elsewhere. Fifteen percent of the Bhutanese are vegetarians, and meat is banned for two months of the year. During the ban, hotels and butchers store up meat, and some argue that the bans prompt even more consumption than might otherwise take place. Buddhist monks have rescued cattle from slaughterhouses, and the Bhutanese raised a strident cry of protest when the World Health Organization, fearing an outbreak of rabies many years ago, insisted on shooting dogs throughout the country. Today, there is a large dog sanctuary near Thimphu, started by Ms. Tashi Payden and colleagues. And, elsewhere, dogs roam the cities and villages at their ease, having been sterilized, inoculated and, usually, quite loved.

293

The Ura valley and monastery adjoins Thrumsingla National Park with its red pandas, barking deer, Bengal tigers and tragopans (horned pheasants). The forest is dense with larch (*Larex griffithiana*), named after the first European botanist to visit Bhutan in the 1830s. The yellow flowering shrub, *Piptanthus nepalensis*, emerges in profusion beside the blue-flowering *Rhododendron hodgsonii* and a second white one, *R. arboreum*. But it is a demur and enchanted forest bog at the eastern end of the Thrumsingla Pass amid fir, hemlock and bamboo, where the campanulate (bellshaped) flowers of *R. kesangiae* blossom in all of their glowing dignity. This species was discovered soon after the Bhutanese National Floral project got underway in 1975 and was named in honor of the Queen Mother Ashi Kesang Choden Wangchuck.

One of the world's greatest waterfalls is Namling, in the heart of Thrumsingla. Its fully unexplored canyon of mixed evergreen deciduous forest and broadleaf presents an utterly tantalizing, if unapproachable Other World of biological splendor. We look for a point to rappel down into the canyon, but the logistics are far beyond our present circumstances. And, none of us are keen to intrude upon that which has never been disturbed.

Such untouched beauty abounds, not just in topographical superlatives, but also in the human spirit whose generosity manifests along this road to the Far East. Here are smiles that do not exist elsewhere in the modern world; care for dogs, cats, cows and goats who meander with a grace and confidence reflecting their own natures and that of the human civilization that engages in the dance of life in their sovereign company. It is civilization without the vile trappings of industrial blight.[11] We take in this new nature, if you will, with quiet wonder and a sense that we must never leave.

One sees evidence of this human restraint in the worldly, docile eyes of a cow as the moon rises over Mongar and the gentle bovines graze in the near dark or sleep comfortably wherever they wish. In India, with its overnight freeway system from Delhi to Mumbai, cows and goats, sheep and dogs, monkeys and others are justifiably bewildered and at risk. Not so in Bhutan, where the animals are assured of their near inviolability. Buddhists in Bhutan will not kill an animal, as a rule, though have no problem eating the meat of dead cows or fish. With nearly 17,000 tourists to Bhutan in 2006, not counting many more Indian tourists who are allowed to drive across the border, some are beginning to worry that the dignity and grace, which characterizes Bhutan to this day, will succumb to the pressures of too much tourism and development. Others have less concern, noting that the Fourth King and his brilliant array of hand-picked Ministers and other government leaders, all of whom have embraced ecological sustainability as in no other nation in history, together harbor reasonable economic dreams within human scale, not outside it.

But the concerns escalate with the 2008 free election in Bhutan, the first Democratically-elected governing body in the nation's 100 years of monarchy. By mid-2007, all of these Ministers had resigned; while two—the Minister of Agriculture and the Home Minister—had been chosen to represent two competing parties in the upcoming election. The latter, Lympo Jigmi Thinley, would become Prime Minister.

Bhutan dates back at least to the 8th century. Only in 1907 was the nation unified politically under the first of five Wangchuck kings. Now, the winds of change can be felt in ecological terms. As road refurbishing continues between Paro and Thimphu

at a feverish rate, Thimphu Valley is turning into an elegant assemblage of new buildings where once (as when Michael first visited the country in the winter of 1975) farmers grew their rice, potatoes and assorted vegetables without the slightest competition from modernity.

The fallout from this nascent development can be felt in stark environmental terms. It was thought that there were as many as 1,000 white-bellied herons left in Bhutan, India and Bangladesh. Now, a revision of the data suggests that fewer than 200 are holding on, maybe a couple dozen in Bhutan. Survey work in the country's southeast is still to be undertaken. The species is now Critically Endangered, along with the pygmy hog; while a known 25 mammals in Bhutan are Endangered or Vulnerable.[12] The single riparian habitat upon which this rare heron depends throughout the year was owned by a monastery. The sand was coveted by developers. It took Bhutanese scientist Rebeccah Pradhan's love of these birds and longtime support from the Royal Bhutanese Society for the Protection of Nature to forcefully protest the proposed destruction of one particular bend in the river. Here Bhutanese monks were confronted by a modern dilemma. Through perseverance, a convergence of government authorities were induced to bow to ethical and biological considerations, as rarely happens these days. The fact there are a dozen birds in crisis in Bhutan is in itself astonishing. But the birds are not the only ones in trouble. Other developmental confrontations are looming for Bhutan.

We spot a rufus-necked hornbill and a paradise flycatcher along the river canyon leading to the imposing Trashigang Dzong. We pass through a mesic system punctuated by unexpected succulents—euphorbias and agave—in this low altitude canyon and a small hydroelectric plant on the Dangmechu, which in turn flows into the Manas, the biggest river in eastern Bhutan. At least 40% of the country's external income comes from her sale of hydropower to India. With serious concern growing over the melting of the Himalaya, a vast calamity hovers above much of Central Asia. With so many hanging lakes likely to overflow (at least 200 according to a United Nations study of "outburst floods" in the region[13]) and with an abundance of fragile water-dependent ecosystems, the prospects for Bhutan are terribly serious. The country has managed to forgo the destruction of watersheds, continuing to maintain almost three-fourths of its forests intact. But what about a future where water can no longer be depended upon for soft-energy revenues? Here is a nation that is a positive net carbon sequester. Saying "No" to gold or forest extraction or other ecologically devastating money-making opportunities will be the challenge. But without that income from small hydroelectric sales, Bhutan will be at great risk.

Another scenario draws her out of her isolation and into the rampant turmoil of global dependency. Bhutan's approximately 640,000 residents and her benign government policies have probably fostered the smallest per capita ecological footprint in the world. The country's Fourth King is a wise leader, an ecological visionary who is deeply loved by his people, so much so that most Bhutanese feel that a democratic election is not necessary. The King nonetheless decided it was time for change. But outside forces have begun eyeing the nation, just as the so-called "Asian haze" has spread further and further north across India towards Bhutan. Just as the world looks to Bhutan for wisdom, Bhutanese have had to regroup before the awesome challenge of climate change. No one quite knows how to do it, although pilot studies are in

place to cope with the potential of overflowing lakes. The bickering of nations at the Bali conference in December 2007, did not help, however.

On this magnificent May morning, there is little reason for pessimism among glorious slopes of red cotton (*Bombax cieba*) whose flowers are favorites of the great barbet birds. The *Jacaranda mimosafolia* is in full bloom. Clouds are gathering, and there is hope of a rainstorm later in the day. As we ascend another pass, the unmistakable signs of an alpine world suddenly emerge in the guise of a yak staring right at us. He is 30 paces away but could cover that distance in all of three seconds.

Much has been written of yaks, the gentle giants of the Himalayas, of which there are approximately 16,000 in the Merak/Sakteng area at any given time.[14] Pema Mashok, in charge of livestock for the village of Sakteng, joins the expedition at the Chaling road-head above the Gamrichu River that descends towards the outlying village of Rangjung. Our route will take us in an easterly loop from Chaling to Merak to Sakteng to Jokhar. The village of Jokhar is at a mere 1,700 meters, whereas Sakteng lies at over 3,500 meters. Along the way, yaks will everywhere be our companions with their Brokpa herders. Our expedition of 15 people ascends far above the village of Chaling, to where maize is being cultivated, plowed and one-month old seedlings transplanted. Soon, among more rhododendron, we see yellow-bellied flowerpeckers (*Dicaeum melanoxanthum*) working the nectar-giving forests, as the slope steepens interminably toward the high peaks above.

The forest offers a first glimpse of Bhutanese interdependency in an unexpected manner, namely daphne trees (*D. bholua*) whose processed paper is still used for writing traditional Buddhist scriptures. Recent pressures upon its use have resulted in an alarming high rate of extirpation of the plant, one more indication that there are growing imbalances.

Six hours of climbing lead us into a primeval copse of oak, *Quercus griffithii*, tortured by ghostly ice slab, wind and rain. Abundant rhododendrons thrive in this atavistic high altitude garden. We have entered the paradise of Sakteng Wildlife Sanctuary amid a drizzle and distant thunder, atop the pass locally named Mindulaptsa, at 3,380 meters. In this hidden world of absoloutely protected habitat, 650 square kilometers in extent, are found black bear, red panda, three species of deer, common leopard, red fox, hundreds of bird species, with more to be discovered. And—most mysterious of all—the yeti.

This is the only sanctuary in the world created to protect the yeti (called the Abominable Snowman by those who ignorantly fear him).[15] Off in the east appears a huge alpine peak. It is the home of the Brokpas' sacred female deity, Aum (or Ama) Jomo (or Jumo), who resides within the 4,505 meter high mountain, above a spectacular river valley. The valley is aswarm in the color of tens-of-thousands of large rhododendron trees that sway like prayer flags in the gusts of wind. Fifteen different species—yellow, pink, red, blue, white, and purple—their scientific nomenclature can be recited with lyricism in the presence of so much magic: *R. arboreum*, *keysii*, *kesangiae*, *wallichii*, *campylocarpum*, *thompsonii*, and *cinnabarnium*. We also see silver fir, juniper, larch, poppy (*M. superba*, *M. simplicifolia*, *M horridula* and *M. peniculata*), aster and an invasive white clover brought in over the centuries on the hooves of bovines. This valley of biological wonders, the Damngo Jang with its Nyera Ama Chhu River and countless *chhunbab* (waterfalls) strikes an appearance of halos in the mist, of rain curtains glowering over the hundreds of meandering yaks as we slowly approach the

village of Merak, our first destination. Ruddy shelducks (*Tadorna ferruginea*) are bathing in the river. A black stork walks contentedly. Black bulbuls (*Hypsipetes leucocephalus*) are everywhere calling. A wild dog attacks us, but stays back in the end, defeated by something in his blood other than fear. He is defending his friends the birds and knows in his heart that we are no threat. He's just sporting. Anyway, we make it clear that we are impressed by his lonely bravado. Tandin stays behind, marking altitudes for every species of rhododendron he finds. To his amazement, the white *kesangiae* is here in all her resplendence. This flower is 150 miles further east than it has ever been recorded and, thus, a new discovery.

It is after 8:30 P.M. and darkness prevails. By headlight, a figure looms, waiting for us on the steep trail with a thermos of hot tea. It is a Brokpa villager who has been sent by the Park Ranger, Mr. Dhono, who awaits us three kilometers further in the village of Marek. By 9:30 that night we straggle into camp. The rest of the expedition members seem unconcerned by the nearly 40 kilometers of difficult trekking in one day. We later learn that locals frequently trek 80 kilometers a day, surmounting numerous passes in thin air while carrying enormous loads: an Olympean feat elsewhere in the world.

In the cold morning, we awake by 5:00 A.M. to gaze from our hillside guesthouse above the four hamlets of Merak, Gengo, Khashiding and Khilpue, which collectively

account for the 268 households and 1,200 Brokpa of the Merak village area. These are yak herders whose ancestors journeyed here under terrible circumstances hundreds of years before. Those who stayed on the Indian side in Arunachal wear black jackets and speak Brami Brokpa. Here the jackets are red. All aspire to have corrugated aluminum roofs, large sheets to replace traditional stone and wood, which the government of Bhutan has begun providing in order to discourage the illegal practice of tree girdling, which had solved two problems for the Brokpa. By imperceptibly cutting around the base of trees, the trees die quickly and the wood is used for building material while providing more and more grazing land. Now that this is a Wildlife Sanctuary, very few trees may be cut. The conflict for a culture which has made itself dependent on yaks for butter, cheese, wool and meat could not be more emphatic. Brokpa cheese is particularly memorable. They call it *zuede* or *yeatpa*. It is fermented in cowhide for a month until it becomes moldy and rotten. Certainly it is an acquired taste, but the Bhutanese and the Brokpa, particularly, love it.

We meet early in the morning with two distinguished herders of Merak, 55-year-old Tashi Chozom and her 44-year-old husband, Jurmi, who is the bloc clerk. Together they have thirty yaks, which they have just brought in from higher pastures. Jurmi calls some to come to him, speaking the Brokpa eastern language known as Sharchogpa. His calls transliterate roughly, "BeBeBe, Sobsobsob, banthebag . . . ." And they come—first Sarah, then Chuta, Cacchung, Doetung, Rabgey and Langa. They are named, says the astoundingly hearty Jurmi, for "the sheer pleasure of their names." He feeds them salt and flour, and they slump down on the grass in bliss, listening

attentively to our conversation. Our presence in Merak has not excited inordinate notice despite the fact that few visitors have come from the outside world. Everyone is far too busy to worry about us, though this couple born in Merak have made some time to chat. Jurmi says he can't imagine living anywhere else. He loves animals, especially the yak, stays over in Merak throughout the harsh winter (most do not, going down to shared homes at much lower altitudes), and he harbors the hope that his son and daughter become teachers or livestock managers. He wishes they will one day see a Yeti, as his own parents and their parents, like so many among the Brokpa, have seen. Now, he fears that too many people (several thousand Brokpa) and yaks have disturbed the shy Yeti, and perhaps it is extinct. He prays this is not so because he deeply loves the Yeti and knows it is the symbol of true wilderness in Bhutan.

Jurmi is not Tashi's only spouse. Brokpa society, like much of Himalayan culture used to be, remains polyandrous and in some cases polygamous, as well. The reasons are largely ecological in origin, owing to a short growing season and the necessity of curtailing large families because of finite food supplies. While certainly frowned upon in this deeply spiritual nation, abortion in Bhutan is nonetheless permitted under certain circumstances, particularly if the mother is at significant risk.[16] But traditional polyandry, at least in Merak, is on the wane. There are presently only three households where two husbands share a wife's workload; and only one where the woman enjoys the assistance of three husbands to help raise the children, graze the yaks, goats and sheep and help out with countless other tasks that spell survival. Life is difficult here.

When Dr. Ugyen Tshewang first visited with a pathologist friend from Queensland University, there had been rumors of a strange ailment affecting the yak and leaving them ridden with lesions and debilitated, though there were no reported mortalities. Upon investigation, Dr. Ugyen determined low yak hemoglobin counts but could discern no mites or parasites under the microscope. In the meantime, he found himself called upon to become a dentist and OBGYN. He protested that, as a vet he really was not allowed to perform such extra-curricular procedures as pulling teeth. But the Brokpa were desperate, and Dr. Ugyen is a true Buddhist. Using ara, a strong alcoholic beverage made of buckwheat, heartily consumed by the Brokpa, he applied pliers to remove rotten teeth and employed considerable common sense and medical training to deliver healthy babies. He concocted a lotion to help with eye problems and one old woman's chronic rheumatism. The elixir contained crushed ginger, garlic and chilis. He had utilized it as an anti-inflammatory in horses and a half-milliliter worth enabled one elderly Brokpa to climb the mountains again.

But the yaks were getting worse. Dr. Ugyen returned a year later, this time to find four dead yak. Post-mortems revealed severe liver sclerosis. The animals had become jaundiced and emaciated. Chemical analysis of tissues revealed a toxic alkaloid substance coming from a *Senecio* genus plant consumed by the yaks in the winter when their preferred *komsa* and *libi*, two native grasses among a half-dozen, as well as the invasive clover which they adore, were deep under ten to twenty feet of snow. The yaks were gorging on the killer plant.[17]

The yaks have other problems, of course. They are ultimately killed by the Brokpa whose aversion to this melancholic cycle is apparent, and some will simply not do it. Buddhism bids them to avoid flesh, and most Bhutanese and Tibetan Buddhists refuse to take part in the killing, delegating the unholy deed to a Tibetan caste who concede the inevitability of death and allow themselves to be engaged in butchery. There is one entire village of migrants to Bhutan that are known to be butchers. A yak is killed after three or four years by those eligible to carry out the sorry task. If left alone, the animal would survive between 15 and 25 years in the wild. The animal brings between US$400 to 500 (or 15 to 20,000 ngultrums, nu's for short). On average a Brokpa earns the value of approximately one yak per year by most wages. In the meantime, the female yak (*chuk*) will typically produce three liters of milk twice a day for eight months of the year. Her calf needs a half liter to survive. The rest is converted to cheese (*chura*) and yak butter (*mar*). The yak's fur is turned into hats: the Brokpa shamu, or *Tsipee cham*, with its unique five trails that ward off evil in all directions while they ingeniously vent water drops when it pours. The hats breed fungi and must be periodically aerated. Scarves (*nyaray*), black woollen cloth (*mekyem*), bags (*phachung*) and rope (*getha*) are also made from yak fur.

Like the Todas of India's Nilgiris, here is a tribe that consumes milk products humanely and sustainably. Few cultures on earth have learned how to do it.

Jurmi reiterates that he cannot imagine life without yaks. If he were to be deprived of his own, he says he would work for someone else who did have yaks. He must be around them. It is a true love affair that only those who have lounged in deep native grasses in the company of yaks for an afternoon under cobalt Himalayan heavens can truly understand.

Bhutan has 12 known sub-breeds of yak and those in the Far East show much higher genetic diversity than those in the West.

The Bhutanese government gives registered pasture land to the Brokpa. The arithmetic has long been worked out: one yak requires approximately three acres of grazing land. Jurmi can legally use roughly 500 acres but there are problems, and they have to do with wealthier Brokpa with more yaks, which encroach upon smaller landholdings, as well as an insufficient quantity of pasture land for the total number of yaks. We meet with Jurmi's friend Lam Rinchen, chairman of the local farmers' group, who takes time away from fixing an oily-looking pump to sit on the ground of his courtyard and talk these matters through with us. He explains the difficulties faced by modern Brokpa very forcefully. There are two thousand residents of Merak. One would never realize this as the village, on the steeply inclining side of a deep valley, subject to cold wind and major storms, sits totally exposed at an altitude of well over 10,000 feet. Most of the adults are up in the higher, windswept meadows with their animals. In April, white potatoes are planted and harvested with luck in July and August, along with cabbage, cauliflower, red onion, radish, rice, maize, wheat, garlic and spinach. There are over 500 varieties of rice in Bhutan, red being the predominant one. In winter, most people go down to Radi, Phongmey and other much lower villages in the Trashigang District. In Arunachal, primarily in Tawang, they trade their butter and cheese for better prices than in Bhutan. Arunachal Brokpa sell their chilies on the Bhutanese side. Salty dried fish is purchased in northern India. There are no fish in the Brokpa rivers, and the explanation given by some is that their Goddess Am Jumo—who came from Tibet and was a consort of the famous 8th

century Guru Rinpoche, Saint Padmasambhava—became enraged that the Brokpa dared to eat fish, which she considered sacred. She rescued all the fish and so no more are found in Brokpa waters. Of course, the contradiction leaps out at you: why did not Am Jumo also protect the yak? Was she partial to freshwater vertebrates? In the meantime, the number of Brokpa acquiring even more animals increases, while the amount of land that can be utilized under the Sakteng Wildlife Sanctuary rulings works against these added agricultural burdens on the habitat. Lam Rinchen is happy about the fact his village lies within the nation's newest protected area. He loves the wildlife. But he also admits that it is difficult to make fences if they cannot cut down trees. Brokpa need to be trained in pasture management, he says, given the new restraints imposed by sanctuary stature. There is a veritable "population explosion" he admits, and with no new inputs of wood for building materials, there are going to be issues: house repairs, fire wood requirements and fencing of property.

This latter issue is particularly troubling for Lam Rinchen. He explains that it is "human nature" that causes the problem. One fellow has 20 yaks and heaps of pasture; another has 100 yaks and little land. It just happens that way. If the small landholder cannot fence off his land, those 100 yaks will wander over and help themselves.

Even the limited supply of wood allowed by the Ministry of Agriculture, which controls the Forest Department that is responsible for the national park system, is insufficient and extremely expensive by Brokpa standards. One acre of fencing, utilizing the fir that is thick and easily split into many poles, costs them in 2007 about

1,000 ngultrums per tree, depending on the board feet size. Native bamboo is placed between the poles (no wire). Such fencing lasts for 75 years, but it is increasingly proving to be an expense beyond the means of many Brokpa.

Such conflicts have aroused some controversy in Bhutan, particularly in light of the new democracy, with its potential for runaway capitalism in a country unaccustomed to riches and bound by visionary conservation principles that do not make modernization readily available to indigenous people like the Brokpa. Obtaining a balance is by no means simple. One anonymous editorialist comments upon proportions: 72% of the country is covered in forest, while another 16% is comprised of alpine peaks or rivers. Broken down differently, 80% of the country's *habitable land area* is forested, but a mere 4% of that land actually supports people living there or utilizing it for grazing or agriculture or both. That is due largely to the extreme topography. Actual registration of agricultural units constitutes a mere 2.5% of the nation's territory "on which 79% of the population depends for subsistence," which correlates with the extreme difficulty of farming on sheer slopes. The authors thus question whether the country's commitment to a minimum of 60% forest cover is actually in the nation's best interest given that the Buddhist Mahayana "Middle Path" has always been Bhutan's approach to life. Such commentary devolves into a false dichotomy between pressure to increase what is perceived as a higher quality of life (modernization) versus the maintenance of the world's highest standards of biodiversity conservation.[18]

This perceived conflict is also inherent to Bhutanese history and religion. The country's main religious sect is known as Drukpa Kagyupa, which dates to the 17th century leader from Tibet, Zhabdrung, a unifier of the nation. His dream of a roaring thunder dragon and transport of a vertebrae of the sacred King of Tibet, Trisong Detsen, to Bhutan (the relic is now housed in Punaka Dzong) are legendary. Bhutan's national bird, a raven (*Corvus corax*), guided the Zhabdrung across forbidding landscapes and today figures in the coat of arms for the monarchy. Also in the 17th century Geshe Tenzin Rabgye built the cliff monastery Taktsang (the Tiger's Den), a remarkable national monument and by all accounts the most beautiful place on Earth in which to meditate. All these ties to Buddhism accumulate into an ethical aesthetic at once spiritual and ecological that cannot be matched.[19] Yet, Buddhism is not without its own contradictions. There have been wars, and most Bhutanese are not vegetarian despite Buddha's counsel on the subject. The Je Khenpo—the country's spiritual leader who spends six months of the year at Punakha Dzong, the other six at Tashichhodzong in Thimphu—is an ardent animal rights activist who goes to various slaughterhouses and buys freedom for the animals. Many of the country's locals resist eating meat on auspicious days, and yak herders are typically loathe to kill one. Moreover, most Bhutanese emanate a sense of profound love of all animals. It is in their art, their religion, their daily lives. There is little known Bhutanese poaching although Chinese and Indians have been steadily implicated in offences aimed at the valuable musk deer and Chinese caterpillar fungus. "A kilogram of musk pods can fetch up to US$50,000 in major destination countries such as Japan."[20] Guns are allowed to be used only if a wild boar, for example, marauds in a farmer's backyard, causing irreparable harm. There is virtually no crime in Bhutan, and while the country has had to cope with a Nepalese immigration crisis in the South, few countries in the world can claim immunity from similar systemic glitches.

This calls into question the unfairness of holding Bhutan to a higher standard than other nations. What is true is that Bhutan has literally resisted the temptation of cashing in on its natural resources. With approximately 5,000 monks in the country, 2,000 temples and/or monasteries and a deeply abiding spirituality in all matters, the nation is ethically sovereign. Her aristocracy bespeaks of modesty, not hubris. And for the last hundred years her Kings and Queens have been among the great minds and exemplars of restraint. The Fourth King, who without precedent abdicated at the age of 51 and retreated to what has been described as a log cabin above Thimphu, while leaving in place a remarkably sustainable blueprint for his people, has no leadership peer in any country. That His Majesty Jigme Singye Wangchuck has not yet received a Nobel Peace Prize is puzzling. His Majesty was resolved that Bhutan should become democratic, that church and state should separate and the monks leave Parliament. With such wise inspiration, Bhutan shows a side of human nature that bodes well for the future of our species should it follow Bhutan's example. In a true sense, Bhutan is a living laboratory for what is possible in human communities. This is why natural and social scientists have closely followed the trends in this remarkable country. They speak of a philosophical modernity that might manage to retain all that is emotive and fair about our past, without jeopardy to the commonweal; a democratic sanctuary where humans and nature are sensitively integrated.

The night prior to our departure, five young women perform dances for our expedition and sing songs of love and yak herding. There is much drinking.

Crossing from Merak to Sakteng requires an ascent up the Nyakchungla Pass, 4,100 meters. The climb is severe, but only a few hours duration. We find two endemic rhododendrons here, including a novel white form of *R. arboreum*. In addition, *R. wightii* is thriving outside its known distribution. At 3,500 meters are gorgeous blue *Primula edgeworthii*. A large-billed crow (*Corvus macrorhynchos*) greets us from the trees. Atop a stupa sits a red-billed chough (*Pyrrhocorax pyrrhocorax*) enjoying a moment of calm sunlight. Darting to and fro are blue-fronted redstarts, both male and female (*Phoenicurus frontalis*). Suddenly, a drizzle passes through on a dark, purple cloud. A storm literally erupts upon the mountain. Trees on the east side of the pass are plastered to the ground and withered from the wind. Clearly, such sudden storms are the norm up here.

Now, a revelation befalls us: there is an opening in the stormy skies far to the north and we gaze in wonder at unknown peaks rising higher, even, than any mountains in Bhutan. No one has ever seen them from here before. That includes every local we subsequently ask. That is because these peaks, which show themselves for all of two minutes, dusted in storm cloud and haze, are none other than Namche Barwa and Gy-

ala Peri's massif, where the great flowing Tsangpo (Brahmaputra River) turns tortuously south and heads from the 15,000 foot Tibetan plateau into Arunachal Pradesh, pouring out at Dibrugarh 150 miles away at low jungly elevations in India, a 13,000 foot descent. In its torrential labyrinth is rumored to exist a great waterfall. The gorge carved out by its fury, sometimes less than 100 feet wide and three times deeper than the Grand Canyon, was first explored in earnest by the great British turn-of-the-century botanist, Francis Kingdon-Ward. The mountains hover around 26,000 feet in an area the Brokpa call "Bumla." For a few seconds we are spellbound.

Sakteng appears 30-odd kilometers away from Merak in a river valley affording more protection from the elements but still at an altitude over 10,000 feet. As in Merak, locals meet us with strong alcoholic beverages and tea. The ceremonies attending upon our arrival confer a cosmic kind of welcoming uncommon in the 21st century. It is at once clear that Sakteng seems to be a slightly more wealthy community than Merak with a high-end civil servant's administrative building very much resembling a temple and an enormous playing field for soccer. Moreover, most of the roofing is

now corrugated aluminum. Standing in the center of the village is a gigantic oak (*Quercus semecarpifolia*). Nearby, a male scarlet finch (*Haematospiza sipahi*) preens himself in a gash of warm sunlight, surrounded by orange staff sergeant (*Athyma cama*), chocolate pansy (*Junonia iphita*) and the playful antics below of an endemic squirrel, one of many in the region. Like squirrels everywhere in the world, he trots up to our boots, stands on his heels and questions us about our arrival.

We speak with one 63-year-old householder, Pasang. He has yaks, a daughter and three grandchildren and by all accounts is supremely happy. He was born in Sakteng and never leaves. There is no television in his world, but he does have a radio, the same radio that would broadcast the coming election debates among candidates. "I need about 15,000 ngultrums a year to live on," he says, roughly US$380. He built his own home thirty years ago at a cost of about $1,000. He makes his own clothes, boots, jackets and hats and is proud of that fact. And, he adds that he has clean drinking water, firewood and grazing lands. What else does a man need in life? Three times a year he goes to the temple or Lakhang at the mountain hosting his deity the goddess Am Jumo, and there makes prayer or puja in April, August and October. The prayers are basically for wellbeing, and specifics, like a good harvest of buckwheat in spring.

We ask Pasang if he has ever seen a yeti, the male being known as *depo*, the female, *depmo*.

"Fifty years ago my neighbor was killed by a yeti one January, in the midst of heavy snowfall. The man was on his way back from the monastery up the hill. It was dark. We found the huge footprints all around. But, no corpse."

A half-dozen of his friends have seen the same kind of prints between Merak and Sakteng. His own parents told him that years ago another man disappeared from Merak, taken by a female yeti. Many years later that man reappeared with huge clumps of hair on his hands. And, his grandmother actually saw the yeti in the mountains just up above the village.

For his part, Lam Rinchen was very clear about the animal. Five years ago in winter, he saw extraordinary footprints on the Nyakchungla (mountain pass). The heel, he says, was two inches, leading to a broad main foot. The prints were 100 feet apart, that's the part which puzzles him. Perhaps there were numerous yeti traveling together, but snowfall filled in most of the prints? he wonders aloud. But make no mistake: "They were yetis, I am certain of it. Each print slightly over a foot long. If it were a Tibetan blue bear, there would be no heel. I know very well the bear's print. These were yeti."

Like Jurmi and Lam Rinchen in Merak, Pasang has mixed feelings about the Wildlife Sanctuary. After all, the forest is their livelihood and so many restrictions do not make life easeier. The soft rhododendron wood they cut for the approximately 36 square feet of wood used for fuel in their stoves costs them about 800 ngultrums. They need two such cords per month. The Forest Service subsidizes them with 1000 ngs per month. But, this is also expensive for the government, given the fact there are 21 small hamlets within the Sakteng Sanctuary and several thousand herders. Notwisthanding the difficulties, Pasang concludes, since the government has created the Sanctuary, it must be a good thing.[21]

The government is also looking at eco-tourism in the area for the future, and proposals are being floated around. The Brokpas are innocent bystanders in such mat-

ters. The wildlife, it must be added, even more so. These are the things that most trouble Bhutan's future, as ecosystems are catapulted towards whatever destiny has in store for them. The coming democracy is for and by the people. But, is it also for all the animals?

We cross the Sakteng river, the Gamrichu, in search of rare flowers and birds. Some in our expedition are actually worried about confronting the yeti, as we are climbing up rarely explored steep valleys. The river below has its own hauntings, for this is where the deceased are dispatched to the other world. Unlike Tibetan Buddhist celestial rituals, as stipulated in the Book of the Dead (the chopped up corpses left out for raptors), here in Sakteng a priest officiates, taking the body and submersing it in the river for up to six days. Then the body is chopped up into pieces and those pieces are sent down river. It is a beautiful river with thundering waterfalls and gorges through some of the finest forest in the world, spilling out a hundred miles to the west in lower mountain valleys.

All in all, the Brokpa are fine people: pragmatic, funny, sweet. There is no apparent ecological fervor on their part, just the necessary day to day tasks that will guarantee a little pleasure in life, amid hardships with which most people outside eastern Bhutan would find impossible to cope—from tigers and mad dogs to lice, fleas and brown leech infestations. The leeches are huge, about 1.5 inches in length. Children's heads are shaved to help impede unpleasant outbreaks at school. Money is scarce. The wind, rain and snow and constant trekking to get anything make for strong bodies and temperaments but it is a very, very difficult life. Yet, the Brokpa obviously treasure their surroundings, which they do not consider isolated in any sense. After all, in Sakteng geog, or district, there are some 364 households. Everyone, of course, knows everyone else.

Key indicators of interest for our biological assessment are bryophytes, vascular (flowering) plants and birds. The latter are particularly difficult to film, though far less problematic to identify acoustically. Basic physical characteristics are crucial to gaining insights among such high and dark canopies as those of the Sakteng Wildlife

310

Sanctuary. The speed of the birds, a function of their high metabolic energy output and requirements for sufficient nutrition above 10,000 feet, defies easy documentation. Keys to rapid glimpses are available in sources as the guidebooks by Grimmett, Inskipp and Inskipp.[22] Those clues include: the bird's eye stripe, supercilium, eye ring, lore, culmen, upper and lower mandibular shape, size and type, the moustachial and submousatachial streaks, and the malar stripe. The feather regions present yet another source of marvel at evolutionary perfection. The feathers typically extend from the bird's crown to its tarsus, taking in the ears, chin, throat, nape, breast, belly, back, rump and tail. All birds are blessed with an enviable layering of plumage, as intricate and beautiful as any great Impressionist canvas and commonly referred to as coverts, which includes lesser and greater, primary, median, secondary, tertial and scapular. Where wings midway make their dominant structural turn is called the carpal joint, much like a human elbow. Raptors particularly may give some clue to their identity, even whilst silhouetted 15,000 feet above a pair of peering binoculars, by the nature of that joint. Feather density, discernible to some extent at a glance, may provide another measure of the bird, from the penguin with its vast range of plumage, down to smaller birds like the sparrow which may have 2,000 separate feathers.

With such general points in mind the steep, mixed broadleaf, deciduous/coniferous forests of easternmost Bhutan confront the visitor with a cacophony of avian music, shimmering phantoms fleeting betwixt shadowed flowers, usually no lower than fifteen meters above the understory. The hill partridge (*Arborophila torqueola*) emits its long-suffering song, nearly in sync with the double whistling rufous-throated partridge (*A. rufogularis*). Two blood pheasants (*Ithaginis cruentus*), silent and intent on their feeding, race into a nearby thicket. On a large *Rhododendron barbatum* leaf, beside an enormous fir tree whose circumference measures 25 feet, huge white splattering appears, perhaps the gift of some large Accipiter like the golden eagle. Everywhere are the raucous mountain bulbuls and sound of fulvous-breasted woodpecker (*Dendrocopos macei*). The common hoopoe (*Upupa epops*) alights momentarily in a clearing before several yaks charge downhill toward us. Something has spooked them. A bear? A leopard? No tiger has been seen here for several years, but who knows.

Coucals and barbets are in the forest nearby. Swiftlets (*Collocalia brevirostris*) dive-bomb something unseen, revealing their presence for a split second. The same goes for the lovely speckled wood pigeon (*Columba hodgsonii*) whom we see for one breath. There are yellow-billed blue magpies (*Urocissa flavirostris*) darting on the path before us, racing through the grass and clover while thousands of feet above, a pied harrier (*Circus melanoleucos*) circles gracefully, flapping its wings but once. Two oriental turtle doves, the eastern Himalayan species (*Streptopelia orientalis agricola*), feed nearby.[23]

But identifications become all but impossible with the constant advent of shrikes, minivets, shortwings, flycatchers, niltavas, robins, chats, treecreepers, tits, hill mynahs, prinias, possibly white-eyes, and untold numbers of the passer (sparrow) and warbler families, some of the genus *Tesia*. We count at least three laughing thrushes, each more exotic than the last.

Amid this fanfare, four birds stand still, to our astonishment: the red-billed chough (*Pyrrhocorax pyrrhocorax*), black (fish-tailed) drongo (*Dicrurus macrocercus*), the human-adoring large-billed crow (*Corvus macrorhynchos*) and the white-collared

312

blackbird (*Turdus albocinctus*). Several of us discuss the omnipresent redstart. Or is it the *Phoenicurus frontalis* with the gorgeous blue front, or the orange-, or yellow-bellied flowerpecker, both of the *Dicaeum* genus and both said to be distributed throughout the northeastern Himalayas? Such is the wearying excitement of those whose bird-obsessed brains are easily stirred by the rich displays. We lay awake imagining the lives of this poignant proliferation of little individuals, abetted by the massive ten-volume work by S. Dillon Ripley and Salim Ali[24] published between 1968 and 1975 that covers some 1,200 bird species of the Himalayas, India and Pakistan. Many new birds have been discovered since that time like the tiny Nepal wren babbler found in 1991 and two *Garrulax* genus laughing thrushes discovered about the same time.[25] Within the past twelve months, just a few hundred miles east of Sakteng in Arunachal, another babbler was discovered.

That bird was photographed but nothing more, in keeping with what has become the new ethic. In Audubon's day, the killing of a hundred birds within a few hours was considered normal. Throughout the last several hundred years conservation meant sacrifice. Museums and ornithologists, concerned with DNA, continue to take samples, which we and others wholeheartedly reject in favor of non-violent methodologies. Alexander Skutch, the great 20th century ornithologist based at his own mountainside laboratory in Costa Rica for many years, wrote of his approach, a strictly compassionate and utterly efficacious one, which he declared was the only sane method of science for civilized human society. Back in the late 18th century, the Indian painter/naturalist Shaikh Zayn al-Din had similarly rejected all violence towards birds, as an aid to studying them, or for any other purpose. Dr. Ugyen at NBC agrees and has turned down applications from respectable scientific organizations throughout the world that asked to come to Bhutan to collect and kill "sample" organisms. That is neither the Buddhist way nor is it an appropriate scientific approach in the 21st century. Nonetheless, Bhutan will probably be challenged with respect to future bioprospecting opportunities and may need to consider the best ethical practices in pursuing acceptable compromises that can benefit the economy in principally benign ways.

Our inability to photograph birds, for the most part, has given those of us on this expedition a far greater appreciation and love of these elusive beauties. We do not have the slightest chance of knowing them, only the hope of catching a glimpse of them through heavenly forests. That must suffice and indeed proffers more joy than can be conveyed in words. The odd dove, woodpecker or rose finch grants us a few seconds before the camera, thus providing more than a sufficient gift in these wilds.

As difficult as it may be to photograph birds in the massive moist hemlock and fir canopies of eastern Bhutan, the flora presents a generous spectacle to the enquiring heart. Tandin, the world's expert on Himalayan ferns, has counted ten thus far, including magnificent *Lepisorus* and *Gleichenia* genera. In addition, he has recognized more than 30% of all known rhododendrons in the country right here in Sakteng.[26] Two large juniper species (*Juniperus recurva* and *J. squamata*) and one hemlock (*Tsuga dumosa*) provide hospice in the mountain world for a wealth of biological abundance. But there is also mountain maple and the gorgeously configured Bhutan pine (*Pinus bhutanica*). Wild rose (*Rosa sericea*) adorns the landscape, along with orchids (*Pholidota pallida* and *Dendrobrium nobli*). Himalayan cobra lilies, violets, bracken fungi, tall Wallich's wood fern (*Dryoptrris wallichiana*), epiphytic oleanders and large stands of

bamboo (*Borinda grossa*)²⁷ grace this little universe. The Brokpa word for bamboo is *sak*. *Teng* means "land." Hence the name Sakteng for the land of bamboo.

In surveying this abundance, what emerges without constraint or contradiction is the realization of unparalleled habitat integrity whose emblematic purchase on the imagination begs the world to remain in this state of romantic grace. Here innocent children bow and wave deferentially before the advance of a stranger, declaring in quiet unison, "Good afternoon, Sir!"

The astonishing biodiversity is mirrored throughout Bhutan. At the Bumdeling Wildlife Sanctuary in the far northeast, beginning at the town of Trashi Yangtse along the sacred river below, 130 separate dragonfly species were recorded in just 10% of the preserve—a place where approximately 150 rare cranes arrive in late autumn. The Bhutanese encompass this abundance in their language, Dzongkha. Tandin translated for us some key terms: environment (*takor natang*); nature (*ranjin natang*); one who loves nature (*ranjin natang lu gami*); compassion (*nyingje*); nonviolence (*zoepa*); sanctuary (*gyalyong linger*); wildlife (*ridag semchen*); renewable (*larjung*); protect and preserve (*sung chop*); Gross National Happiness (*Gyalyong Gakyid Pelzom*); bird (*jha*); animal (*semchen*); yeti (*meegoe*).²⁸

There is no word, as yet, for ecology, conservation or sustainability, as such, though the government is working along with Benin, Costa Rica, Holland and Denmark to promote sustainable development, alternative energy and ICDP, or Integrative Conservation and Development Programs. Bhutan even sent a delegation to the 1992 Rio Summit to encourage such policies and eventual partnerships.²⁹

For 1,200 years the world of Drukyul, the country of the thunder dragon (species unknown), has been nurtured by a passion for the spiritual life, honed by the necessities and austerities imposed in the steepest, most inaccessible topography of any nation. These trials, beginning with those recorded during the three visits from Tibet of the great Guru Rinpoche Padmasambhava in the 8th century, helped fuel a way of life

that has been consistently dignified, gracious, generous and firm in its commitment to ranjin natang or nature.

Following the Zhabdrung's unification of the country during the 17th century (what had been a concatenation of extraordinary monastic fortresses or dzhongs that proved too difficult for even Mongol battalions to conquer), Bhutan exercised its Middle Path of Mahayana Buddhism. This unified Bhutan succeeded in expelling a British military invasion in the 1860s. It did not allow tourists until the winter of 1974/75 (when Michael first had the privilege of visiting). The nation's exclusivity and high altitude inaccessibility have been her saving grace, along with her cultural commitment to conservation, which enabled her to retain one of the highest concentrations of primary, pristine habitat by proportion to country size (at 36,394 square kilometers) of any nation, a steadfast achievement embodying the universal goal of conservation biology. Only Suriname and—because of the inaccessibility of her boreal forests—Canada enjoy a similar status.

Leaving Sakteng, we wait on the road for a calf to suckle her mother (Bhutan is alone among countries in continuing to afford the bovine a high degree of autonomy and dignity) while a troop of capped langurs feed on ficus trees in advance of the approaching monsoon rains. The sheer prolific nature of Bhutan continues to reveal herself along the one roadway. Blood pheasants, a satyr tragopan, a monal pheasant, macaques and yellow-billed magpies, oaks, magnolias in bloom, grey langurs, endless rhododendrons, shrikes (genus *Lanius*), grey bush chats, black drongos, Eurasian blackbirds, slaty-backed flycatchers, mountain bulbuls, and the ever present large hawk-cuckoo (*Cuculus sparverioides*) whose lonely, melancholic wail echoes across the landscape of huge canopy, all accompany our passage back towards the west of the country. And there, on a hillside, is a small wild rooster who in every respect conforms to some exotic, undocumented cross of the wild Sri Lankan junglefowl (*Gallus lafayetti*), the Himalayan junglefowl and the gorgeous peninsular Indian grey jungle-

fowl (*Gallus sonneratii*). In other words, these magnificent birds, chickens by any other name, are also wild—the chicken/pheasant equivalent of a macaw.

Every glance yields to the enquiring mind an irrepressible exuberance of life whose infinite details will never, must never lose their mystery. This mandate inheres within all the great sanctuaries of the world.

In Bhutan, a great challenge will be the continued spiritual expression of her ecological blueprint. This Bhutan Biological Conservation Complex with its total of 21 protected areas and corridors, beginning with Royal Manas and gazetted during the 1980s and 1990s—a gift of the Earth, said His Majesty—are nearly all inhabited by indigenous people. The wellbeing of those rural denizens of the parks and reserves is critical to the continued success of the conservation network. Conflict avoidance will require accommodation of the needs of people who have very little in terms of conventional income generation. People like Jurmi and his family. The altitudes in SWS say it all: regeneration of seedlings on slopes in excess of 45 degrees does not happen.[30] That is just one basic window looking out over the severity of the life embraced by alpine nomads. Their future depends on sustainable teamwork with nature, which turns easily to hardship and is anything but romantic. So these two worlds of perception must meet. Buddhism is their common language, but survival may be more basic.

Bhutan's goals hinge upon finding income without imposing on the core areas of preservation, where people continue to eek out their venerable livelihoods. The building of a road, politically motivated, would be a disastrous incursion into Sakteng. Solar panels for year-round electricity would not. It is a delicate balance. Bhutan confronts the same conservation challenges as other nations. The liberalization of tourism offers no guarantee of sustainability. Big hotels and intrusive tour groups will damage wildlife and interfere with tradition. The *1995 Forest and Nature Conservation Act* listed all of Bhutan's known endangered species. Their protection is of paramount importance to lawmakers within the country but so is viable human infrastructure.

There are countless solutions and compromises being proposed all the time. A new house in Merak or Sakteng might require as many as 100 blue pines. An application and permit for a new house can take two-to-three years. Pine versus spruce (which species are likely to support more native biodiversity and in what proportions?); hard wood versus soft; building versus heating; access to the forests; new roads, new codes of practice and of protection and the ever looming goal of 30,000 megawatts of hydroelectric generation in a country currently generating 2,000 megawatts: these issues confront a nation that has only just embraced democracy for better or worse. By 2020 all households will be connected to a natural electrical grid or to community solar power, say authorities. With a 2% population growth rate and Total Fertility Rates (TFRs) between two to three children per couple (TFRs of four to five in rural Bhutan), potential problems are written in bright lights. Sixty-five percent of all Bhutanese are between the ages of 15 and 25, at the height of their reproductive years. Unemployment, intellectual brain drain (not yet considered to be a problem) and the need for additional colleges throughout the nation are all challenges the new democracy must address that can only serve to further tighten the screws on continued conservation success.

His Excellency Chief Justice Sonam Tobgye believes that His Majesty the Fourth King's conservation ethic will never be eclipsed; that his decree on forest conservation was a "singular and brave act." When it was announced, people tended to think of forests as a resource to be cut and sold. The King closed down saw mills and propagated the belief, consistent with Buddhism, that nature must be conserved. People listened, says the Chief Justice. And today the results are discernible: over 200 mammalian and 770 known bird species in the country (based on actual sightings) and an average of 300 new plant species being identified in Bhutan every year since 2002. In addition, there are 115 to 150 tigers living in "contiguous distribution" with as many as 81 "breeding adults," which suggests a "viable population that can serve as a vital gene pool for future conservation efforts."[31]

Throughout the country's 20 districts, more and more people are being trained to respect and identify species. At NBC, specialists are hired to go out into rural areas and provide farmers with new methods of enhancing yield in sustainable manners. Dr. Ugyen is even looking at a microbial repository for the country. Bhutan cannot compete in the manufacture of competitive bulk foods with her neighbors India and China, but she recognizes and is pursuing the fact that the Land of the Thunder Dragon can excel at niche marketing, particularly in the organic sector. In fact, the Gasa District will be the first organic district in the country.

This versatility, coupled with the most contemplative and pro-active conservation efforts in the world, make all of Bhutan a unique sanctuary and an unprecedented international emblem of spiritual ecology at work.

CODA

On a plane somewhere in Asia, en route to the United States, looking down through broken cloud cover, we see patches of green and brown, patches of white, and scratches and inorganic blotches suggesting the presence of humans. But we also see gigantic visual lures of emptiness, holes that are not holes, but caesuras free of human intervention, where nature has been left alone, or is recovering. Images of a 21st century planet whose destiny is contested: not because of little birds or squirrels or silently grazing yaks, but because of people like ourselves, flying on gas-guzzling airplanes, wandering the Earth like lost souls trying to understand what is happening.

Each humbling immersion into wilderness, that blessed moment in the presence of the Other, remains a most dominant, inexplicable force in our personal lives. We try to reach out in often clumsy, though well-intended ways, hoping to be of service, to partake of the sheer wonderment of interspecies collaborations. And to do something—*anything*—to alleviate the stress and pain bearing down upon so many of the last vestiges of Eden. We want somehow to merge with that blind Arcadian ideal of nature our species has persistently nurtured, despite its often contradictory behavior. To be at peace and connected with these remarkable sanctuaries and communities we have been privileged to visit—not just scientifically, but emotionally. That reunion rejects categorical definition. We want the myriad echoes, memories and images to be themselves, unqualified, free.

We debated this impulse with respect to photo captions, and, notwithstanding abundant Latin nomenclature throughout the text, have opted for a counterbalancing impressionistic palette, "photo-liberation" (with the exception of the paintings, and images of those human friends who were so helpful and generous throughout the many research trips and expeditions).

Despite the human turmoil in this world and its inordinate power over the rest of the Creation, we are hopeful, even optimistic, knowing that such special people are out there. They are working assiduously to safeguard these incredible oases with all their denizens, and by collective aspiration must ultimately succeed at restoring ecological balance and refurbishing this sanctuary, our one earth. Our home.

NOTES

THE LOVE AND PROTECTION OF INNOCENCE

1 *See* www.Scandinavica.com/culture/nature/sweden.htm

2 *See* "Protected Areas," http://atlas.nrcan.gc.ca/site/english/maps/environment/ecology/protecting/protectedareas

3 The North Carolina Zoo, in the Uwharrie Mountains near Asheboro, has been a strong partner of the Alligator River National Wildlife Refuge in efforts to restore a critically endangered population of one of two native wolves in North America. The zoo has maintained a program of breeding and re-introducing *Canis rufus gregoryi* to the wild. *See* www.nczoo.org/animal_id/na_red_wolf.cfm; see also www.fws.gov/alligatorriver/redwolf.html

4 *See* "Conservation Designations," http://www.naturenet.net/status/; see also Jenny Coates, "Dartmoor, England: Preserving an Ancient Man-Made Wilderness," www.gonomad.com/alternatives/0608/dartmoor.html; see "Calke Park designated National Nature Reserve," September 17, 2004, www.english-nature.org.uk/News/story.asp?ID=638; and "5m lottery boost to conserve Epping Forest's medieval past," Heritage Lottery Fund, www.hlf.org.uk/English/InYourArea/London/CaseStudies/Epping+Forest.htm.

   The categories become even more complicated when one considers such an unlikely place as a huge oil refinery compound—Petrotrin in Pointe-à-Pierre, south of the Trinidad in the Caribbean nation of Trinidad and Tobago—where dedicated ornithologists with the Wild Fowl Trust have for forty years provided a refuge and a breeding site for such rare species as the black-bellied whistling tree ducks and the country's national bird, the scarlet ibis.

5 http://www.iucn.org/themes/ssc/redlist2006/redlist2006.htm.

6 The Alliance for Zero Extinction (AZE) offers one important approach to understanding protection of threatened species, as well as the stakes involved. AZE's combined analytical assemblage includes assessments by 53 conservation organizations that have chosen as high priorities those 595 sites across the planet where an estimated 794 species (as of December 2005) are most at risk of going extinct. The prioritizing comes in the wake of revelations concerning the patterns of accelerated extinctions during the past 500 years, with 250 extinctions known to have occurred during that period, and 1,500 extinctions predicted in the next one to five decades, at current trends. The goal of AZE is to provide so rich a data bank at local levels that governments, communities and private donors will feel the irresistible impulse to favor and implement protection. *See* http://www.sciam.com/article.cfm?articleID=000E29B2-967D-1DC1-94E2809EC5880108. *See also* Russell A.

Mittermeier, Patricio Robles Gil, Michael Hoffmann, John Pilgrim, Thomas Brooks, Cristina Goettsch Mittermeier, John Lamoreux and Gustavo A. B. Da Fonseca, *Hotspots Revisited: Earth's Biologically Richest and Most Endangered Terrestrial Ecoregions*, Preface by Peter A. Seligmann, Foreword by Harrison Ford, Mexico: Cemex, 2004, p.29-31.

7 The vast majority of plants found in gardens, swamps, forests and jungles (over 450,000 species thus far identified) are known as vascular plants. In addition to sunlight, what keeps them alive is their system of tissues, which provide them the ability to receive and process water, sugar and mineral salts. They are so critical to the Earth's life support that they have been deemed to be the core criteria for determining the 35 hotspots listed to date. This is because a large number of endemic vascular plants translates to an equally large number of resident protozoa, insects, amphibia, reptiles, birds and mammals. They are interdependent, and this web of life (spiritual traditions like Jainism have so described it for millennia) can be ascertained in the hotspots. Lose such areas and we shall suffer untold consequences. Evolution itself, fueled by these biological deep lineages, would change course, possibly for the worse. The "worse" could be defined as a vast diminution of species, as well as humans' ability to survive in a world where critical resources seem to vanish overnight. One expression of this denuded horizon is the cracked desert of the Sudan, stressed by drought, resource constraints and an overabundance of humans and ungulates. In Eastern Brazil's Atlantic Rain Forest, less than 7% of wilderness remains of an area that once comprised pristine ecosystems covering the size of three Californias. Similarly, less than 10% of Madagascar's indigenous biological communities endure amid poverty, slash and burn agriculture, and huge regions eroded in the aftermath of human endeavors to survive. And in India, the conflicts between humans and other species have all but doomed the Bengal Tiger, and the fewer than 200 remaining Gir Asiatic lions in a region where pastoralists and their 15,000 cattle, goats and sheep compete with the big cats for survival. *See* "India tries to balance tiger protection with rights of forest dwellers," by Raymond Thibodeaux, www.kansascity.com/news/world/story/373149.html. *See also*, "Parks 'failing Africa's wildlife'" http://news.bbc.co.uk/go/pr/fr/-/hi/sci/tech/6972416.stm.

8 ibid.

9 *See* Russell A. Mittermeier, Patricio Robles Gil and Cristina Goettsch Mittermeier, *Megadiversity: Earth's Biologically Wealthiest Nations*, Mexico: Cemex, 1997, pp.17-37.

10 *See* C.H. Sekercioglu, S.R. Loarie, F.O. Brenes, P.R. Ehlich and G.C. Daily, "Persistence of Forest Birds in the Costa Rican Agricultural Countryside," *Conservation Biology*, Vol. 21, No. 2, 2007, pp.482-494.

11 *See* J.R. Rohr, C.G. Maha, and K.C. Kim, "Developing a Monitoring Program for Invertebrates: Guidelines and a Case Study," *Conservation Biology*, Vol. 21, No. 2, 2007, pp.422-433.

12 *See Global 200 World Wildlife Fund: Places That Must Survive*, by Fulco Pratesi, White Star, 2007; *See also* www.panda.org/about_wwf/where_we_work/ecoregions/about/index.cfm.

13 *See* www.unesco.org.

14 *See* http://whc.unesco.org/pg.m?cid=3115. *See* Marco Cattaneo and Jasmina Trifoni, Translated by Timothy Stroud, *World Heritage Sites: Nature Sanctuaries*, UNESCO, Italian National Commission, Milan: White Star Publishers, 2003, pp.382-387.

15 *See* www.unesco.org/mab / for UNESCO Biosphere Reserves. In addition, 150 nations signed the Convention on Biodiversity at the Rio Summit in 1992, with the goal of rescuing the planet from further biodiversity loss, and alleviating poverty to help achieve that goal. To date, at least 188 countries (excluding the U.S.) have ratified the CBD, and many have undertaken BAPs, or Biodiversity Action Plans. *See* http://www.biodiv.org/convention/default.html.

16 www.fws.gov/refuges/habitats/endSpRefuges.html.

17 *See* www.fws.gov/Refuges/generalInterest/factSheets/

18 *See* Ruth Rudner, *Our National Parks*, Photography by David Muench, Foreword by Tom Kiernan, President, National Parks Conservation Association, Portland: Graphic Arts Books, 2005.

19 Conservation currencies, varying valuations of nature, are often non-binding. One example is the Convention on Wetlands, signed in the Iranian city of Ramsar in 1971. To date 1,651 specially designated sites in 154 countries cover 149.7 million acres. But the Convention is non-binding.

20 *See* Population Reference Bureau 2006 World Population Data Sheet: Threatened and Endangered Animal Species: www.prb.org/DataFind/datafinder7.htm.

21 *See* http://www.unep-wcmc.org/wdpa/. *See also* http://www.staff.amu.edu.pl/~zbzw/ph/pnp/swiat.htm.

22 *See* Scott Norris, "Evolutionary Tinkering," *Conservation In Practice*, Published by the Society for Conservation Biology, Vol. 7, No. 3, July-September 2006.

23 *See* "Leveraging Science for Conservation," Center for Applied Biodiversity Science at Conservation International, Newsletter, June 2003, p. 2. *See also* Craig R. Groves, *Drafting A Conservation Blueprint: A Practitioner's*

Guide to Planning for Biodiversity, Foreword by Malcolm L. Hunter Jr., The Nature Conservancy, Washington, D.C.: Island Press, 2003.

24 See the new "encyclopedia of life" project at www.eol.org/home.html. See also Joshua Reichert, Director of Environmental Division, Pew Charitable Trusts, "One by One, the World Is Becoming a Lonelier Place," Los Angeles Times, March 15th. See also, J. Michael Scott, Dale D. Goble, and Frank W. Davis (Eds.), The Endangered Species Act at Thirty: Conserving Biodiversity in Human-Dominated Landscapes, Vol. 2, Washington, D.C.: Island Press, 2006.

25 Dominique Browning and the Editors of House & Garden, The New Garden Paradise: Great Private Gardens Of the World, New York: W.W. Norton & Company, 2005.

26 E. O. Wilson, The Creation: An Appeal to Save Life on Earth, New York: W.W. Norton & Company, 2006, pp.108-109.

A LITTLE BIRD IN THE LARGEST PROTECTED AREA ON EARTH

1 See http://en.wikipedia.org/wiki/Mount_Saint_Elias.

2 See www.byzantines.net/saints/st%20elias.htm.

3 See Travels In Alaska, by John Muir, Introduction by Edward Hoagland, The Modern Library, New York, 2002, pp.109-112. See also John Muir: Nature's Visionary, by Gretel Ehrlich, National Geographic, Washington, D.C., 2000, pp.196-197.

4 pp.533-545, National Audubon Society Field Guide To Birds, Western Edition, by Miklos D. F. Udvardy, Revised by John Farrand, Jr., Visual Key by Amanda Wilson and Lori Hogan, Alfred A. Knopf, New York, 1994: A Chanticleer Press, Inc. Publication. See also Kittlitzs's Murrelet (Brachyramphus kittlitzii), summer plumage, Source: Plate 1, p.44a, Painting by John L. Ridgway, and Robert Ridgway, Report Upon Natural History Collections Made I Alaska Between The Years 1877 and 1881 by Edward W. Nelson, Ed. by Henry W. Henshaw, No. III, Arctic Series of Publications Issued In Connection With The Signal Service, U.S. Army, Washington: Government Printing Office, 1887. Interestingly, Nelson writes, "The first example of this rare bird known to exist in any American museum was secured by the writer in Unalaska Harbor the last of May, 1877. The birds were in company with S. atiquus and B. marmoratus, and like the latter were not shy. Their habits appeared to be the same, all feeding upon small crustacea. These three species kept about the outer bays all the last half of May, but about the first of June became scarce, as they sought their breeding places. Since my capture Mr. Turner has taken another specimen in the Aleutian Islands, and the species may be found more common there when the islands have been more thoroughly explored." p.44.

5 Alaska's Giant of Ice and Stone: Wrangell-St. Elias National Park, by John G. Mitchell, National Geographic, March 2003, p.64.

6 Exploring The Alaska-Yukon Bordercountry, Photography and Sidebars by John W. Page, NorthWord Press, Minocqua, Wisconsin, Alaska Natural History Association, 1994, p.119. See also "A Geologic Guide to Wrangell-Saint Elias National Park and Preserve, Alaska," U.S. Geological Survey Professional Paper 1616, U. S. Department of the Interior, U.S. Geological Survey, Denver, Colorado, 2006.

7 Ahtna Athabaskan Dictionary, by James Kari, Alaska Native Language Center, University of Alaska Fairbanks, 1990, p.493. See also Alaska Park Science: Connections to Natural and Cultural Resource Studies in Alaska's National Parks, National Park Service, U.S. Department of Interior, Alaska Support Office, Anchorage, Alaska, 2003. See also, Mammals of Alaska, Alaska Geographic Guides, The Alaska Geographic Society, Anchorage, Alaska, 1996. For the park's plant diversity, see "Native Vascular Plants of Wrangell-St.Elias National Park & Preserve," compiled by Mary Beth Cook, Alaska Natural History Association, Anchorage, Alaska, 2002. (The Latin names for this volume are based upon Flora of the Yukon, by William J. Cody.) See also, Alaska Trees & Wildflowers, by James Kavanaugh, Illustrated by Raymond Leung, Waterford Press, 2001; and Field Guide to Alaskan Wildflowers, by Verna E. Pratt, Alaskakrafts, Inc., 1989.

8 See http://icybayadventures.blogspot.com/. See also Guide to the Birds of Alaska, Robert H. Armstrong, Alaska Northwest Books, 4th Edition, 2006, "Alcids" pp. 176-187. See also, Field Guide to Bird Nests and Eggs of Alaska's Coastal Tundra, by Timothy D. Bowman, U.S. Fish and Wildlife Service, Anchorage, Alaska, published by Alaska Sea Grant College Program, University of Alaska, Fairbanks, Alaska, 2004.

9 Kathy Kuletz, "Kittlitz's Murrelet: A Glacier Bird in Retreat," May 3, 2004. www.alaska.fws.gov/media/murrelet/overview.pdf; see also Birding Community E-Bulletin, "In the words of researchers John Piatt (USGS) and Kathy Kuletz (USFWS), 'The fate of the Kittlitz's Murrelet may hinge on the fate of Alaska's glaciers...'" www.refugenet.org/birding/febSBC07.html; see also www.birdlife.org/datazone/species/index.html?action=SpcHTMDetails.asp&sid=3310&m=0; and www.defenders.org/globalwarming/meltdown/navigating-the-arctic-meltdown-chapter-6.pdf. See also, Alaska Park Science: Scientific Studies on Climate Change in Alaska's National Parks, National Park Service, U.S. Department of Interior, Alaska Regional, Office, Anchorage, Alaska, 2007.

10 See "Extinction and Population Scaling" by William E. Kunin, in Scaling Biodiversity, Edited by David Storch, Pablo A. Marquet, and Majes H. Brown, Foreword by Robert M. May, Cambridge University Press, 2007, p.396. See also, "Accuracy of Bird Range Maps Based on Habitat Maps and Habitat Relationship Models," by Barrett A. Garrison and Thomas Lupo, in Predicting Species Occurrences: Issues of Accuracy and Scale, Edited by J. Michael Scott, Patricia J. Heglund, Michael L. Morrison, et. al., Island Press, Washington, D.C., 2002, pp.367-375.

A CITY CALLED SAINT FRANCIS

1 "Centennial Perspective from Alaska Maritime NWR," www.fws.gov/refuges/centennial/centAlaska.html.

2 See The Farallon Islands: Sentinels of the Golden Gate, by Peter White, Scottwall Associates, Publishers, San Francisco, 1995, p.1. The chart referenced was drawn by Sebastian Viscaino. The "seven dots" were called "Frayles." It is remarkable that Viscaino got seven dots right, but forgot to mention San Francisco Bay.

3 See Birds of Northern California, by David Fix and Andy Bezener, Lone Pine Publishing, Auburn, WA, 2000.

4 See "Farallon National Wildlife Refuge," by Joelle Buffa and Eileen McLaughlin, Tideline, Vol. 22, No. 1, Spring 2002, p.1.

5 See Pacific Coast Ornithology, www.towhee.net/history/chronology.html.

6 See Golden Gate National Parks: A Photographic Journey, by Christine Colasurdo, Golden Gate National Parks Association, San Francisco, 2002.

7 See "Picturesque California: How westerners portrayed the West in the age of John Muir," by Sue Rainey, Common-Place, Vol. 7, No. 3, April 2007.

8 See John Muir: Nature's Visionary, by Gretel Ehrlich, National Geographic, Washington D.C., 2000, pp.136-137.

9 See Offshore: Paintings of the Farallones, essays by Philip E. Linhares, Peter Selz and Claire Peaslee, with paintings by Jerrold Ballaine, Tony King, Jack Stuppin and William Wheeler, California Academy of Sciences, 1997.

10 See Muir Woods, by James M. Morley, Published by Smith-Morley, San Francisco, 1991, Revised Edition, pp.4-7.

11 ibid., p.6.

12 See Pacific Coast Mammals, by Ron Russo and Pam Olhausen, Nature Study Guild, 1987. See also Local Birds Of Marin County: Quick Guide, Local Birds, Inc., Woodside, CA, 2002.

13 See Golden Gate Park, by Christopher Pollock, Encyclopedia of San Francisco, San Francisco Museum & Historical Society, 2003.www.sfhistoryencyclopedia.com/articles/g/goldenGate-park.html.

14 See California Coastal Access Guide, The California Coastal Commission, University of California Press, Berkeley, Sixth Edition, 2003. See Alfred L. Kroeber, Handbook of the Indians of California, Washington, D.C.: Bureau of American Ethnology Bulleton No. 78, 1925. See also Malcolm Margolin, The Ohlone Way: Indian Life in the San Francisco-Monterey Bay Area, Heyday Books, Berkeley, CA, 1978.

15 See "National Wildlife Refuge System: A Visitor's Guide: Celebrating a Century of Conservation," U.S. Fish & Wildlife Service, http://refuges.fws.gov/

A VISION OF URBAN ARCADIA: CENTRAL PARK

1 *Central Park: A History and a Guide*, Second Edition Revised, by Henry Hope Reed and Sophia Duckworth, Clarkson N. Potter, Inc., New York, 1972, p.3.

2 *See The Park And The People: A History of Central Park*, by Roy Rosenzweig and Elizabeth Blackmar, Cornell University Press, 1992, pp.20-21.

3 *See Frederick Law Olmsted: Landscape Architect 1822-1903*, Edited by Frederick Law Olmsted, Jr. and Theodora Kimball, G.P.Putnam's Sons, The Knickerbocker Press, New York and London, 1928, pp.538-539. For the earliest images of Central Park, see the Thirteen Annual Reports of the Board of Commissioners on the Central Park, William C. Bryant & Co., New York, 1857-1870, the first report of which was by Egbert L. Vielé, the chief designer and planning engineer for the park.

4 Reed and Duckworth, op.cit., p.2.

5 *See* "City of New York," by Mayor Michael R. Bloomberg and Commissioner Adrian Benepe, Central Park Conservancy Annual Report 2006, p.3.

6 ibid., p.11.

7 *Central Park*, Preface by Elizabeth Barlow Rogers, Commentary by Marie Winn, Aperture Foundation, New York, 1995.

8 *See* "New York City Public Art Curriculum," www. blueofthesky.com/publicart/works/balto.htm.

9 *See Central Park Wildlife: An Introductiont to Familiar Species Found in New York City's Central Park*, A Pocket Naturalist Guide, by James Kavanaugh, illustrations by Raymond Leung, Waterford Press, China, 2006.

10 *See* "Elusive Coyote Is Captured in Central Park," by Maria Newman and Janon Fisher, *The New York Times*, March 22, 2006

11 *See* "Satan's Boletus," http://waynesword.palomar.edu/plfeb98.htm. *See also*, "Tom Volk's Fungus of the Month for December 2004 - *Daldinia concentrica*, the coal fungus, carbon balls, cramp balls, or King Alfred's cakes," TomVolkFungi.net and http://botit.botany.wisc.edu/toms_fungi/dec2004.html.

12 *See* "Bioinvasion: From Old World to New," by Chad Cohen, National Geographic Society, January 23, 2001. *See* nationalgeographic.com.

13 ibid., p.3.

14 *See* http://waynesword.palomar.edu/plfeb98.htm#carbon.

15 *See* Marie Winn, *Red-Tails in Love, Updated Edition*, Vintage Books, Random House, New York, 2005.

16 Go to www.centralparknyc.org.

17 *See* Cal Vornberger, *Birds of Central Park*, Foreword by Marie Winn, Harry N. Abrams, Inc., Publishers, New York City, 2005.

18 *See* "The City Naturalist: Observing Birds," by Leslie Day, www.nysite.com/nature/birding.htm. Numerous bird-specific websites provide "insider" goings-on; details, and geography to better serve the passionate birdwatchers in the Park. They include, http://mariewin.server304.com/index.htm; http://www.palemale.com/; http://palemaleirregulars.blogspot.com/; http://urbanhawks.blogs.com/urban_hawks/; and for other parts of the greater New York area, http://www.jknaturegallery.com/. This perfect biological egalitarianism has been challenged, of late, by one New York City lawmaker who fears a public health hazard and would like to rid New York of pigeons, fining anyone who feeds them $1,000. In 2003 the City "briefly employed" a hawk "to scare pigeons" but it apparently went after a Chihuahua and the initiative was shut down. *See* "New York mulls $1000 fine for feeding pigeons," by Edith Honan, from Reuters, in *The New Zealand Herald*, www.nzherald.co.nz/category/story.cfm?c_id=500834&objectid=10475806

19 *See* John K. Howat, *Frederic Church*, Yale University Press, New Haven and London, 2005, p.83.

20 ibid., p.86.

21 *See* Cal Vornberger, *Birds Of Central Park*, Foreword by Marie Winn, Harry N. Abrams, Inc., New York City, 2005, p.203. *See also* Cal's *Pocket Guide* version of the same book, inside the back flap.

22 ibid., p.54.

23 ibid., p.110.

PASTURE OF GREAT SPIRITS: FARM SANCTUARY

1 *See Voices from the Underground: For the Love of Animals*, by Michael Tobias, New Paradigm Books, Pasadena, CA, 1998, p.33.

2 *See* "A Conversation with Gene Bauston," by Marla Rose, July 1999, www.veganstreet.com/community/bauston.html.

3 Tobias, op.cit, *Voices from the Underground*, p.41.

4 ibid., p.66.

5 *See* "Farm Sanctuary 2006 Annual Report," "Highlights," www.farmsanctuary.org/about/annual_06.htm.

DR. RUSSELL MITTERMEIER AND THE LAST GREAT TROPICAL RAIN FOREST

1 *Hours of Gladness*, by M. Maeterlink, Translated by A. Teixeira De Mattos, Illustrated by E. J. Detmold, London: Allen & Co., 1912, p. 13.

2 They are the black spider monkey, the red howler monkey, the brown capuchin, the weeper capuchin, the Guiana squirrel monkey, the golden handed or red handed tamarind, the white faced saki and the Northern bearded saki.

3 *See* the Introduction for a discussion of "hotspots."

4 *See* Population Reference Bureau data on the country at: www.prb.org/Countries/Suriname.aspx.

5 *See* "The Difficult Flowering Of Suriname: Ethnicity And Politics In A Plural Society," by Edward Dew, Vaco N. V., Uitgeversmaatschappij, Paramaribo, 1996, p.4.

6 *See* "Conserving Earth's Living Heritage: A Proposed Framework for Designing Biodiversity Conservation Strategies," by Russell Mittermeier, Conservation International, Washington D.C., 2004.

7 *See* "The Central Suriname Nature Reserve: Republic of Suriname," CI, Paramaribo, 2002, p.6.

8 *See* www.stinasu.sr/; www.unesco.org/en/stateparties/sr; www.thesalmons.org/lynn/wh-suriname.html; and www.ci-suriname.org/csnr/eng/Protected_Areas_Programme.htm. *See also* www1.nhl.nl~ribot/English/indexpl5.htm.

9 *See* Francois Haverschmidt and F.G. Mees, *Birds of Suriname*, Vaco Uitgeversmaatschappij, Paramaribo, 1994; see also *Birds of Northern South America: An Identification Guide*, 2 vols., by Robin Redstall, Clemencia Rodner, and Miguel Lentino, Yale University Press, New Haven, 2006.

10 *See* http://news.mongabay.com/2007/0604-suriname.html.

11 *See* U.S. Department of State overview of Suriname's economy at, www.state.gov/r/pa/ei/bgn/1893.htm; For carbon sequestration values in Suriname and elsewhere, see http://news.mongabay.com/2007/0813-deforestation.html.

12 op. cit., http://news.mongabay.com.

THE IBERIAN WOLF SANCTUARY

1 *See* WolfPrint, Special edition on Portugal, UK Wolf Conservation Trust, Issue 20, Summer 2004. www.ukwolf.org. *See also*, "Walking With Wolves," www.abc.net.au/rn/talks/europe/stories/s51209.htm; "Archives 2005" www.euroloup.com/revuedepresse2005.htm; Coexistence News, No.1, September 2005; www.wolfology.com; and "Restoring Europe's Wolves," by Luigi Boitani, International Wolf, Vol. 9, No.4, Winter 1999, www.wolf.org/wolf/learn/iwmag/1999/wnt99/wnt99a3.asp.

2 *See* "Equisave: The Miranda Donkey," www.equisave.eu/equisave_races.php?i=4

3 For more information on the AssociaçÐo Para a PreservaçÐo do Burro "Burricadas", *See*: http://burricadas.org/.

4 *See* "Lynx on comeback," *New Zealand Herald*, November 8, 2007, www.nzherald.co.nz/category/story.cfm?c_id=500834&objectid=10474657

THE MANY LOVES OF BRIGITTE BARDOT

1 "Seal Hunting 2006," May 1, 2007, www.fondationbrigittebardot.fr/site/fbb_a.php?IdPere=&Id=314.

2 "Alaska's aerial wolves hunting," October 2006, www.fonationbrigittebardot.fr/site/fbb_a.php?IdPere=&Id=284.

3 *See* FBB l'info-journal, No.'s 46, 52, 53, and 54. www.fondationbrigittebardot.fr.

4 *See* "Biodiversity and Protected Areas: France," http://earthtrends.wri.org, p.1. *See also,* "France: Overview," "Status and Trends of Biodiversity," www.cbd.int/countries/default.shtml?country=fr.

5 *See* www.nationmaster.com/country/fr-france/agr-agriculture; see also OECD Statistics, at: http://stats.oecd.org/wbox/viewhtml.aspx?queryname=314&querytype=view&lang=en

6 Four major works on early French landscape aesthetics are critical reading: *Royal palaces and chateaux in Paris and its surroundings, Lorraine and the Loire region,* by Israel Sivestre, Paris, 1666-1669; *Recueil de sept suites gravées,* by Gabriel Perelle, Paris, ca.1690; *Description des nouveaux jardins de la France et de ses anciens chateaux, mêlée d'observations sur la vie de la campagne et la composition des jardins,* by Alexandre Laborde, Paris, Delance, 1808-1814; Cabinet du Roi. *Vues des maisons royales et des villes conquises par Louis XIV,* by Jean Marot et al., Paris, 1680.

7 *See* www.animalinfo.org/country/France.htm. *See also,* "Total number of endangered vascular plant species and the share of endangered tree species and other endangered vascular plant species in forests," http://dataservice.eea.europa.eu/atlas/viewpub.asp?id=1811; and www.eu-wildlifetrade.org/html/en/wildlife_trade.asp

8 *See* "National Threatened Species Listing Based on IUCN Criteria and Regional Guidelines: Current Status and Future Perspectives," by Rebecca M. Miller, J.P.Rodriguez, A.A.-Fowler, et al., *Conservation Biology,* Vol. 21, No. 3, June 2007, p.685. The science assessing endangered species does not concern itself with the so-called domestic species of the kind Brigitte Bardot and her colleagues are working to protect. In the recent report, "State of the World's Animal Genetic Resources" by the UN Food and Agriculture Organization, much is made of the fact that about 20% of farm animal breeds throughout the world are headed toward extinction. The widely-touted statistic that more than nine billion people by the year 2050 will need huge amounts of livestock products, ignores the greater truth that humans do not require meat consumption. It is culinary choice, not biological imperative. For farm animals, not only are their breeds disappearing with the advance of mechanized, homogenized factory farming, but each individual animal will likely be slaughtered. When such legislation as the Endangered Species Act (ESA) in the United States is analyzed, a species is seen to be in trouble if it is quantified as being "at risk 'in all or a significant portion of its range'." A recent study makes it clear that a definition of "significant portion" has never been clarified. That is also the case with farm animals who are also subject to "critically endangered" status. The French love their pets, but like others globally, think nothing of partaking of meat and fish and other products manufactured by all those cruel methods Ms. Bardot and team are persistently agitating against in Brussels. That's where agricultural policies, transport, slaughterhouse practices and hunting traditions are debated; and laws for the Europen Union engineered. *See* "A Biological Framework for Evaluating Whether a Species Is Threatened or Endangered in a Significant Portion of Its Range," by Robin S. Waples, Peter Z.B. Adams, James Bohnsack and Barbara I. Taylor, *Conservation Biology,* Vol. 21, No. 4, pp. 964-974. One other looming threat that will clearly impact all such organizations as Ms. Bardot's, and their efforts to help the animals, is a recent U.S. decision to permit the cloning of animals for slaughter. *See* "Cloned meat and milk are safe to eat, FDA says," by Karen Kaplan, *Los Angeles Times,* January 16, 2008, pp.A1, A19. While the approximately 97 million U.S. bovines bound for slaughter each year are not all candidates for cloning, this FDA greenlight on the process signals yet another level of hell for our mammalian brethren who will be genetically created, reared in confinement, then slaughtered for human consumption.

GUT AIDERBICHL: REMARKABLE OASES OF COMPASSION

1 "Die Zeitschrift für Förderer und Freunde von Gut Aiderbichl," (Monthly Magazine), www.gut-aiderbichl.com.

A REFUGE FOR BEARS

1 "The Bear Den," by Don Middleton, 1996. *See* www.7thfloormedia.com/projects/exwork/best/bearden/evolve.htm.

2 *See* Findings of the Group of Experts on Large Carnivore Conservation to the Bern Convention: Council of Europe; Oslo, Norway, June 2000. The most comprehensive analysis of the European brown bear's status, distribution, and options for the future was written in 2002 by John D. C. Linnell, Norwegian Institute for Nature Research, Daniel Steuer & Petra Kaczensky, Vauna, formerly the Munich Wildlife Society, John Odden, Department of Zoology, Norwegian University of Science and Technology, and Jon E. Swenson, Department of Biology and Nature Conservation, Agricultural University of Norway. *See* their downloadable document and extensive bibliography, "2002 European Brown Bear Compendium: Wildlife Conservation Issues: Technical Series Number 004A," Publication Series Editor: William Wall, Senior Scientist for Wildlife Conservation, Safari Club International, Dept. of Wildlife Conservation, Herndon VA, 2002.

3 ibid.

4 "Status survey and conservation action plan: Bears. Gland, Swizerland: IUCN Publications, by C. Serveheen, S. Herrero, and B. Peyton, 1999. *See also,* "Final draft action plan for conservation of the brown bear (*Ursus arctos*) in Europe," by J.E. Swenson, N. Gerstl, B. Dahle, and A. Zedroser, Strasborg: Council of Europe, 1999.

5 *See* "Rescuing Orphan Bear Cubs," www.ifaw.org/ifaw/dfiles/file_178.pdf.

6 "Management strategy to handle welfare problems of captive brown bears (*Ursos arctos*): Case study on captive brown bears in Georgia, August 2006," NWS-I-2006-21, p.29, by Annemarie Garssen for her Masters Programme in Natural Resources Management at Utrecht University. Garssen did field research for 5 1/2 months at Alertis and 3 weeks in Georgia. At NACRES, her team supporters were Irakli Shavgulidze, Bejan Lortkipanidze and Mari Shikhashvili.

7 "A Bear Forest in the Netherlands," by Koen Cuyten. *See:* www.alertis.nl

8 Garssen, op. cit.

9 Cuyten, op. cit.

10 *See* "Status and Trends of Biodiversity," www.cbd.int/countries/default.shtml?country=nl. Three Dutch initiatives complement the Bear Sanctuary: the National Ecological Network, the Nature Conservation Act, and Natura 2000.

PROTECTING THE LAST OLD FORESTS OF EUROPE

1 *Remarkable Trees of the World,* by Thomas Parkenham, W.W. Norton & Company, New York, 2002, p.26.

2 *See The Afterlife of a Tree,* by Andrzej Bobiec (Editor), Jerzy M. Gutowski, Karol Zub, Paweł Pawlaczyk, and William F. Lauadenslayer, WWF Poland & Foundation of Environmental and Natural Resources Economists, Bialystok Poland, 2005, p.12.

3 *See Mythic Woods: The World's Most Remarkable Forests,* by Jonathan Roberts, Foreword by Thomas Pakenham, Weidenfeld & Nicolson, London, 2004, pp. 20-29.

4 *Tree: A New Vision of The American Forest,* by James Balog, Sterling Publishing, New York, 2004, p.54.

5 *Landscape and Memory,* by Simon Schama, Alfred A. Knopf, New York, 1995, p.29.

6 Carmen de Statura, Feritate ac Venatione Bisontis, ca. 1520, ibid., p.38.

7 *See* "Newfound Fossils Reveal Secrets of World's Oldest Forest," by John Roach, National Geographic News, http://news.nationalgeographic.com/news/2007/04/070418-oldest-trees.htm. *See also,* "How plants conquered the land," by Hans Steur, www.xs4all.nl~steurh/eng/old1.htm. *See also,* "Molecular basis for the evolution of xylem lignification," by Gary Peter and David Neale, *Current Opinion in Plant Biology,* Vol. 7, Issue 6, December 2004, pp.737-742.

8 *World Heritage Sites: Nature Sanctuaries,* by Marco Cattaneo and Jasmina Trifoni, Translated from Italian by Timothy Stroud, White Star Publishers, Vercelli, Italy, 2003, p.20.

9 Private discussion with Dr. Okołów.

10 *See The Białowieʑa Forest Saga,* by Simona Kossak, MUZA SA, Warszawa, 2001, p.260.

11 *Pan Tadeusz or The Last Foray In Lithuania, A Tale Of The Gentry In The Years 1811 And 1812 Translated Into English Verse With An Introduction by Kenneth R. Mackenzie*, Sixth Edition, Lomianki, 2007, pp.134-135.

12 See *Gallery of Polish Painting*, Edited by Ewa Micke-Broniarek, Translated by Joanna Holzman, National Museum, Warszawa, 2006.

13 J. Brincken *Mèmoire Descriptif sur la Forêt Impèriale de BiałłowieÐa en Lithuanie*, Varsovie, 1828.

14 ibid, Brincken.

15 Kossak, op. cit., p.292.

16 Bobiek, et al., op. cit., p.9.

17 ibid., p.18.

18 ibid., p.79.

19 See *Puszcza Białowieska*, by Pawel FabijaÐski, Instytut Wydawniczy Kreator, Białystok, 2006, p.8.

20 ibid.

21 See *Bialowieza National Park: In A Nutshell*, by Czesław Okołów, Bialowieski Park Narodowy 2007, p.14.

22 For one of the very best of these, see *Puszcza Białowieska, Cztery Pory Roku: The Białowieska Primeval Forest Four Seasons*, by Włodzimierz ŁapiÐski, TECJA-Verbum, 2000.

23 They are the black (*Dryocopus martius*), great-spotted (*Dendrocopos major*) green (*Picus viridis*), lesser-spotted (*Dendrocopus minor*), grey-headed (*Picus canus*), middle-spotted (*Dendrocopos medius*), three-toed (*Picoides tridactylus*), and white-backed (*Dendrocopos leucotos*) woodpeckers, as well as the highly unusual Eurasian wryneck (*Jynx torquilla*).

24 For the best in avian audio from Bialowieza, see the three volume "Polskie Ptaki," Solitan 2006, Poland; and the two-volume "Głosy ptaków Polski," by Zdzislaw PalczyÐski, 2003, www.otop.org.pl.

25 See *The Strict Nature Reserve*, by Bogdan Jaroszewicz, and Czesław Okołów, p.15.

26 See *Bialowieza National Park: In a Nutshell*, by Czesław Okołów, Bialowieski Park Narodowy 2007.

27 See the list of leaf types from the back-cover of *The Palace Park*, by Amelia Kawecka, Bialowieski Park Narodowy, Chief Consultant Czesław Okołów, 1999.

28 See *Vegetation Dynamics in Temperate Lowland Primeval Forests: Ecological Studies in Bialowieza Forest*, by J.B. Falinski, Springer-Netherland, 1986. It is worth pointing out that Falinski's work is considered to be the greatest ecological study ever produced in Bialowieza—the result of nearly five decades of study. A further note that speaks to the government's high level of economizing, the National Park has no budget to acquire the actual book but, rather, a xerox copy of it.

29 See *Puszcza Białowieska*, by Wojciech SobociÐski, Wydawca, Studio Fotografii Przyrodniczej HAJSTRA, Warszawa, 2003.

30 See "We Must Not Cut Down Old Trees," A Film/Slide Presentation Appeal on CD, WWF Poland, Warsaw, 2007.

31 See *The Hwozna Protective Forest Area*, by Bogdan Jaroszewicz, Chief Consultant, Czesław Okołów, Bialowieski Park Narodowy, 1999.

32 See "Protect birds: What is NATURA 2000?" by Tomasz Cofta, http://birds.poland.pl/protect/article,What_is_NATURA_2000,id,92892.htm

33 See *Biebrza: ptasi raj*, by Tomasz Kłosowski, MULTICO Oficyna Wydawnicza Sp. Z.o.o., Warszawa 2003.

34 See *Rospuda*, by Zofia Pilasiewicz, Photographed by Piotr Malczewski, Prezes Bernard Banaszuk, Bialystok, 2007. See also "Poland: Commission pursues legal action for violation of nature directives," www.viabalticainfo.org/Poland-Commission-pursues-legal. See also www.europa.eu/rapid/pressReleasesAction. do?reference=IP/06/1757&forma, Brussels, Dec.12, 2006. See also, "Poland's reckless approach to natural treasure lands it in European Court of Justice," www.viabalticainfo.org/Poland-s-reckless-approach-to. See also, "Natura 2000 vs. management of Baltic's natural areas," Minister of Environment Prof. Jan Szyszko, Warsaw, May, 2007. See also, "First National Report To the Conference Of The Parties To The Convention On Biological Diversity," Ministry of Environment Protection, Natural Resources and Forestry of the Republic of Poland; Sponsored by the United Nations Environment Programme Global Environment Facility, Warsaw, Poland 1997.

35 See *The European Bison: Forest Emperor*, Bialowieski National Park, Bialowieza 2005, p.3.

36 See *Poland BiałowieÐa Primeval Forest of Europe*, By Christian Kempf, Translated by William Roche and Thierry Lux, adapted by William Roche, SETEC-TOUR, Bialystok, 1997, p.61.

37 See *Kraina Ðubra: The Land Of The Bison*, by Wojciech SobociÐski, Wydanie I, Drukarnia, Tolek, Mikołów, globalna wioska, Patronat: Bialowieski Park Narodowy, 2004, p.19.

38 See *The Nature Guide to the Bialowieza Primeval Forest: Poland*, Crossbill Guides, by Dirk Hilbers, edited by Dr.te Boekhorst, B. Kwast, M. Seifert, C.Hilbers, R. Hilbers, B. Redekopp, and K. Lotterman, Crossbill Guides Foundation, Nijmegen, The Netherlands, and KNNV Publishing, Utrecht, Netherlands, 2005, p.70.

39 SobociÐsk etal., op.cit., p.109.

40 See "*The European Bison: Forest Emperor*," Bialowieski National Park, Bialowieza 2005, p.15.

41 SobociÐsk etal., op.cit., p.19. See also *Ðubr*, by Andrzej Stachurski and Jan RaczyÐski, AFW Mazury nd..

42 Personal conversation with Tomasz Wesolowski.

FOR THE LOVE OF WILDLIFE: MARIETA VAN DER MERWE AND FAMILY

1 See www.peaceparks.org

2 See "Caring for Creation: Vision, Hope and Justice," Social Statement of the Evangelical Lutheran Church in America, August 28, 1993 Kansas City, Missouri. Action Institute for the Study of Religion and Liberty, Grand Rapids, Missouri.

3 *For the Love of Wildlife*, by Chris Mercer, Vine House Distribution, 2003.

4 Some of the flagship species at Harnas:
   Cheetah (*Acinonyx jubatus*)
   Leopard (*Panthera pardus*)
   Bat-eared fox (*Otocyon megalotis*)
   Black-backed jackal (*Canis mesomelas*)
   Caracal (*Caracal caracal damarensis*)
   Lion (*Panthera leo*)
   Springbok (*Antidorcas marsupialis*)
   Kudu (*Tragelaphus strepsicerus*)
   Oryx (*Oryx gazella*)
   Hardebeest (*Alcelaphus buselaphus*)
   Eland (*Taurotragus oryx*)
   Purcupine (*Hystrix africaeaustralis*)
   Warthog (*Phacochoerus aethiopicus*)
   Vervet monkey (*Cercopithecus aethiops*)
   Chacma baboon (*Papio ursinus*)
   Wild dog (*Lycaon pictus*)
   Brown hyena (*Hyaena brunnea*)

5 See Michael A McCarthy and Hugh P. Possingham, "Active Adaptive Management for Conservation," *Conservation Biology*, Vol. 21, No. 4, 2007, p.957. The crisis factor in African conservation is especially severe. See "Parks failing Africa's wildlife," September 3, 2007, http://news.bbc.co.uki/1/hi/sci/tech/6972416.stm.

HOWARD BUFFETT AND THE WORLD OF THE CHEETAH

1 Some of the better known and/or significant conservation areas include: the Ben Alberts Nature Reserve, the Borakalalo National Park, the Chamberlain Bird Sanctuary, De Wildt Cheetah Research Centre, D'Nyala Nature Reserve, the Lapalala Wilderness, Loskop Dam Nature Reserve, Mabusa Nature Reserve, Marakele National Park, Masebe Nature Reserve, Mdala Nature Reserve, Mkhombo Nature Reserve, the Percy Fyfe Nature Reserve, Pilanesberg National Park, the Pretoria National Botanical Garden, the Rhino Bushveld Eco-Park and the Witvinger Nature Reserve. For a complete list and descriptions, see Judy Beyer, Alan Duggan, and Brian Johnson Barker (Eds.), *Reader's Digest Illustrated Guide to the Game Parks & Nature Reserves of South Africa*, The Reader's Digest Association South Africa, Cape Town, 1997, pp.76-93.

   Further South, The Kogelberg Biosphere Reserve in the heart of the Cape Floristic Province Hotspot, is

South Africa's first UNESCO sanctioned world Biosphere preserve, hosting 100,000 ha, 1,300 endemics per 10,000 square kilometers, for a total of 9,087 plants, of which 6,218 are endemic to the country. As Chris Burlock describes in *The Oldest World Record*, this remarkable region, an hour from Cape Town, has embodied the internationally-critical reserve concept: "core areas" of absolute pristine ecosystems; "buffer zones" of non-impactful scientific research and ecological classroom experiences, and "transition zones" where communities who find themselves suddenly living in or beside a UNESCO designated area must work with the various agencies, and scientists to make sure they don't starve to death. *See The Oldest World Record*, Indwe, September 2006, pp.102-104.

2 Howard Buffet, "Sharing Responsibility to Make the World Safer," Global Partnership Forum October 4, 2006, p.3.

3 *See* "Chinese Tigers Learn Hunting, Survival Skills in Africa," by Leon Marshall, National Geographic News, http://news.nationalgeographic.com/news/2005/03/0302_050302_tiger_africa.html/

THE ORIGINAL GARDEN OF EDEN

1 *See* Population Reference Bureau data for Yemen, www.prb.org.

2 *See* "Important Bird Areas in the Middle East," Compiled by M. I. Evans, BirdLife Conservation Series No. 2, BirdLife International, Cambridge, England, 1994, pp. 380-81. *See also*, R.F. Porter, S. Christensen, P. Schiermacker-Hansen, *Field Guide to the Birds of the Middle East*, Illustrated by A. Birch, J. Gale, M. Langman, and B. Small, T & AD Poyser, London, 1996.

3 *See The Periplus of the Erythraean Sea: Travel and Trade in the Indian Ocean By a Merchant of the First Century*, Translated from the Greek and Annotated by Wilfred H. Schoff, Longmans, Green and Co., New York, 1912.

4 *See* Bruno A. Mies, "Bottle-Trees and Heat on Socotra (Yemen): A Big-Foot Story: A Temperature Study of *Adenium Socotranum* (Apocynaceae) and *Dendrosicyos Socotrana* (Cucurbitaceae)," *Cactus and Succulent Journal* (U.S.), Vol. 71 (1999), No.2, p.60.

5 I.B. Balfour, "The Botany of Sokotra," *Transactions of the Royal Society of Edinburgh* 31: 1-446.

6 H.O. Forbes (ed.), *The Natural History of Sokotra and Abd-el-Kuri*, Special Bulletin of the Liverpool Museums, Henry Young & Sons, London, 1903.

7 Douglas Botting, *Island of the Dragon's Blood*, Hodder and Stroughton, London and Wilfred Funk, Inc., New York, 1958.

8 *Ethnoflora of the Soqotra Archipelago*, Designed By Diccon Alexander, Edited By Ruth Atkinson, The Royal Botanic Garden Edinburgh, 2004.

9 *Socotra: A Natural History of the Islands and their People*, by Catherine Cheung and Lyndon DeVantier, Science Editor Kay Van Damme, Odyssey Books & Guides, Hong Kong, 2006.

10 "*Thelopsis paucispora*, a new lichen species from Socotra (Yemen)," Othar Breuss and Matthias Schultz, *The Lichenologist* (2007), Cambridge Journals, http://journals.cambridge.org/action/display/Abstract. *See also* "Checklist of lichens and lichenicolous fungi of Socotra (Yemen)," November 2004, www.biologie.uni-hamburg.de/checklists/middleeast/yemen_socorta_l.htm.

11 "Dermaptera of the Socotra Archipelago, with the description of a new species," by Fabian Haas, Hans Pohl and Wolfgang Wranik, *Fauna of Arabia*, Vol. 20, pp. 409-419, May 9, 2004.

12 From private correspondence with Michael Scholl and Sultan, Dubai Expeditions, April, 2007.

13 *See* "Four new bird species in Yemen from Socotra," S. J. Aspinall, R. R. Porter and O. Al-Saghi, OSME, *Sandgrouse*, Vol. 26, No. 1, Spring 2004, pp.48-50. The birds, seen between 1999 and 2001, were a long-tailed cormorant, yellow bittern, Madagascar pond heron and Amur falcon.

14 Cheung and DeVantier, op. cit., p.330.

15 ibid., p.76.

16 *See* "Socotra Island xeric shrublands (AT1318)", www.worldwidlife.org/wildworld/profiles/terrestrial/at/at1318_full.html.

17 Cheung and DeVantier, op. cit., p.137.

18 *Socotra: An Introduction to the Natural History of the Islands and their People*, by Catherine Cheung and Lyndon DeVantier, Socotra Conservation Fund (SCF), Hadibo, Yemen, 2004, p.27.

19 Cheung and DeVantier, op.cit., p.169.

20 ibid., Cheung and DeVantier, p.136.

21 From unpublished UNDP-GEF-EPA data, in "Saving Socotra: The Treasure Island of Yemen," by Edoardo Zandri, UNDP Programme Manager, Socotra Conservation and Development Program, Principal Contributors Catherine Cheung and Salah Hakim, January, 2003, p.15.

22 Adnan al-Qaisy, "Street medicinal herbs could be harmful," *Yemen Observer*, January 20, 2007, Vol. X, No. 7, p.7.

THE BIRTH OF AN ORYX:
AL AREEN WILDLIFE SANCTUARY

1 *See* Population Reference Bureau for Bahrain at www.prb.org.

2 *Wildlife of Bahrain*, by Mike Hill, Miracle Publishing, Manama, 2003.

3 *See* "Conservation in Bahrain," by Halal Abdulrahman, www.eef.org.bh/cnsrvnbhr.htm.

4 *See* "Traffic Blamed for Air Pollution in Bahrain," by Sara Sami and Tariq Khonji, *Gulf Daily News*, October 15, 2006, www.arabenvironment.net/archive/2006/10/106334.html.

In terms of the country's struggle with globalization and the attempt to sustain an indigenous spirit, both ecologically and with respect to urban planning, see "Bahrain proves it's a small world after all," by Daniel Altman," *International Herald Tribune*, October 17, 2007, p.11.

5 Hill, op. cit., p.181.

6 ibid., p.1, from the Foreword by the Vice President, National Commission for Wildlife Protection, H. H. Shaikh Abdullah Bin Hamad Al Khalifa.

7 *See* Marijcke Jongbloed, "Comeback of the Unicorn," Al Sindagah, September-October, 2005, p.2, www.alsindagah.com/septoct2005/oryx.html.

THE PRECIOUS SANDS OF AL MAHA:
THE DUBAI DESERT
CONSERVATION RESERVE

1 The seven Emirates are Abu Dhabi, Dubai, Ras al-Khaimah, Sharjah, Ajman, Fujairah, and Umm al Qawain.

2 *See* Marijcke Jongbloed, "Comeback of the Unicorn," Al Sindagah, September-October, 2005, p.2, www.alsindagah.com/septoct2005/oryx.html.

3 *See* "Environment and Wildlife," United Arab Emirates Yearbook 2006, p.289.

4 *See* Daniel Bardsley, "Cancer cure from desert: Camels Used To Generate Antibodies to Treat Prostate Tumours," *Gulf News*, February 10, 2007, p.3.

5 *See* "Visitor's Guide," Dubai Desert Conservation Reserve, p.11.na.

6 Jongbloed, op.cit., p.2. *See also, Wild About Mammals: A Field Guide to the Terrestrial Mammals of the UEA*, by Marijcke Jongbloed, Robert Lleellyn-Smith and Moaz Sawaf, Arabian Leopard Trust, 2002, Dubai.

7 *See A Photographic Guide to Birds of the Middle East*, Photography by David Cottridge, New Holland Publishers, 2006, London; *Important Bird Areas in the Middle East*, Compiled by M. I. Evans, BirdLife International, Cambridge UK, 1994; *The Comprehensive Guide to the Wild Flowers of the United Arab Emirates*, by Marijcke Jongbloed, with G. R. Feulner, B. Böer, and A.R.Western, Environmental Research and Wildlife Development Agency, Abu Dhabi, 2003; and *Wild About Reptiles*, by Marycke [sic] Jongbloed, with JNB "Bish" Brown, Environmental Research and Wildlife Development Agency, Barkers Trident Communications, London, 2000.

8 *See Dubai 24 Hours*, by Michael Tobias, Motivate Publishing, Dubai, 2003, p.43.

VEGETARIAN ECOLOGY IN RAJASTHAN

1 *See* M. R. Nielson, "Importance, cause and effect of bushmeat hunting in the Udzungwa Mountains, Tanzania: implications for community based wildlife management," *Biological Conservation*, Vol. 128, pp. 509-516, 2006, cited by Jon Fjeldså, "How Broad-Scale Studies of Patterns and Processes Can Serve to Guide Conservation Planning in Africa," *Conservation Biology*, Vol. 21, No. 3, p.665.

2 *See* www.esamskriti.com/html/new_essay_page. asp?cat_name=quanda&cid=422&sid=102. *See also*, Michael Tobias, *World War III: Population and the Biosphere at the End of the Millennium*, Santa Fe: Bear & Company, 1994, pp.136, 141, 313. *See also*, Michael Tobias, "The Anthropology of Conscience," *Society & Animal Forum: Journal of Human-Animal Studies*, Vol. 4, No. 1: www. psyeta.org/sa/sa4.1/tobias.html.

3 *See* Tripti Pandey, Foreword by H.H. Maharja of Jodhpur, *Pushkar: Colours Of The Indian Mystique*, Kowloon, Hong Kong & Bookwise PVT. LTD, New Delhi: Timothy J. Scollary, Cheltenham Investments Ltd, 2004, pp.18-21.

4 *See* Dr. Prithvi Raj, *Pushkar: A City oF Peace And Spirituality*, Ram Publishers, 2006.

5 *See* Praveen Mathur and Nimit R. Chowdhary, "Environmental Degradation at Pushkar Valley [India]: Restrain Tourism Or Promote Tourism?" *Acta Universitatis Palackianae Olomucensis Facultas Rerum Naturalium, Biologica*, Vol. 37, 1999, p.121.

A TRIBE THAT WORSHIPS FLOWERS & BUFFALO

1 Henry S. Salt, *The Call of the Wildflower*, London: George Allen and Unwin Ltd, 1922, p.12.

2 Leonardo Da Vinci, Translated by John Francis Rigaud, *Treatise on Painting*, London: George Bell & Sons, 1897, p.2.

3 Immanuel Kant, Translated by J. W. Semple, *The Metaphysic of Ethics*, Edinburgh: T. & T. Clark, 1869, pp. 106-107.

4 Sunjoy Monga, *Wildlife Reserves of India*, Mumbai: India Book House PVT LTD, 2002, p.8.

5 Shashwat Chaturvedi, "The Last Roar" June 27, 2007, Data Quest, http://dqindia.ciol.com/content/ egovernance/2007/207062701.asp.

6 *See* www.cbd.int/countries/profile.shtml?country=in

7 Shashwat Chaturvedi, op.cit.

8 "Cull Of The Wild," May 21, 2007, *India Today*, p.75.

9 Michael Tobias, *World War III: Population and the Biosphere at the End of the Millennium*, Santa Fe: Bear & Company, 1994, p.122.

10 These include Nagarhole National Park, Karnataka-Bandipur Tiger Reserve/National Park, Mudumalai Wildlife Sanctuary, Silent Valley National Park, Wynaad Wildlife Sanctuary, the mountainous Nilambur, Siruvani and Tamil Nadu/Coimbatore Central Reserve Forests, and Mukurthi National Park. Corridors include Annamalai National Park and the Parambikulam.

11 *See* "Restoring the Toda Landscapes of the Nilgiri Hills in South India," *Plant Talk: Supporting Plant Conservation Worldwide*, No. 44, April 2006, www.plant-talk.org, p.29.

12 *See* Dr. V. S. Vijaya and Ranjit Daniels, "The Nilgiri Biosphere Reserve: a review of conservation status," Working Paper No. 16, 1996, p.5, M S Swaminathan Research Foundation, Madras UNESCO South-South Cooperation Programme and SACON, Sálim Ali Centre for Ornithology and Natural History, www. unesdoc.unesco.org/images/0011/001137/113753e0. pdf. Sponsored by the Rajiv Gandhi Institute for Contemporary Studies, and published as part of Protecting Endangered National Parks 1, 1995. *See also*, R.J.R. Daniels, "The Nilgiri Biosphere Reserve and its role in conserving India's biodiversity," *Science* Vol. 64, 1993, pp. 706-708. *See also*, "Fauna of Nilgiri Biosphere Reserve," edited by the Director, Zoological Survey of India (Fauna of Conservation Area Series 11), Calcutta, 2001. In addition, R J Ranjit Daniels, *Amphibians of Peninsular India*, India Academy of Sciences, Universities Press (India) Private Limited, 2005; and *The Book of Indian Birds*, 13th Edition, by Sálim Ali, Bombay Natural History Society, Oxford University Press, 2002.

13 Vijaya and Daniels, op. cit., pp.13, 18. The authors cite previous work by M.P. Nayar, "Endemic flora of Peninsular India and its significance," *Bulletin of the Botanical Survey of India*, Vol. 22, pp. 12- 23, 1983. *See also*, K.S. Manila, *Flora of Silent Valley Tropical Rain Forests of India*, Calcutta: The Mathrubhumi Press, 1988; and K.Subiwwianyam and M.P.Nayar, "Vegetation and phytogeography of the Western Ghats," *Ecology and Biogeography in India*, pp. 178-196 (cd) Mani, M. S. The Hague, 1974.

14 Ajith Kumar, Rohan Pethiyagoda, and Divya Mudappa in Russell Mittermeier, et.al., *Hotspots Revisited*, Cemex, 2004.

15 *See Hotspots: The Feature Film Documentary*, A Dancing Star Foundation Production, 2007.

16 *See* R. Prabhakar, and M. Gadgil, "Nilgiri Biosphere Reserve: Biodiversity and population growth, Survey of the Environment," *The Hindu*, pp.31-37, 1994.

17 Vijaya and Daniels, op. cit.

18 *See* Dr. Tarun Chhabra, "A Journey to Nyoolzn: A Toda migration," *The India Magazine of her People and Culture*, February, 1995, pp.62-71.

19 *See* S. Kumar, et al., "Genetic variation and relationships among eight Indian riverine buffalo breeds," *Molecular Ecology*, Vol. 15, March, 2006, p.593.

20 M. Maeterlink, Translated by A. Teixeira De Mattos, *Hours of Gladness*, Illustrated by E. J. Detmold, London: Allen & Co, 1912, p.167.

21 Chhabra, op. cit., "Restoring the Toda Landscapes..." p.30.

22 ibid, p.30.

23 *See* Dr. Tarun Chhabra, "Balmy balsams: The endangered *Impatiens*, endemic to the upper Nilgiris, offers an excellent illustration of phytogeography," *Frontline*, Vol. 23, Issue 26, Dec. 2006. www.frontline.in/ stories/20070112000706600.htm. p.6.

24 *See* Dr. Tarun Chhabra, "A Journey to the Toda Afterworld," *The India Magazine of her People and Culture*, September, 1993, pp. 7-16.

25 Chhabra, op. cit., "Restoring the Toda Landscapes...", p.29.

26 *See* Sálim Ali and S. Dillon Ripley, *Handbook of the Birds of India and Pakistan*, Ten Volumes, Sponsored by the Bombay Natural History Society, Bombay, London, New York: Oxford University Press, 1968.

27 *See* W.E. Marhsall, *A Phrenologist Amongst the Todas, or, The Study of a Primitive Tribe in South India*, Gurgaon, Haryana: Vipin Jain for Vintage Books, 1989. *See also*, W.H.R. Rivers, *The Todas*, 2 volumes, Jaipur, India: Rawat, 1986 (originally published in 1906); and A. Walker, *The Toda of South India: A New Look*, New Delhi: Hindustan Publishing Corporation, 1986.

28 *See* Michael Tobias, "The Anthropology of Conscience," *Society & Animal Forum: Journal of Human-Animal Studies*, Vol. 4, No. 1: www.psyeta.org/sa/sa4.1/tobias.html.

WAT PHRA KEO: ECOLOGICAL AESTHETICS

1 Boaz Englesberg, "Stalling the Wildlife Trade," *Action Asia*, January/February, 2007, pp.36-38.

2 Mark Graham and Philip Round, *Thailand's Vanishing Flora and Fauna* Bangkok: Finance One Public Company Ltd, 1994.

3 *See* www.cbd.int/countries/profile.shtml?country=th.

4 ibid.

5 ibid.

6 Belinda Stewart-Cox, *Wild Thailand*, Photographs by Gerald Cubitt, Produced in association with the Seub Nakhasathien Foundation, London: New Holland Publishers Ltd; Reprinted by Asia Books, 1997, p.38.

7 L. Bruce Kekule, *Thailand's Natural Heritage: A Look at Some of the Rarest Animals in the Kingdom*, Bangkok: WKT Publishing Co Ltd, 2004, p.222.

8 *See* "Endangered Species," in Jim Thompson, *Thailand: A Traveller's Companion*, Archipelago Guides, Editions Nouveaux-Loisirs, Bangkok: Jim Thompson Thai Silk Company, 1994, p.124. *See also* "Thailand's Biodiversity Action Plan," as stipulated under the U.N. Convention on Biological Diversity: www.cbd.int/countries/default. shtml?country=th.

9 *See The Story of Ramakian: From the Mural Paintings along the Galleries of the Temple of the Emerald Buddha*; and *The Temple of the Emerald Buddha and the Grand Palace*, both published in Bangkok: Sangdad Publishing Co, Copyright 0-2674-7184.

10 *See* Santi Leksukhum, *Temples of Gold: Seven Centuries of Thai Buddhist Paintings*, Photographs by Gilles Mermet, Translated from the French by Kenneth D. Whitehead, Bangkok: River Books, 2000. Of more recent interest and importance are the annual exhibitions of contemporary Thai painters at the Queen's Gallery in Bangkok where many of the finest Buddhist interpretive works are on display. *See The 29th Bua Luang Exhibition of Paintings*, Bangkok: Bangkok Bank Foundation, 2007

THE BUTTERFLIES OF KUALA LUMPUR

1 From Wallace, *The Maylay Archipelago*, cited by Yong Hoi-Sen in *Malaysian Butterflies: An Introduction*, Kuala Lumpur: Tropical Press Sdn. Bhd., 1983, p.11.

2 ibid., p.12 quoted in Hoi-Sen.

3 This fact is mentioned in Myriam Baran and Gilles Martin, Translated from the French by Simon Jones, *Butterflies of the World*, New York: Harry Abrams, 2006, p.117.

4 ibid., p.8.

5 Hoi-Sen, op. cit.

SINGAPORE'S HEART & SOUL: BUKIT TIMAH NATURE RESERVE

1 Quoted by William Warren, *Singapore: City of Gardens*, Hong Kong: Periplus Editions Ltd, 2000, p.153.

2 ibid.

3 Population Reference Bureau, DataFinder, www.prjprbdata/wcprbdata7.asp?DW=DR&SL=&SA=1

4 *See* Choo-Toh Get Ten, Dr. C.J. Hails, Bernard Harrison, Dr. Wee Yeow Chin and Wong Kew Kwan, *A Guide to the Bukit Timah Nature Reserve*, Singapore: Singapore Science Center, 2000, 5th printing. *See also* Dr. Peter K. L. Ng (Ed.), *A Guide to the Threatened Animals of Singapore*, Singapore: Singapore Science Center, 1998; Hugh T.W. Tan (Ed.), *A Guide to the Threatened Plants of Singapore*, Singapore: Singapore Science Center, 1998; Peter K.L. Ng (Ed.), *Freshwater Life in Singapore*, Singapore: Singapore Science Center, 2000; Veronique Sanson, *Gardens and Parks of Singapore*, New York: Oxford University Press, 1992.

5 Sanson, op. cit., p.51.

6 *See* Cheah Jin Seng, *Singapore: 500 Early Postcards*, Singapore: Editions Didier Millet, 2006.

7 *See* Joseph R. Yogerst and R. Ian Lloyd, *Singapore: State Of The Art*, Singapore: R.Ian Lloyd Productions, 2006.

FORESTS OF ETERNITY: ULU TEMBURONG NATIONAL PARK

1 The country at present produces roughly 200,000 barrels of crude oil per day from a largely discrete complex of "4,000 reservoirs, over 200 offshore structures, more than 700 production wells and 1,200 pipelines stretching over 2,400 kilometers." *See* Wani Gapar, "The Challenges," *The Brunei Times*, Brunei Darussalam 23rd National Day Special Supplement, February 24, 2007, p.3.

2 *See* E.L. Caldecott, J.D. Caldecott, and G. Davison, "Protected Areas of the World: A Review of National Systems," World Conservation Monitoring Centre, 1992, pp.1807-1820. htlp://books.google.com/books?isbn=2831700930. *See also* http://aseanbiodiversity.org/cgi-bin/abiss.exe/sql?SID=875871&sql=ctry/lawdetails&law_pk=104.

3 *See* "A Garden City with Green Pockets," na. *Borneo Bulletin*, February 23, 2007, p.12. In 1987, as much as 81% of the country was assessed as being in a natural vegetative state. By 1999 that percentage had dropped to 75%, according to K.M. Wong and A.S. Kamariah, writing in "Forests and Trees of Brunei Darussalam," Tree Flora of Brunei Darussalam Project, 1999, p.12. Now, it is 71 to 72%. If, in 20 years nearly 10% has been lost, this trend underscores the Government of Brunei's need to be especially watchful.

4 *See* Population Reference Bureau, PRB Country Profiles, Brunei, calculated as of 2005. *See also*, www.brunei.gov.bn/index.htm (The Government of Brunei Darussalam); and www.bedb.com.bn (Brunei Economic Development Board)

5 The three nations have pledged to double the protected areas of Borneo to 84,950 square miles (220,000 sq. km).

6 *See* Junaidi Payne and Charles M. Francis, *A Field Guide to the Mammals of Borneo*, Illustrations by Karen Phillipps, Kota Kinabalu: The Sabah Society, 2005.

  For other databases on Bornean biodiversity see Natural History Publications (Borneo) Sdn. Bhd., www.nhpborneo.com. These include: *A Guide to the Dragonflies of Borneo*, and works on rafflesia, fungi, orchids, nepenthes, slipper orchids, the genus Paphiopedilum, Coelogyne, gingers, phasmids, crocodiles, snakes, turtles, swiftlets, and proboscis monkeys. *See also* Nick Garbutt and J. Cede Prudente, *Wild Borneo: The Wildlife and Scenery of Sabah, Sarawak, Brunei and Kalimantan*, Preface by Sir David Attenborough, Cambridge: The MIT Press, 2006.

7 *See* "The Noel Kempff Mercado Climate Action Initiative: A Carbon Credit Market Pilot Project in Bolivia," by Richard Bruneau, B.Sc, Servicio Nacional de Areas Protegidas de Bolivia, La Paz, June 15, 2000. *See* www.augustana.ca/rdx/bruneau/documents/Noel%20Kempff%x0Mercado%20Carbon%20Sequestration.pdf

  A wealth of current literature exists on the various carbon offset theories, equations, and sequestration markets. *See* www.ecobusinesslinks.com/carbon_offset_wind_credits_carbon_reduction.htm. *See also* the Congressional Budget Office report on CO_2 Emissions at: www.cbo.gov/ftpdoc.cfm?index=6148&type=0. *See also*, "Maximizing Benefits from the Clean Development Mechanism: Developing country supply of carbon sinks and technology transfer projects," by Richard Bruneau, INAF 5702: International Environmental Affairs, http://unfccc.int/resource/docs/2006/sbsta/eng/misc05.pdf. *See also* "Nations take a singular stand to save standing rain

forests," by David Greising, Chicago Tribune, December 18, 2007, p.A8.

8 *See* Mohan Srilal, "Good life is under threat in Brunei," Asia Times, July 27, 2000. www.atimes.com/se-asia/BG27Ae02.html.

9 Wong and Kamariah, op. cit., p.18.

10 *See* P.S. Ashton, *Manual of the Dipterocarp Trees of Brunei State*, London: Oxford University Press, 1964. *See also* A.D. Poulsen, I.C. Nielsen, S. Tan, and H. Balslev, "A quantitative inventory of trees in one hectare of mixed dipterocarp forest in Temburong, Brunei Darussalam," in D.S. Edwards, W.E. Booth and S.C. Choy (Eds.), *Tropical Rainforest Research: Current Issues*, Dordrecht: Kluwer Academic Publishers, 1996, pp.139-150.

11 *See* S.J. Davies and P. Becker, "Floristic composition and stand structure of mixed dipterocarp and heath forests in Brunei Darussalam," *Journal of Tropical Forest Science*, Vol. 8, pp. 542-569, 1996.

THE EXTENDED FAMILY OF DR. BIRUTÉ GALDIKAS: TANJUNG PUTING NATIONAL PARK

1 For the three definitive books by, or about, Dr. Galdikas, see her powerful autobiography, *Reflections of Eden: My Years with the Orangutans of Borneo*, Boston: Little, Brown and Company, 1995; Biruté Galdikas with Nancy Briggs, *Orangutan Odyssey*, Photographs by Karl Ammann, New York: Harry N. Abrams, Inc, 1999; as well as the remarkable book: Sy Montgomery, *Walking with the Great Apes: Jane Goodall, Dian Fossey, Biruté Galdikas*, A Peter Davison Book, Boston: Houghton Mifflin Company, 1991.

2 ibid., quoted on p.275 of Sy Montgomery's *Walking with the Great Apes*.

3 *See* "Speciation and Intrasubspecific Variation of Bornean Orangutans, *Pongo pygmaeus pygmaeus*," by Kristin S. Warren, Ernst J. Verschoor, et al., *Molecular Biology and Evolution*, Vol. 18, pp. 472-480, 2001.

4 Alfred Russell Wallace, *The Malay Archipelago: The Land of the Orang-Utan and the Bird of Paradise: A Narrative of Travel with Studies of Man and Nature*, London: Macmillan And Co, 1906, 10th edition, p.69.

5 Junaidi Payne and Charles M. Francis, *A Field Guide to the Mammals of Borneo*, with illustrations by Karen Phillipps, Kota Kinabalu: The Sabah Society, 2005, p.228.

6 ibid., pp. 223–231.

SACRED BIODIVERSITY ACROSS KYOTO, JAPAN

1 *A Guide to the Lake Biwa Museum: Lakes and People: Toward a Better, Symbiotic Relationship*, A Publication of the Lake Biwa Museum, November, 2003.

2 ibid.

3 *See* Michael Tobias, *After Eden: History, Ecology & Conscience*, Slawson Communications, San Diego, 1984.

4 Gisei Takakuwa, *Japanese Gardens Revisited*, Photographs by Kiichi Asano, Rutland and Tokyo: Charles E. Tuttle Company, 1973, p.116.

5 *See* www.biodiversityhotspots.org/xp/Hotspots/japan/ conservation.xml. *See also* http://www.biodic.go.jp/ english/rdb/rdb_f.html.

6 "Unique And Threatened Biodiversity," www. biodiversityhotspots.org/.

7 ibid. *See also* Shinji Takano, (Ed.), *Birds of Japan in Photographs*, Tokyo: Tokai University Press, 1981.

8 *See* Sylvia A. Johnson, *Mosses*, Photographs by Masana Izawa, A Lerner Natural Science Book, Minneapolis: Lerner Publications Company, 1983, p.37.

9 *See* Zennoske Iwatsuki and Masana Izawa, *Yama-Kei Field Books*, Japan, 1996.

10 *See* http://www.pfaf.org/database/plants. php?Aphananthe+aspera.

11 For general descriptions, and fine photography, see Mizuno Katsuhiko, *The Courtyard Gardens of Kyoto*, Kyoto: Suiko Books, 1996; Mizuno Katsuhiko, *Gardens in Kyoto*, Kyoto: Suiko Books, 2002; and Tom Wright and Mizuno Katsuhiko, *Zen Gardens: Kyoto's Nature Enclosed*, Kyoto: Suiko Books, 1990. For more in-depth information, the most definitive Japanese garden book is undoubtedly the two-volume, Josiah Conder, *Landscape Gardening in Japan*, Printed by the Hakubunsha, Ginza, Tokio, 1893. A revised edition by the same title was published in 2002 by Kodansha International, Tokyo, Foreword by Azby Brown.

12 *See* http://www.u-tokyo.ac.jp/public/archive_e.html.

THE PARADISE OF SAKTENG: BUDDHIST ETHICS AND CONSERVATION IN BHUTAN

1 *See* Dr. S. Sathyakumar and Dr. B.S. Adhikari, "Vegetation, Bird and Mammal Surveys in Sakteng Wildlife Sanctuary, Bhutan," Submitted to WWF, Bhutan & Nature Conservation Division, Royal Government of Bhutan, by Wildlife Institute of India, Dehradun, India, March, 2005, pp.iii-iv.

2 In addition to Dr. Ugyen Tsewang, World Environment Foundation Head, Preston Scott made the critical entrées and Mr. Dorji Tshering, Director of the National Library facilitated access to Lynpo Thinley, Home Minister and subsequent candidate for Prime Minister.

3 *Biodiversity Action Plan for Bhutan 2002*, Ministry of Agriculture, Royal Government of Bhutan, Thailand: Keen Publishing, 2002. *See also* Tashi Wangchuk, P. Thinley, K. Tshering, C. Tshering, D. Yonten and B. Pema, with S. Wangchuk, *A Field Guide to the Mammals of Bhutan*, Art Coordinated by Kama Wangdi, Thimphu: Department of Forestry, Ministry of Agriculture, Royal Government of Bhutan, 2004.

4 *See* Dr. Ugyen Tshewang, "Biodiversity Conservation and Management Initiatives in Bhutan," National Biodiversity Centre, Ministry of Agriculture, Thimphu, Serbithang, Royal Government of Bhutan, www. dancingstarfoundation.org. *See also*, "Royal Bhutan Gene Bank, National Herbarium and Royal Botanical Garden Inaugurated," www.moa.gov.bt/newsdetail. php?newsID=130&from=archive; and "Promoting Biodiversity Conservation in the Kingdom of Bhutan," pp.6-7, *Stewards' Watch*, Vol. 2, No. 1, Fall 2001, World Foundation For Environment And Development. *See* Dr. Ugyen Tshewang, "Biodiversity Conservation and Management Initiatives in Bhutan," National Biodiversity Centre, Ministry of Agriculture, Thimphu, Serbithang, Royal Government of Bhutan, www. dancingstarfoundation.org. *See also*, "Royal Bhutan Gene Bank, National Herbarium and Royal Botanical Garden Inaugurated," www.moa.gov.bt/newsdetail. php?newsID=130&from=archive; and "Promoting Biodiversity Conservation in the Kingdom of Bhutan," pp.6-7, *Stewards' Watch*, Vol. 2, No. 1, Fall 2001, World Foundation For Environment And Development. *See also Biodiversity Action Plan III*, United Nations Convention on Biological Diversity, Royal Government of Bhutan, Thimphu, Bhutan, Spring 2008.

5 *Treasures of the Thunder Dragon: A Portrait of Bhutan*, by Ashi Dori Wangmo Wangchuck, Penguin Books India, 2006.

6 *See* Rebecca Pradhan, *Wild Rhododendrons of Bhutan*, Thimphu, Quality Printers, Kathmandu, 1999.

7 *See* Karma Tenzin, "Wooing the East" *Bhutan Times*, October 7, 2007, pp.1, 16.

8 Bhutan joined the International Postal Union under the guidance of former Ambassador Dasso Karma Letho, then Minister of Communications for Bhutan. It was the now retired Dasso Karma Letho and his daughter, Mrs. Sonam Lhamo, whose Pristine Druk Tours kindly provided the expert and complex logistics to make our expedition possible.

9 Legend has it that a hunter, when once pursuing a deer, shot the terrified animal with an arrow but did not kill her. The wounded deer escaped to a cave in which the great Tibetan Buddhist saint Milarepa was meditating. The hunter tracked the deer to the cave and his subsequent encounter with Milarepa converted him to vegetarianism for life.

10 *See Biodiversity Action Plan for Bhutan 2002*, Royal Government of Bhutan, p.36.

11 *See* Kunzang Choden, DAWA: *The Story of a Stray Dog in Bhutan*, Thimphu: KMT Press, 2004. Stray dogs enliven the night life of Thimphu and most other towns across the country, though recently the issue of what to do with so many canines has reached parliamentary attention. *See* Ugyen Penjore, "Stray free by December 2007," by Kuensel Online, www.kuenselonline.com/modules.php? name=Name&file=article&sid=8623.

12 Those species include, "Golden Langur, Capped Langur, Dhole/Wild Dog, Red Panda, Bengal Tiger, Snow Leopard, Asian Elephant, One-horned Rhinoceros, Asiatic Water Buffalo, Hispid Hare, Ganges River Dolphin, Assamese Macaque, Sloth Bear, Himalayan Black Bear, Smooth-coated Otter, Fishing Cat, Marbled Cat, Clouded Leopard, Asiatic Golden Cat, Swamp Deer, Gaur, Serow, Takin, Mouse-eared Bat [and] Sikkim Rat." Red List of Threatened Species, IUCN, 2006, cited in Draft Text of Biodiversity Action Plan for Bhutan 2008, BAPIII, September 2007, National Biodiversity Center, Serbithang, Bhutan.

13 *See* "Global warming message from Mount Everest" by Barry Rutherford, http://hubpages.com/hub/Global_ warming_message_from_Mount_Everest; and "The sons of Hillary and Tenzing speak out about climate change: 'Believe us, it's a reality'," by Cahal Milmo and Sam Relph, July 6, 2007, ibid.

14 The offspring of a chuk, or female yak (*dri* in common Tibetan parlance), and the Tibetan (non-yak) bull is known as a chouie or dzomo, and will frequently be killed at three weeks or so with a single bullet to the head. The reason proffered for this very un-Buddhistic action is that the milk will have been degraded in quality, though no known genetic explanation backs up this logic. *See* "Reproduction in female yaks (Bos grunniens) and opportunities for improvement," by X. Zi., *Theriogenology*, Vol. 59, Issue 6, page 1303. *See also*, "Reproduction In The Yak," FAO Corporate Document Repository, www.fao.org/DOCREP/006/AD347E/ad347e09. htm. *See also* "Merak Gewog Ninth Plan 2002-2007," www. pc.gov.bt/fyp/Gewogs/tg_Merak.pdf.

15 *See* Kunzang Choden, *Bhutanese Tales of the Yeti*, Bangkok: White Lotus Press, 1997.

16 *See* "Bhutan: Abortion Policy," www.un.org/esa/ population/publications/abortion/doc/bhutan1.doc.

17 Interestingly, a similar story comes from Easter Island, where an American vet discovered an invasive plant killing the native horses. For a superb overview of yak life in Bhutan, see "Yak Production Systems In Bhutan," by Tashi Dorji, Ministry of Agriculture, Bumthang, Bhutan, www.fao.org/ag/agP/agpc/doc/Proceedings/Tapafon02/ tapafon3.htm

18 *See RNR*, *Renewable Natural Resources Newsletter*, May/June 2006, Vol. xx, No. 112, p.2, "Forest cover: Perception and Science," anonymous editorialist.

19 *See* Francoise Pommaret, Translated by Elisabeth B. Booz, *Bhutan*, New Delhi: Timeless Books, 2003, pp.61-63.

20 BAPIII, op. cit., Introductory Chapters, "Wildlife Poaching."

21 Similar feelings and challenges have been described in other inhabited Bhutanese national parks. *See* "Striking a Balance between Conservation and People: The Jigme Dorji National Park," www.unvolunteers.org/Infobase/ articles/1999/99_06_01BTN_thimphu.htm.

22 Richard Grimmett, Carol Inskipp and Tim Inskipp, *Guide to the Birds of the Indian Subcontinent*, Christopher Helm Identification Guide Series, Christopher Helm Publishers, LTD London, revised Reprint, 2001.

23 For a fine description of the Columbiformes, see Salim Ali and S. Dillon Ripley, *Handbook of the Birds of India and Pakistan*, Vol. 3, Stone Curlews to Owls, Bombay: Oxford University Press, 1969, pp.76-162.

24 *Handbook of the Birds of India and Pakistan.*

25 Grimmett, Inskipp and Inskipp, op. cit., p.11.

26 Our colleague Tandin Wangdi from the National Biodiversity Centre recognized the following Rhododendron species: *R. arboreum*, the normal red one, as well as a white one; *R. keysii*; the endemic *R. kesangiae* white form, the pale lilac-like *R. wallichii*, the red *R. thomsonii*, the small yellow *R. campylocarpum*, the white *R. lanatum*, the yellow *R. wightii* at 3940 meters, the highest one ever seen in full flower, the small shrubby *R. setosum*, used by the Brokpa for incense, *R. falconeri*, not in flower, the red *R. kendrickii*, the white *R. maddenii*, the white *R. triflorum*, the red *R. hodgsonii*, the small pink *R. glaucophyllum*, and *R. barbatum*, not in flower but showing off its distinctive peeling bark. *R. pogonophyllum*, not seen since 1937 where it was recorded at 4,200 meters clinging to a rock, could easily be rediscovered here, defying its "presumed extinct" status. Conservation biologists never lose hope.

27 *See* A.J.C. Grierson and D.G. Long, *Flora of Bhutan Including a Record of Plants from Sikkim*, 9 Volumes, Edinburgh: Royal Botanic Garden, 1983, with WWF assistance.

28 Translations by Tandin Wangdi, Personal Discussions. At the Bhutanese Government level, all of these concepts are diffused throughout the administrative hierarchies and a multilayered approach to conservation. The Ministry of Agriculture is charged with taking care of the nine protected areas and genetic corridors, though the day-to-day work falls to the Director General of Forests under whose aegis is the National Conservation Department that is focused on issues of wildlife. The Deputy Minister takes up issues pertaining to Environmental Impact Assessments (EIAs) for road building and other large earthmoving enterprises and also contends with pollution and climate change. The Royal Society for the Protection of Nature is a Bhutanese NGO that has effectively served as a watchdog. Dr. Ugyen's previous administrative mandate at NBC lay within the Agriculture Ministry and is charged primarily with flora, livestock and, most critically, the Biodiversity Action Plan, as stipulated under the United Nations International Conventional on Biological Diversity.

29 *See* "Sustainable Development Agreement, Bhutan," Sustainable Development Secretariat, Thimphu, Bhutan. *See also*, Karma Ura and Karma Galay (Eds.), *Gross National Happiness and Development*, Thimphu: The Centre for Bhutan Studies, 2004.

30 *See* Dr. S. Sathyakumar and Dr. B.S. Adhikari, "Vegetation, Bird and Mammal Surveys in Sakteng Wildlife Sanctuary, Bhutan," Submitted to WWF-Bhutan & Nature Conservation Division, Royal Government of Bhutan, by Wildlife Institute of India, Dehradun, India, March, 2005, p.28. *See also* www.moa.gov.bt/moa/main/index.php for Vol. 1, No. 5, February 6, 2002.

31 BAPIII, op. cit.

PHOTO CAPTIONS AND CREDITS

All images photographed by the authors Michael Tobias and Jane Morrison, except where noted below.

PEOPLE & HISTORIC ART AND PHOTOGRAPHY

PAGE IX
Her Majesty Ashi Dorji Wangmo Wangchuck, Queen of His Majesty the Fourth King of Bhutan

PAGE XVI
Henry David Thoreau, in 1855, from Frontispiece, *Walden, Or, Life in the Woods*, With An Introduction By Bradford Torrey, Illustrated with Photogravures in Two Volumes (First Illustrated Edition), Houghton, Mifflin And Company, Boston and New York, 1897, Private Collection

PAGE 2
Thomas Hill, "Muir Glacier," 1889, Anchorage Museum at Ramuson Center

PAGE 3
Kittlitz's Murrelet (*Brachyramphus kittlitzii*), summer plumage, Source: Plate 1, p.44a, Painting by John L. Ridgway, and Robert Ridgway, from *Report Upon Natural History Collections Made in Alaska Between the Years 1877 and 1881*, by Edward W. Nelson, Edited by Henry W. Henshaw, Government Printing Office, Washington D.C., 1887, Plate 1, Facing page 44, Private Collection.

PAGE 19
Joelle Buffa, Supervisor of the Farallon National Wildlife Refuge, San Francisco Bay National Wildlife Refuge Complex

PAGE 20-21
Albert Bierstadt, 1830-1902, "California Spring," 1875, Fine Arts Museums of San Francisco

PAGE 21
John Muir, ca. 1902, Private Collection

PAGE 34-35
Frederic Edwin Church, 1826-1900, "Heart of the Andes," 1859, The Metropolitan Museum of Art

PAGE 37
Cal Vornberger, Photographer

PAGE 42
Gene Baur, President, Farm Sanctuary

PAGE 53
Dr. Russell Mittermeier, President, Conservation International

PAGE 59
Dr. M. John Tjie Fa, Minister of Land Planning and Forestry, Suriname

PAGE 69
Professor Francisco Fonseca, President, Grupo Lobo

PAGE 72
Filipa Marcos, Research Associate, Grupo Lobo

PAGE 74
Diogo Pimenta, Associação Para a Preservação do Burro - Burricadas

PAGE 80
Brigitte Bardot, President, Fondation Brigitte Bardot

PAGE 92
Michael Aufhauser, President, Gut Aiderbichl

PAGE 109
Koen Cuyten, Bear Welfare and Facility Management, ALERTIS, Fund for Bear and Nature Conservation

PAGE 120
Tomasz Wesolowski, Professor, Department of Avian Ecology, Wroclaw University

PAGE 125
"Wisent," drawing by Leonard Chodzko, ca.1833, Private Collection

PAGE 128
Professor Czeslaw Okolów, Senior Scientist and former Director of Bialowieza National Park

PAGE 144
Marieta van der Merwe, President, Harnas Wildlife Foundation

PAGE 145
Morgan Ruth Howells, Marieta van der Merwe's granddaughter

PAGE 147
Howard G. Buffett, President, Howard G. Buffett Foundation

PAGE 155
Howard and Devon Buffett

PAGE 177
Sager Khamis, Public Relations & Environment Media Director of the National Commission for Wildlife Protection, Kingdom of Bahrain

PAGE 213
Dr. Tarun Chhabra, President, Edhkwehlynawd Botanical Refuge (EBR Trust)

PAGE 224
Emerald Buddha, Art Media, Bangkok, Thailand

PAGE 242
UPPER LEFT, MIDDLE LEFT: from Museum Display Bukit Timah Nature Reserve, Singapore

PAGE 256
Dr. Biruté Galdikas, President, Orangutan Foundation International and Husband Pak Bohap

PAGE 276
Dr. Hiroyuki Akiyama, Museum of Nature and Human Activities

PAGE 282
Michiko Kohri, Translator

PAGE 291
UPPER RIGHT: Tandin Wangdi, Senior Biologist, National Biodiversity Centre
LOWER RIGHT: Her Majesty Ashi Dorji Wangmo Wangchuck, Queen of His Majesty the Fourth King of Bhutan

PAGE 300
LOWER LEFT: Jurmi and Tashi Chozom

PAGE 318
MIDDLE LEFT: Lyompo Sonam Tobgye, Chief Justice of Bhutan
LOWER LEFT: Dr. Ugyen Tshewang, Former Director of National Biodiversity Centre, currently Governor, Trashiyangtse Dzongkhag
RIGHT: Tashi Payden Tshering, Executive Director, RSPCA

PAGE 319-321
Other dear friends and new acquaintants

PHOTOGRAPHS BY, AND COURTESY OF, THOSE OTHER THAN THE AUTHORS

PAGE VI
UPPER LEFT MIDDLE: Jesse Irwin, U.S.Fish and Wildlife Service ("USFWS")
LOWER LEFT MIDDLE: Cal Vornberger
LOWER MIDDLE RIGHT: Fondation Brigitte Bardot
LOWER RIGHT: Gut Aiderbichl

PAGE VII
UPPER LEFT: Koen Cuyten, Alertis

PAGE XIV
LOWER RIGHT: Paul Jansen

PAGE XVII
LOWER RIGHT: Brent Beaven

PAGE XVIII
UPPER RIGHT: Ryan Ingram

PAGE XIX
UPPER RIGHT: Michael Scholl

PAGE 4
LOWER LEFT: Nick Hatch

PAGE 5
LOWER RIGHT: Mason Reid

PAGE 8
UPPER LEFT: Michelle Kissling, USFWS
MIDDLE LEFT: Michelle Kissling, USFWS

PAGE 9
ALL THREE PHOTOS: Jonathan Felis

ACKNOWLEDGMENTS

Many people, organizations, agencies and governments were extraordinarily generous in terms of time, expertise, and collaboration. To all of them, as well as so many other associates throughout the world who have assisted this project in some manner, we offer our utmost gratitude.

IN THE U.S.A.

ALASKA: Anchorage Museum; Kathleen Hertel, Director, Museum Library and Archives; Tracy Leithauser, Museum Librarian; Alsek Air Service, Inc.; Les Hartley, Chief Pilot; US Fish & Wildlife Service, Juneau Office; Michelle Kissling, Wildlife Biologist; Wrangell Mountain Air; Natalie Bay; Wrangell-St. Ellias National Park and Reserve; Meg Jensen, Superintendent; Smitty-Parratt, Chief of Interpretation; and Mason Reid, Park Ranger.

FARALLONES: San Francisco Bay National Wildlife Refuge Complex; Joelle Buffa, Manager and Supervisor of the Farallon National Wildlife Refuge; Russ Bradley, Ornithologist, Point Reyes Bird Observatory; Fine Arts Museum of San Francisco; Susan J. Grinols, Director of Photo Services and Imaging; and Mick Menigoz, Captain of the Superfish.

MUIR WOODS: The U.S. National Park Service; John Muir National Historic Site; Muir Woods National Monument; Harold Wood, Chair, Sierra Club John Muir Education Committee; and Trish Richards, Holt Atherton Library.

FARM SANCTUARY: Gene Baur, President and Co-Founder and Jeff Lydon, Executive Director, and his wife, son, and daughter

NEW YORK CITY: The Central Park Conservancy; Regina V. Alvarez, Director of Horticulture and Woodland Management; Doug Blonsky, President; Cal Vornberger, Photographer; Metropolitan Museum of Art; and Julie Zeftel, Image Librarian.

IN EUROPE

AUSTRIA: Gut Aiderbichl; Michael Aufhauser, President; and Christian Dutz.

FRANCE: Fondation Brigitte Bardot; Ghyslaine Calmels-Bock, Executive Director; Annaig Lamoureux, Assistant to Christophe Marie; and Christophe Marie, Coordinator.

HOLLAND: Alertis Fund for Bear and Nature Conservation; and Koen Cuyten, Bear Welfare and Facility Management Director.

POLAND : Bialowieza National Park; Mr. Eshe Dackiewicz, Wisent Breeding Program Director; Małgorzata Karas, Managing Director; Dr. Renata Krzysciak-Kosinska, Head of the Research Unit; Dr. Professor Czeslaw Okolów, Senior Park Scientist; Mateusz Szymura, MSc.,

Scientific/Educational Outreach, Natural History Museum, Bialowieza National Park; and Dr. Tomasz Wesolowski, Department of Avian Ecology, Wroclaw University.

PORTUGAL: Iberian Wolf Recovery Centre (IWRC); Francisco Fonseca, President; Filipa Marcos, Research Field Associate; Association for the Study and Protection of Donkeys and Cattle (AEPGA); Diogo Pimenta, Director, Associação Para a Preservação do Burro-Burricadas; and Ana Bacelar, Volunteer, Writer.

IN AFRICA

NAMIBIA: Harnas Farm; Marietta van der Merwe, President; Marlice van Vuuren; and Cecelia Venter.

SOUTH AFRICA: Howard G. Buffett Foundation; Howard Graham Buffett, President; Devon Buffett; and Trisha Cook, Secretary to Howard Buffett.

IN THE MIDDLE EAST/PERSIAN GULF STATES

KINGDOM OF BAHRAIN: Public Commission for the Protection of Marine Resources; Sager Khamis, Public Relations & Environment Media Director; Dr. Ismail M Al-Madani, Vice President and General Director; and Dr. Adel M. Al-Awadhi, Director of Protection Areas.

YEMEN: Museid Alansi, Airport Service Manager, Sheraton Sana'a; Ehab Abdul Malek Eshaq, Yemen Airways; Socotra Archipelago Conservation and Development Program (SCDP); Salem Daheq Ali, Unit Director, Community Development and Decentralization; Dr. Paul Scholte, Chief Technical Advisor, United Nations Development Program (UNDP); Fuad Ali, Team Leader, Economic Growth; Tariq Syed; Ramzi Rassi; Michael C. Scholl, President, White Shark Trust; and Sultan Been Mejren.

U.A.E: Al Maha Desert Resort & Spa; Tony Williams, Vice President; the kind staff at Al Maha; Greg Simkins, Staff Scientist, Photographer; and Ryan Ingram, Staff Scientist, Photographer.

IN ASIA

BHUTAN: The Royal Government of Bhutan; His Majesty Jigme Singye Wangchuck, Fourth King of Bhutan; Her Majesty Ashi Dorji Wagmo Wangchuck, Queen of the Fourth King; Dr. Ugyen Tshewang, Founding Director of the National Biodiversity Centre, currently Dzongdag, Trashi Yangtse; Lyompo Sonam Tobgye, Chief Justice, Royal Court of Justice; Preston Scott, Executive Director of the World Foundation for Environment & Development (WFED); The Former Honorable Minister of Home and Cultural Affairs, Lyompo Jigmi Thinley, leader of the

Druk Phuensum Tshogpa (DPT) and newly elected Prime Minister of Bhutan; Dorjee Tshering, Director National Library of Bhutan; Nim Dorji, Former Director, Sustainable Development Secretariat; Singay Dorji, National Biodiversity Centre; Benchen and Tashi Khenpo, Lingkor Tours & Treks; The entire staff of Bhutan's National Biodiversity Centre, particularly Tandin Wangdi, Senior Scientist, Chief Botanist for Expedition; Rinchen Yangzom, National Herbarium; Pristine Druk-Yul Tours & Treks, Dasho Karma Letho, Managing Director; Mrs. Sonam, Director; Yamu Gallay, Expedition Associate; Vijay Moktan, Executant, World Wildlife Fund, Bhutan; Ugen P. Norbu and the entire *Biodiversity Action Plan III* team; Tashi Payden Tshering, RSPCA-Serbithang; Rebecca Pradhan, Ornithologist, Royal Society for the Protection of Nature; Tashi Wangchuck, Driver and Guide.

BORNEO: Orangutan Foundation International (OFI); Dr. Biruté Mary Galdikas, President; and Nanang Hidayat, Orangutan Tours.

BRUNEI: Dr. Noralinda Haji Ibrahim, Director of Forestry Department; and Bing Salazar, River Guide.

INDIA: Dr. Tarun Chhabra, President of EBR Trust; and Ramneek Singh Pannu, Co-Director EBR Trust.

JAPAN: Conservation International (CI); Yasushi Hibi, Director Japan Program (CI); Hiromi Tada, Associate, Japan Program (CI); Dr. Hiroyuki Akiyama, Museum of Nature and Human Activities; Michiko Kohri, Translator; Dr. Tomoki Nishimura, Curator Lake Biwa Museum; Dr. Yoshitaka Ooishi, Laboratory of Landscape Architecture, Division of Forest and Biomaterials Science, Kyoto.

IN SOUTH AMERICA

SURINAME: Conservation International Suriname (CI); Dr. Russell A. Mittermeier, President, Conservation International, Washington D.C.; Ella Outlaw, Assistant to Dr. Mittermeier, Conservation International, Washington D.C; Wim Udenhout, Executive Director, Conservation International, Suriname (in Paramaribo), and Former Prime Minister of Suriname, and Ambassador to the U.S.; Annette Tjon Sie Fat, Technical Director; Reggy Nelson, Conservation International, Suriname; Dr. James Watling, Suriname Site Scientist, Tropical Ecology Assessment & Monitoring, Conservation International, Suriname; Dr. M. John Tjie Fa, and staff, Minister of Land Planning and Forestry, Suriname.

IN THE PACIFIC REGION

NEW ZEALAND: Brent and Kari Beaven; The Pat and Derek Turnbull Family; New Zealand Department of Conservation; Craig Potton; Robbie Burton, Craig Potton Publishing, Nelson.

FOR DANCING STAR FOUNDATION

Donald Cannon, Vice President, Finance and Operations; Karine Dinev-Hackett, Executive Assistant, Research Associate; Maral Ohanian, Accounting; Samantha David; the entire staff at the DSF Sanctuaries in the U.S.; DSF colleagues Dr. Patrick Fitzgerald, Geoffrey Holland, and Robert Radin. Additional friends of the Foundation, Marek and Gosha Probosz, Michael Bostick, and particularly Dr. Marc Tobias and Betty Tobias.

FOR THE SMITHSONIAN CENTER
FOR FOLKLIFE AND CULTURAL HERITAGE

Kevin Blackerby, Development Officer; Richard S. Kennedy, Deputy Director; Richard Kurin, Director;

FOR COUNCIL OAK BOOKS

Laura Wood, Editor and Associate Publisher; Carl Brune, Designer; and the entire staff at Council Oak Books, Paulette Millichap and Sally Dennison, Publishers.

A DANCING STAR FOUNDATION BOOK

First edition, firsting printing, 2008

Printed and bound in China by Global PSD

Cover and interior design by Carl Brune

ISBN 978-1-57178-214-4

LIBRARY OF CONGRESS CATALOGING-IN-PUBLICATION DATA
Tobias, Michael.
 Sanctuary : global oases of innocence / Michael Tobias & Jane Gray Morrison.
    p. cm.
 "A Dancing Star Foundation Book."
 Includes bibliographical references.
 ISBN 978-1-57178-214-4 (hardcover)
 1. Wildlife refuges. 2. Animal sanctuaries. I. Morrison, Jane Gray- II. Title.

QL82.T63 2008
333.95'416--dc22

2008001757